A Bride's Passage

A Bride's Passage

SUSAN HATHORN'S
YEAR UNDER SAIL

Catherine Petroski

NORTHEASTERN UNIVERSITY PRESS
Boston

Northeastern University Press

Library of Congress Cataloging-in-Publication Data

Petroski, Catherine.
A bride's passage : Susan Hathorn's year under sail / Catherine Petroski.
p. cm.
Includes bibliographical references and index.
ISBN 1-55553-298-5 (cloth). — ISBN 1-55553-297-7 (pbk.)
1. Hathorn, Susan L. — Diaries. 2. Women — Maine — Diaries. 3. Transatlantic
voyages — History — 19th century. 4. Maine — Biography. I. Title.
CT275.HNM456P48 1997
910.4'5 — dc20 96-32145

Designed by Janis Owens

Composed in Garamond #3 by G & S Typesetters, Austin, Texas.
Printed and bound by Thomson-Shore, Inc., Dexter, Michigan.
The paper is Glatfelter Supple Opaque Recycled, an acid-free stock.

MANUFACTURED IN THE UNITED STATES OF AMERICA
01 00 99 98 97 5 4 3 2 1

To Henry

Contents

AUGUST
Jode's Slippers / *112*

SEPTEMBER
Homeward / *131*

OCTOBER
Hathorn Block and Richmond House / *146*

NOVEMBER
The Nest / *164*

DECEMBER
Swift Ships / *174*

APPENDICES

Illustrations

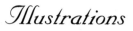

Introduction

❦

Susan Lennan Hathorn's twenty-fifth year, 1855, was one of singular events in her life—the first year of her marriage to a dashing young sea captain named Jode Hathorn, her first ocean voyage and trip to a foreign country, the birth of her first child. Fortunately 1855 is also the year she wrote every day in a diary, and just as fortunately, Susan Hathorn flourished in Maine in the mid-nineteenth century, where the cherishing of literacy and family were values that helped both inspire and preserve her diary of 1855. It is a document that follows the transformation of an intelligent but somewhat giddy and pretentious bride into a serious and mature woman, and it is a document of love which confronts the separation that the wife of a seagoing captain knows she must accept.

Throughout her diary's pages, Susan Hathorn reveals herself as a woman who is by nature, circumstance, and education simultaneously typical and atypical of her time. Born into a farming family in central Maine, Susan Lennan seemed imbued with a questing spirit, seeking the world beyond the few hundred hilly, rocky acres on which she grew up. More highly educated than most women of her day, having attended Mary Lyon's revolutionary Mount Holyoke Seminary, Susan would indeed travel the world, but, like most women (and men) of her time, she would continue to live nearly all her seventy-six years in her native town. Family would always remain at the center of her attentions, as is evidenced in the array of Hathorns, Lennans, Browns, Rings, Smalls, and Bickfords who people her diary's pages.

Until its midcentury maritime boom, the Maine town of Richmond on the west bank of the Kennebec River had been a farming community. Susan's father, James Lennan, came from Georgetown, a town on the opposite side of the river, where he was born in 1796, the fourth of David and Agness Lennan's ten children.[1] The Lennans were farmers and remained so even as maritime industries flourished in Richmond—no Lennans appear in business directories or records relating to maritime work.[2] Several generations of Susan's mother's family, the Hildreths,[3] had lived and farmed in the Gardiner–West Gardiner area, where Lucy and James Lennan settled after their marriage. Respectable, hardworking people, Susan's branch of the Lennan-Hildreth families nonetheless did not prosper. Recorded real estate deeds trace a steadily declining balance in the Lennans' holdings, as parcel after parcel left family hands.

The James Lennans' farm sat on the east side of the Post Road running from Portland to Augusta, Maine; its farmhouse was a wood-shingled, center-chimney cape that faced west, halfway up a wooded rise. It was in all likelihood here that on September 7, 1830, Lucy and James's second daughter was born, and her name was recorded as "Susannah Hildreth Lennan" in the Vital Records of Gardiner. At the time of Susan's birth, her sister Lucy was a week short of turning six, and her brother Hosea was almost three. Her sister Molly would be born when Susan herself was three, and her brother Llewellyn a year and a half after that. Joseph, the Lennans' last child, was born when Susan was eight.[4]

By 1855 when Susan wrote about her family in her diary, her older (and favorite) sister, Lucy, had married Amasa Ring, the boy from the adjacent farm, and they had two children, James and young Lucy.[5] Susan's brother Hosea married Ann Foy in 1851, but their first two daughters had died by 1855.[6] Susan's younger sister, Molly, who like Susan would teach school in Richmond, was never to marry. Her younger brother Llew would not marry until seven years later, in 1862.[7]

The Lennans lived a few miles west of Richmond's center, but the Hathorns lived in the middle of town. The families joined by Susan and Jode's marriage would not appear to have had much else in common, except that long before the Hathorns had anything to do with ships and the sea, they were farmers as well. Much more information is available on the Hathorn family; because of their prosperity and prominence in the community, they left a more voluminous paper trail in the public record. And interestingly, the Richmond Hathorns descended from the "black sheep" side of the Salem, Massachusetts, family that included the author Nathaniel Hawthorne.[8]

Black sheep or not, the Richmond Hathorns did well for themselves. Most lastingly conspicuous of their accomplishments was the 1851 construction of a monumental, clean-lined, redbrick building, the Hathorn Block, at Richmond's waterfront crossroads of Front and Main, where it nestled its four stories against the clay hill rising from the Kennebec.[9] In the Block, Susan's father-in-law, Jefferson, and his brother J. J. operated a "store" (warehouse), and on nearby river frontage that they owned they operated a small shipyard. By the year 1855, the Hathorns had built three brigs—the *Harriet*, the *Importer*, and the *Leo*—and the bark *J. J. Hathorn*. In addition, Jefferson Hathorn owned an interest in the Richmond House, the boardinghouse that he and his wife, Sally, ran and lived in, situated on Main Street adjacent to the Hathorn Block.

But the Hathorns did not come to Richmond, or Maine, with the money to build blocks and ships. Jefferson Hathorn, Jode's father, was born in 1805, the first of four sons born to John Jr., a farmer, and Elizabeth Bickford Hathorn. Jefferson's brother Joseph Jefferson, who would be his business partner and after whom the bark was said to be named, was John and Elizabeth Hathorn's youngest child.

In February 1832, Jefferson Hathorn left the Dresden, Maine, family farm, married Sally Small, and came to Richmond. Their first child, Joseph, known as Jode, was born that December, followed by Sally in 1834, Jefferson Jr. in 1840, and Volney in 1844.[10] During their childhood, Jefferson Hathorn Sr. went to sea, skippering vessels in the coastering and West Indies trade. A frugal man, he reinvested his profits in maritime enterprises, and his brother J. J. (known in Richmond as "Jack") kept a keen eye on these and other interests on land. The brothers' partnership flourished, and during the 1830s and 1840s, the Hathorns began appearing as share-owners in registration papers of Richmond-built ships. In addition, they were accumulating parcels of real estate surrounding the waterfront holdings. As the Lennans' fortunes declined, the industrious Hathorn brothers' were on the rise.

But Susan Lennan Hathorn was herself a woman to be reckoned with, and she left her own kind of paper trail. Besides her diary there are two other documents, written while she was a student at Mount Holyoke Seminary. Susan's extant writings relate to each other in important ways, and taken together they inform us not only about her personal qualities but about the place and time in which she lived. "A Three Years Cruise in the Ship Graduate" (underlines are Susan's) was Susan's final essay for the one academic year she was in residence at Mount Holyoke (1851–52).[11] In choosing to write an allegory likening the educational experience of Mount Holyoke students to a voyage to Europe, Susan expressed a geographic vision of the world of ideas, drawing on the scenes of her Richmond home and revealing if not her plan to marry Jode Hathorn at least an ambition to travel the world. The other document, a letter written to Susan's former student Emily Whitten, described the tightly regimented life Susan encountered at Mary Lyon's Mount Holyoke Seminary for young women.[12] More important, as the more private of the two writings, it reveals several significant qualities in Susan's personality that would play themselves out in her diary three years later.

How Susan Lennan came to attend Mount Holyoke is not known, but the Mount Holyoke of the time would seem an excellent match for her:

> To Mount Holyoke came serious, mature young women. To such students Mary Lyon offered intellectual mastery, inner system, and the hope of faith. She created a total institution that promised to turn outward structure into inner order, transforming New England daughters into 19th century individuals. To do this, Mary Lyon drew on the oldest resource in women's education, the mother-daughter tie, recreating within the seminary a new bond between teacher and student. Mount Holyoke designed its seminary building as a well-governed home, its internal organization allowing the oversight within a strict family and its associations confirming the link between mother and teacher.[13]

However ideally suited she was to the institution, Susan Lennan was not a typical Mount Holyoke matriculant. At twenty-two, Susan was older than most of her classmates when she wrote the "Ship Graduate," and for about four years before entering the seminary, she had led at least a semi-independent life working as a schoolteacher. By the time she wrote her final essay at Mount Holyoke in the summer of 1852, she realized that she herself would not sail on the "Ship Graduate."[14] As early as her January 1852 letter to Emily, who was considering attending Mount Holyoke, Susan suggested that her intention had been to spend just one year there: "Formerly many entered and graduated the same year," she wrote, but "now it is almost impossible."[15]

Susan's letter to Emily confirmed that daily life within the seminary walls was indeed much like that in a large family, with "work" for all. The letter also revealed Susan's shrewdness, as she capitalized on her predisposition to early rising:

> As for the work, we can almost always do what we like. If the work we prefer is light, we must work an hour and a quarter, if harder, only an hour. . . . The first of the term, I used to weigh the bread for the morning's breakfast, and make thick[e]ning for toast . . . now I build the morning fires, which is pretty hard but I like it as I gain time. I get all my work done for the day an hour and a quarter before breakfast.[16]

For Susan's taste, however, the close management of students' time at Mount Holyoke was a bit too restrictive. Noting the seminary students' isolation from townspeople, Susan confided to Emily, "We are in a sort of nunnery." Evidently, seminary living had demanded a change that Susan, accustomed to working and moving about in a community, came to feel was unreasonable.

Nonetheless, Susan herself would acknowledge the strong impression her Mount Holyoke days had made on her, for she would write at one point in her maritime diary, "Concluded the week by putting ward robe in order, after the Holyoke Custom."[17] What portion of Susan's self-

discipline was hers innately and what part Mount Holyoke cultivated
no one can know. But whatever its source, a strong sense of order domi-
nates the 1855 diary of Susan Lennan Hathorn, and clearly those Holyoke days made an indelible impression on her. In Susan's description of
a day's schedule to Emily, one sees the central role of discipline and
order:

> All the pupils must rise at fifteen minutes of five, then a girl goes all
> over the house and rings a large bell, called a rising bell. At six the
> <u>tardy</u> bell is struck, and if you are not up then you must give in
> "Tardy in rising," before all the teachers and the whole school. So it
> is with every thing—you must not be absent from domestic work,
> from table, from school exercises, tardy at table, at domestic work-
> exercises, in rising, in retiring. You must not be absent from church
> nor delinquent in Composition.[18]

Susan not only rationalized specific dormitory regulations but also extended the responsibility, discipline, and order fundamental to the Holyoke system to a universal need:

> You must not leave your <u>fire</u> without putting up the <u>fender</u>. . . . You
> must not leave wood on the Zinc or hearth; nor matches out of [the]
> box, nor must you carry fire unless in a fire pan. . . . You see there is
> nothing that is not necessary in a family of more than two hundred
> and fifty pupils. If we did our work only when we pleased, you see
> we should all starve to death,—and there would be no system about
> the arrangements. As it is, every thing goes on regularly. Everyone
> one has her regular portion to do and is expected to do it. . . . It is
> not very <u>hard</u> to wash down a flight of twenty stairs all painted or to
> wash with a handled mop, a space of painted floor as large as a small
> bedroom, and this is the floor mopping at South Hadley, that I have
> heard folks make so much talk about.[19]

Shipboard order, work, and discipline would not be so very different
from the discipline Mount Holyoke expected its students to develop.
Aboard the *J. J. Hathorn*, Susan would see decks swabbed and holy-
stoned, learn that a fire at sea was more to be feared than any gale, and,

of course, hear the ship's bells that divided and ordered each and every day. More than once during her time at sea, Susan must have recalled the bells system at Mount Holyoke, which she admitted "at first plagued me very much indeed," and which she described for Emily:

> Rise at a quarter of five, do chamber work,—get dressed and head combed and study a half hour before breakfast which is at half past six. . . . At half past eight we have <u>silent</u> study hours begin and you must not speak[,] only at the half hour bells. . . . If we had liberty to talk when we pleased we should not study at all. We must not enter rooms except at the five minutes bell before breakfast and for 15 minutes after—at the five min. bell before dinner till two, or a quarter past—and from the 5 min. bell before supper till 15 minutes after. If we could talk and go to one another's rooms just when we chose, the lessons would generally be <u>minus</u> with many.[20]

As Susan drew Emily a verbal map of the dormitory and discussed the assignment of roommates, she revealed a veteran teacher's grasp of how certain students can affect overall discipline:

> Each one writes a note to the teacher, telling with whom and in what <u>story</u>, not what room, she would like to be put. If they can possibly accommodate you, they commonly do, unless they think two <u>wild</u> ones want to get together, when they try to put a wild one and a steady one together.[21]

In the close quarters of shipboard life, Susan would have an opportunity to observe the interactions among a crew at sea—not very different at all, as her "Ship Graduate" essay presages, from dormitory life at Mount Holyoke.

🦢

We can only speculate about why Susan did not return to Mount Holyoke after July 1852. Had she become discouraged about the impossibility of graduating in just one year, or had she simply run out of money? Was the regimentation and confinement of seminary life too restrictive for a young woman who had tasted independence? Or was she eager to get back to Richmond? Had she, while teaching school, perhaps watched the *J. J. Hathorn* take shape and then slip into the Kennebec in November 1848, bound for distant ports? Had she fallen in love with the Hathorns' oldest son, Jode, and decided to marry him?

Other than Susan herself, no one can really be sure. But we do know that on September 20, 1854, Susan and Jode were married in Richmond. Shortly thereafter they left for Philadelphia, where the *J. J. Hathorn* waited for them. They cleared the port of Philadelphia on October 20 for Savannah, Georgia with a cargo of bacon, hollowware, plows, vinegar, suet, stoves, liquor, furniture, coal, alcohol, hay, pipe, twenty-two tons of "cut Pig Iron," iron bars, copper, nails, "Boiler Flues," plaster, and "1 Locom[o]tive + Tender Complete in 24 ps." with "192 RR[railroad] Wheels. on 96 Axles."[22] In Savannah the bark *J. J. Hathorn* landed its mixed cargo and shipped Georgia timber for Santiago de Cuba.

Thus the Hathorns—husband, wife, and bark—were back at sea as Susan began her diary. With it and the new year, Susan also began embroidering a pair of house-slipper-tops for Jode, the first of many needlework projects she would record throughout 1855. Her diary survives as the daily testimony of a woman who sometimes finds herself in unusual and dangerous circumstances, but one who seeks a reassuring order and meaning in her experience.

Jode invented the phrase "chalk ginger blue" to describe the breathtaking speed of one fantastic day's run on the deep blue Atlantic. He might easily have been describing the fleeting swiftness of the Hathorns' first year of marriage, the story of which his bride, Susan, has left us.

A Bride's Passage

Aboard the J. J. Hathorn

On the evening of Monday, January 1, 1855, Susan Hathorn sits at her husband's desk, opens a new marbled-cover daybook, dips a steel pen in black ink, and in a small, clean, practiced hand writes:

This begins another new year. What strange things may happen ere its close none now know. I have passed it very pleasantly indeed — begun to work a pair of shoes for Jode, and considering how many interruptions I have had through the day, have accomplished considerable.[1]

The desk at which Susan writes is the captain's, aboard the merchant bark *J. J. Hathorn*, at sea between Savannah and Santiago de Cuba. Eager for the unique experiences that await her, Susan is beginning the chronicle of a year of diverse and singular events in her life. As the bride of a young merchant captain, she is making her first trip abroad, and in fact her first ocean voyage ever. During 1855 she will discover the complex, cosmopolitan world of merchant sail, and the pleasures and challenges of domesticity when she returns to Maine.

Susan's New Year's Day continues with concerns even less like those of the parlor, as she turns from needlework to navigation. The *J. J. Hathorn* is having difficulty fixing its position. She reports: "This morning was cloudy and we did not get an altitude until past eleven which was not of much use. The sun did not come out fairly at noon, so we were hardly sure of the latitude."[2] Until it makes landfall, the *J. J. Hathorn* must search among the coral reefs for a safe passage into the Caribbean, hardly an auspicious way to spend a New Year's Day. Though Susan

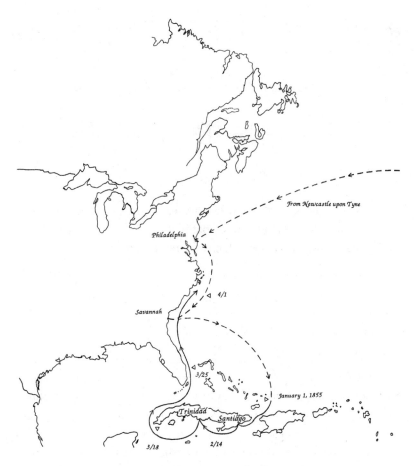

This map approximates the J. J. Hathorn's route and calls in Cuban ports, January
1–April 1, 1855. When the diary begins on January 1, the Hathorns were transiting
the passage between Grand Turk and the Caicos Islands. After stops in Santiago and
Trinidad de Cuba, the J. J. Hathorn sailed around the western end of Cuba, then
traveled on the Florida Current to the east coast of Florida and the Gulf Stream proper.
The broken lines approximate the J. J. Hathorn's travels during the second half of
1854, from Newcastle to Philadelphia to Savannah and on toward Cuba.

never gives their port or date of departure, on January 1 the *J. J. Hathorn* is a long seventeen days out of Savannah, and Susan says they are bound for the Cuban port of "St. Iago" (Santiago).[3] Susan's concern about the *J. J. Hathorn*'s position may be due in part to her naturally apprehensive temperament, but even the most sanguine sailor knew the Caribbean's coral reefs and pirates posed dangers for the unwary.

Susan's good cheer and admiration for her husband's seamanship are evident as she tells how the year's first day ended:

> *Jode had calculated correctly — at three, we made the lighthouse on the Grand Turk. They hoisted a signal which Jode hardly knew how to interpret — but finally concluded it must mean that he should lay by and not attempt to go through the Passage until morning. As soon as he put the ship about, the signal was lowered, which proved he guessed correctly.*[4]

Susan's "Jode" is Captain Joseph S. Hathorn,[5] named as the bark is for his uncle, Joseph Jefferson Hathorn, one of the vessel's original owners. This voyage is notable for Jode, his first as master of the *J. J. Hathorn*, his first as a husband. Married the previous September, Jode and Susan are clearly on their honeymoon, and Jode has exercised the captain's privilege of having his wife sail with him.[6]

Satisfied that the bark is in capable hands, the captain's bride turns to her own pursuits. The life of a seagoing wife holds long days and lonely hours, but fortunately Susan Hathorn has independent interests and resources with which to fill them. As her diary unfolds, Susan reveals herself to be an avid reader—a particular devotee of Sir Walter Scott—and an even more avid needlewoman. Mid-nineteenth-century women viewed "plain" sewing and mending as requisite wifely skills, and for those with the luxury of training and leisure time, "fancy" sewing was a pleasurable, productive accomplishment.[7]

Susan's commitment to needlework goes a step beyond. For her, needlework is a passion, a creative and emotional release that gives an otherwise reticent woman a tangible, unambiguous way to express her affection. Thus, beginning the pair of "shoes" for her husband is a highly significant way for Susan to mark the new year. Susan attacks every

task—even the embroidering of oak-leaf designs on Jode's slippers—
with single-minded zeal. If interruptions hinder her progress, she does
not disguise her impatience. Yet her needlework is something she pur-
sues without self-regard, and she minimizes her achievements: "I have
worked quite steadily all day on the shoes—shall finish one front tomorrow. It is by no means so great an undertaking to embroider a pair,
as I judged it to be."[8] As she fills this marbled-cover book, Susan Hathorn will write one account of 1855 in ink, and, with her yarn and
thread, as Jode's slipper-tops and later more practical projects take
shape, she will fashion a gloss—a second, parallel story—on the first
year of her marriage.

The new year's second morning brings somewhat improved weather—
"Cloudy today, but a most glorious breeze"—and Susan also reports that
the *J. J. Hathorn* has passed a difficult test: "This morning we came safely
through Turk's Island Passage and did not repent laying by last night.
It is not a very safe place to sail through by dark."[9] At 4 P.M. that day,
when the sun comes out at last, Susan enters the first of her many notations of the *J. J. Hathorn's* coordinates. She uses her own style—"long.
was 72″07. Latitude, 20″27."[10] These coordinates place them forty
miles off the northwest cape of Hispaniola, the present day Haiti and
Dominican Republic. They will run for the Windward Passage and follow a southwesterly course between Hispaniola and Cuba. Exhilarated
by their day's progress, Susan says, "If this breeze lasts through the
night, we shall make St. Iago tomorrow! Can now see high land (at
6 P.M.) which we suppose is Tortuga. There is a full rigged Brig in
sight."[11] As the *J. J. Hathorn* safely navigates the Windward Passage, she
is ebullient: "We had a fine breeze all last night—our good ship plows
the waves right merrily."[12] They progress along Cuba's southeastern
coast, where the island's highest range, the Sierra Maestra, meets the sea,
and she writes:

> *This morning, land could be seen upon both sides of us — the tall mountains
> of Cuba close at our right. I never saw anything grander than these moun-*

Morro Castle, part of the Spanish fortification of Santiago de Cuba that began in the sixteenth century, guards the narrow strategic entrance to Santiago Bay. On the rocks at the base of its cliff, as Susan recorded in her diary, the J. J. Hathorn *briefly went aground.*

tains — with the sea breaking up against their bases. Oh! if one could always have such a glorious sun, fine breeze and everything else so favorable, there would be no life in the world, like one "on the Ocean wave." The full moon rose gloriously over the Cuban mountains.[13]

With the favorable breeze, the entrance to Santiago harbor, some two hundred miles west of the passage, is in sight "from the topmast" of the *J. J. Hathorn* by the evening of January 3. In noting the first of several full moons to appear in her diary, Susan's prose seems momentarily liberated from its usual Down-East Maine terseness. She quickly camouflages her excitement over reaching her first foreign port with matters of seamanship: "So we shall heave to for tonight—, and enter the harbor betimes tomorrow."[14]

Susan has learned that a sailing ship's progress relies on the forces of nature, and that one day's glorious breeze is the next day's dead calm. Yet she displays little patience with the delays involved in a vessel's arrival in port. Only four days into her new journal, Susan's rapture over the moonlit mountains evaporates in frustration. The port is in sight, but despite human effort and wishes, the *J. J. Hathorn* cannot reach it. She still notes the dramatic purple sunsets, but she fumes, "Not a breath of wind stirring to send a body on his way." The rough chop of shallow coastal waters complicates even her writing in the diary: "Intended to keep this journal very neatly indeed, but it is so difficult to write, when the ship jumps about so. I fear me, I shall fail."[15]

The *J. J. Hathorn*'s so-near-and-yet-so-far situation puts Susan completely out of sorts. She even complains about her needlework, saying she must stop working on Jode's shoes because she has "used up all of one shade, that I want the most," which obviously would be obtainable if they could just make port. Yet along with her anxious, impatient nature, and even on the hot, frustrating day that follows, Susan possesses an equanimity that forbids her from seeing situations as totally unredeemed:

> *Today has been very showery — considerable rain has fallen, while the sun was shining as brightly as could be. The weather is as hot as dog days. The Thermometer in the cabin, stood above 80°. The sun seemed burning hot. I never saw any thing half so beautiful as this sky here — at sunset, there is a peculiar purple tinge, that lends a coloring to these glorious mountains, that is beautiful beyond description. This afternoon, there were three rainbows at once. I have been as smart as can be today — have worked on the shoe and could complete the front tomorrow, if I only had the needful shade of worsted.*[16]

On the first Saturday of January, the *J. J. Hathorn* lies at the approach to Santiago harbor waiting for a pilot. After the weather, the pilot is the other major variable governing a vessel's arrival in port, and obtaining the services of a harbor pilot in 1855 involved an element of luck and often some maddening delays, especially in the view of no-nonsense

Yankee skippers or their wives. Captains might wait days before a pilot came alongside to offer his services, and even then negotiations might not prove successful. In some ports a captain had to go ashore to engage a harbor pilot, and even then a pilot's expertise was no sure thing. Despite Susan's impatience, the Hathorns' delay is not as horrendous as it might have been; Jode does get a pilot that day. Susan describes Santiago harbor as the pilot takes the *J. J. Hathorn* in:

> At half past three, P.M., one came aboard, and took us in as far as the
> Mor{r}o Castle, when the wind suddenly changed and came in a gust, "dead
> ahead." So the anchor was dropped, and here we are, just under the battle-
> ments of this old feudal castle. I never saw anything like it — I would give
> anything if Lucy could only be here to see it too. . . .[17] As I write, I can hear
> the breakers, just above us, as they dash against the rocks, which look as if
> eaten away by canker. The Light house is very near, and looks beautifully.
> Then the air is so warm and balmy. Oh this is the place to live — a thought
> of winter would never enter one's head.[18]

Thoughts of winter, however, and of home and family—especially her favorite sister, Lucy—clearly *are* present in Susan's head. Compared with the tropical heat, towering island sunsets, and mountain moonrises along the Cuban coast, the first week of January back in Richmond could not be more different, with the frozen Kennebec, snow, and ice under low slate-colored skies. With her adventure of seeing the world momentarily stalled, Susan's expression of homesickness—her longing for her sister—has a peculiarly Victorian cast. She does not simply wish Lucy could see the Morro; she "would give anything if *Lucy could only be here* to see it too." [19] Susan's expression of affection recalls the many mid-nineteenth-century wedding trips that were spent traveling from home to home, visiting relatives.[20] And so to relieve her homesickness, Susan turns to her needlework and works on Jode's shoe "as long as I could for want of worsted, then took the other pattern." [21]

From atop its two-hundred-foot-high bluff, the fortress El Morro guards the entrance to Santiago's natural harbor, an almost landlocked bay on which a settlement was established by Spain in 1514 to serve as Cuba's first colonial capital. The *J. J. Hathorn* is entering the bay in

which U.S. Admiral William T. Sampson would trap and sink Admiral
Cervera's Spanish Fleet a few days after Theodore Roosevelt and his
Rough Riders' heroics on nearby San Juan Hill. But Santiago Bay would
wait another forty years for those events, and the Hathorns are eager to
put in.

🦭

Harbor pilots could be a captain's salvation or his ruin, particularly in
the days of sail. The Saturday Santiago pilot takes them only as far as
the Morro. Because her diary has no printed spaces for Sundays, Susan
initially makes no separate Sunday entries; however, in the entry of
Monday, January 8, she mentions that a pilot, presumably a second, had
come on board on Sunday. Journals of sea captains and their wives make
clear that pilots often extorted bribes and pamperings, and being at
their mercy, captains generally complied. Judging from the Hathorns'
arrival in the port of Santiago—no masterpiece of ship handling—the
pilots' prima donna antics may have been masking a certain measure of
incompetence.

   As their second Santiago pilot weighs the *J. J. Hathorn* anchor and
goes back out to turn around, Susan reports with dismay,

> *In so doing, went in contact with an English brig, loaded with fish, which
> came in after us and anchored close to us. But little damage was done to
> either brig or Barque. By the time we had tacked, all favorable symptoms
> had disappeared and here we seem likely to stay.*[22]

With the *J. J. Hathorn* back outside the harbor, Susan shuts out the problem by finishing the front to Jode's shoe ("It is very showy indeed"). She
is determined to look on the bright side ("It seems as if we had ended
the voyage. I feel as happy and contented in sight of these mountains as
if such were really the case"). But her impatience is not far beneath the
surface, for she concludes, "Should have washed had I thought we should
be here so long."[23]

   When the pilot gives up and disembarks on the following very rainy
and blustery day, Jode throws maritime law to the wind and takes mat-

ters into his own hands. Susan concludes her description with the masterful understatement that one comes to see is her style.

> *Then { Jode and the crew} attempted to get the ship inside the harbor with the small anchor — succeded {sic} nicely until in the very narrowest part of the harbor, when the wind suddenly changed and blew us ashore under the walls of the Mor{r}o. Finally a pilot came to our assistance — also the Captain of the Fort sent his boat to us, and we came off "gallantly" as the Spaniard said, and anchored in the channel in a favorable place. Thought at one time we were "a gone goose," but there was no damage done as we can discover. It would have been a bad job if she had got ashore, as we had no Pilot on board.*[24]

By Wednesday after dinner, a pilot is now back on board, but he has no better luck. Susan describes another collision that

> *put us off against an American ship that had anchored close in the channel, bows on — the Pilot steered so close to her we carried away her jib-boom — said we must do that or go ashore, & that it was unlawful to anchor so. Hope such is the case. The wind died away, so we could not reach the town after all, but had to anchor in the stream once more.*[25]

Besides her needlework, domestic chores and aquatic wildlife provide diversions for Susan. On the eighth, she reports, amazingly, "Saw a dolphin for the first time"; and on the thirteenth, surely in error, she reports seeing "a penguin" from the *J. J. Hathorn*'s deck.[26] At midweek, Susan writes, "Pilot brought me a little cunning kitten,"[27] but since she never mentions the kitten again, perhaps it is just a standard pilot's diversion for a captain's wife.

The day of the kitten's visit Susan starts to do the wash but "skinned my hands—so got Hannah, the stewardess to finish." This is the first mention of Hannah, the cook's wife, of whom Susan will have more to say later. Stewards' and cooks' wives sometimes shipped with their husbands as assistants. Holding a unique place in the all-important chain of shipboard command, a steward reported directly to the captain (whose personal attendant he was), and not to the mates, as other crew members were required to do. Cooks, like sail-makers and carpenters, were part of the shipboard contingent called "idlers," crewmembers who did not stand watch and thereby were outside the usual chain of shipboard command. A steward's or cook's wife would be there to assist her husband, not act as the seafaring wife's personal servant.

Though Hannah finishes the wash, Susan does not entrust to her the ironing of Jode's shirts. Susan would know it is important that Jode look his absolute best in Santiago, for the captain represents the ship's interests in negotiations with port officials, shipping agents, and consignees in port. "I have ironed the shirts, eight of them—had capital luck," she reports.[28] Yet a strict shipboard rule complicates Susan's ironing: the captain's wife is not to be in the galley, which is where the irons are heated. Susan even comments on this logistical problem: "The irons do not hold the heat and by the time I got one towel ironed, had to trudge to the galley for a new flat."[29]

As the *J. J. Hathorn* finally approaches its Santiago berth that Thursday, Susan is treated to her first bevy of foreign customs officials. "All the wise heads of Santiago de Cuba then came off in a royal barge," she quips, "and paid us the honor of a visit.—a part of them spoke broken English." Jode goes ashore and the *J. J. Hathorn*'s bill of health is found to be in order, whereupon Jode reports to the office of the cargo consignee, Mr. Brooks. There Jode learns that the *J. J. Hathorn* needs to be moved about two miles farther "down the river" to unload.

Susan quickly develops a dim view of Cuban bureaucracy: "A custom house officer, who cannot speak a word of English, is to accompany us, and to favor us with his presence, while we are discharging."[30] On that hot Friday when Susan is running back and forth with the irons, she considers the custom of the siesta: "Our police officer betook himself to his bunk forenoon and afternoon—think he enjoyed himself far better than when up."[31]

Jode secures the official docking permit, a hat for himself, and a quantity of mangoes, which he brings back and Susan eats with abandon. The sailors improvise a deck awning for Susan over the ship's aftercabin; finally she has "a beautiful cool place to sit," continue her work on Jode's shoe, and observe the "penguin."[32]

Now that they are in port, Jode and Susan can expect to call on and be called upon by other vessels' masters and their wives. That Friday evening a "Captain Inghram" (Susan later corrects his name to Captain Igan) is the first to pay a visit to the *J. J. Hathorn*, and he invites the Hathorns to accompany him on a sight-seeing trip into the mountains that Sunday.

Unlike the diaries of many whaling captains' wives, Susan's does not make much ado about her religious observations. Ironically, while the outwardly more pious whalers would regularly break the Sabbath to "lower for fish" if their holds were empty, the more secular merchant-men generally observed the Sabbath as a day of rest, in port and at sea. Indeed, until Susan divides her diary space for Monday, March 19, and makes a separate entry for Sunday, March 18, she respectfully confines herself to her book's printed format, which gives spaces for only Monday through Saturday on its two-page-per-week spread.[33]

Thus with no unloading to supervise on Sunday, the Hathorns can accept Captain Igan's invitation, and they set out on a Sunday morning trip to "the Copper Works," which Susan writes about that night:

Had one of the finest times I ever had in my life. The English people were very hospitable — could not do enough for a body. Went on a horse back ride after dinner — managed better than I anticipated. Breakfasted with Capt. Tibbetts — dined at the Harveys — called on Dr. Chi{b}nall's family and spent the night at Mr. Harvey's. This morning, took the Cars[34] for the Ship, where we arrived safely about nine.[35]

Back at the ship on Monday, Susan writes letters to her relatives. A vessel carrying the mail has come in and Jode rows "to town" to collect theirs, but no letters have come for them.[36] This will be a hard-working week for both the *J. J. Hathorn*, landing its cargo, and Susan, who must take advantage of the port to accomplish certain domestic duties. On Tuesday she "had the water hot by half past seven and finished my wash by eleven." After dinner—the midday meal—she exercises the in-port prerogative of the master's wife (the cook likely being ashore on leave) and bakes "two loaves of cup cake, and a host of ginger crackers."[37] A captain's wife needs something fancier than a sea cook can muster to offer her husband's colleagues when they call.

On Tuesday, the sixteenth, Jode has better luck with the mail. Susan reports letters from several family members: their brother-in-law "Brown,"[38] Jode's younger brother Jeffy, and one of Susan's sisters, Molly. The Richmond mail assures Susan and Jode that all is well back home. That afternoon, Captain Igan calls again and proposes a second copper mine trip to the mines at "Coubra" (Cobre); since this trip will be on Wednesday, only Susan will be able to go.[39] That day, she

> got up at five and was all ready for the Cars before Capt Igan. We had a fine ride through the flower decked country — much shorter than the first one to the Cobu {sic} mines. Arrived at Mr. Harvey's at half past eight — found they were not expecting us until night. Spent the day very happily indeed.[40]

In fact, Susan spends most of this week ashore, without Jode, but Penelope-like, she diligently continues working on his shoe-top. She spends one entire day with Dr. Chibnall's wife, teaching her different knitting stitches and doing some crocheting for her.[41] While Susan appreciates the Santiagan hospitality, a bit of Yankee disapproval creeps into her description of the slower-paced Caribbean lifestyle:

> Mrs. Chibnall sent her maid for me at nine. I wore my lawn dress — and the maid took my blue bauge[42] skirt, my sack-collar &c. on her head, and followed after me — this is Spanish fashion. We breakfasted at twelve A.M. and dined at six. They are so indolent, the ladies do not dress until after dinner. Then a Bruce or wrapper is all sufficient, for every purpose.[43]

By the next morning, Susan herself is going colonial. Spending the night at Mrs. Harvey's house, Susan writes that even she did not get up early, contrary to her nature. After a late breakfast the entire household, including Susan, strolls out together to the shops, and she buys a "hair comb" and handkerchiefs. She extends her affinity for doctors' wives when she meets the impressive "Madame Pollard, a Spanish lady who married an English physician. She was very stately and noble looking."[44]

On Saturday Susan rises early and that day experiences her first Spanish *mercado*:

> *It was a curious market place. The women sat flat on the ground and spread*
> *the various articles they had for sale about them. As we passed the church,*
> *peeped in to see the devotees — the virgin's house was very splendid, and the*
> *organ sounded grandly. . . . Through the day, all the time I could get worked*
> *on my shoe. As we were at dinner, Jode made his appearance! The negroes*
> *danced the tumbour in the evening and we walked up a little while to see*
> *them. It was curious and one would not imagine that they had worked all*
> *this 1 week.*[45]

During the week that follows, Susan is in the social swim, visiting
the intriguing "Madame Lavine" and others, but she also continues her
in-port ship-housekeeping chores (airing out of flannels, etc.), and she
hemstitches a handkerchief she had bought in Cobre for Jode.[46] Captain
Igan continues in his role as social director for the visiting captains and
engages a box for them at the theater on Tuesday. The theater party
includes "Mons. and Madame Lavine," Captain Igan, the Harveys, and
the Hathorns. Susan writes:

> *A late night: The plays were beautiful. The first act or whatever it may be*
> *called was of tableaux — representing the gods & goddesses. The 2d, rope*
> *dancing — third standing on one another's shoulders & heads. 4th Dances —*
> *5th A Pantomime.*[47]

The theater party is such a success that the group goes again two evenings later. "The plays were excellent," Susan reports, but this evening is
blemished: "Had my gala plaid shawl and printed Cashmere stolen from
the boat."[48] Moreover, Susan has overdone things a bit—late nights and
island food are playing havoc with her digestive system. She doctors
herself with rhubarb, the common herbal remedy for diarrhea, and reports her affliction in graphic, clinical terms. "Do not feel very well,"
she writes two days later, but "I am still crocheting."[49]

Life in port on the *J. J. Hathorn* has been anything but peaceful among
the crew. During the previous week, Susan recorded "a regular mess in

camp. Mate, Steward & Stewardess at war." Now there are fresh hostili-
ties among the hands, plus an additional complication for the young
new captain to deal with: "Another war in the camp—trouble between
the mates and a Dutchman, one of the sailors. Jode took Bill up to the
hospital as he has been a long while sick." [50]

One month earlier, on December 10, 1854, Jode Hathorn celebrated his
twenty-second birthday. [51] Twenty-two was a young age to shoulder the
responsibilities of a vessel's chief executive officer, husbanding not only
the usual vessel, cargo, and crew but also his new-sailor wife, Susan.
Unmistakably, that Jode's family held the majority of shares in the *J. J.
Hathorn* is relevant to his being named master. Additionally, his being
given the command may have stemmed from an understandable disarray
in the Hathorns' business affairs following the death of Jode's uncle
Joseph Jackson Hathorn in March 1854. However, many nineteenth-
century sailing masters took their first commands in their twenties, and
officers who failed to reach captain by about thirty were often deemed
unlikely to ever do so, and something of a failure. Past that age, an
officer could go as mate, commanding a vessel only in an emergency,
such as a captain's death or incapacitation.

A detailed description of the captain's role appeared in print in 1841.
In that year, Richard Henry Dana Jr., whose *Two Years Before the Mast*
had given American readers an account of "the life of a common sailor
at sea as it really is," published an even more distinctly nonfiction work
titled *The Seaman's Friend*. [52] Dana, a lawyer, described the relationship
between master and men in terms of the most basic legal convention,
the contract: "The master of every vessel of the United States . . . must
make a contract in writing (shipping articles) with each seaman, speci-
fying the voyage, terms of time, &c." [53] Shipping articles of the time are
long on the ship's, owners', and officers' rights and expectations and
prerogatives, and short on the seaman's side of the bargain. From the
seaman's side, ship's articles are not an agreement a person with a choice,
or any bargaining power, would want to accept, but many hands did not

understand, could not do better, or simply wanted to go to sea under any terms.

The captain's authority was absolute and unquestionable, but in return he was expected to see not only to the safe arrival of vessel and cargo but also to the safety and health of his men:

[E]very vessel of seventy-five tons or upwards, navigated by six or more persons in the whole, and bound from the United States to any port in the West Indies, is required to have a chest of medicines, put up by an apothecary of known reputation, and accompanied by directions for administering the same. The chest must also be examined at least once a year and supplied with fresh medicines.[54]

Jode's responsibility for health aboard his vessel would grow increasingly important over the next several months. By the end of January, Jode becomes concerned about his wife's health and about the health of at least one crew member. Susan writes that she is "very feverish indeed at night . . . took two emetics, which threw off the fever, but weakened me badly." With Susan so weak she "can hardly get out of bed," Jode takes an unusual step that Susan describes in her diary: "the men did not work, as I was so nervous." Madame Lavine, who has a reputation for being "very good in sickness," comes to see Susan and "proscribes" for her.[55]

On the following day with Susan improved, the crew resumes unloading the cargo—lumber—surely a noisy business. Jode apparently would like to get out of Santiago as soon as possible, for he breaks another maritime rule—that masters never perform manual labor—as Susan reports he is "at work in the hold with the men."[56] Susan's new friend, Mrs. Harvey, perhaps recognizing that the Hathorns will soon be leaving Santiago, sends for Susan, who is still too ill to go visiting: "Mr. Matthews came down from Cobre to look at the lumber—Mrs. Harvey sent for Jane & myself to go up. Jane returned with him but is coming back Friday."[57]

The crew is working overtime, too, in keeping the relationships among them lively. The "war" the Hathorns found on their return from

The rigging and sails of a typical three-masted bark make it an easily identified vessel. It carries all square sails on yardarms on all masts except the last (or "mizzen") mast, where it carries fore-and-aft sails and there are no yardarms. Mid-nineteenth-century wooden barks, like the J. J. Hathorn, *were usually three-masted; some immense iron barks at the end of the century had as many as five masts.*

the theater has turned into an ongoing conflict. Susan reports "Strange doings in the galley. Stewardess drunk as a beast—thinks her husband so—had a regular fight—." [58] At the close of this entry, Susan casually mentions the good news that inwardly must have thrilled her: "Jode chartered the ship today for Europe." [59]

❧

To what kind of vessel do this young couple entrust themselves for the Atlantic crossing? Many nineteenth-century photographs of ships at anchor and generic paintings of them both amidst dramatic and placid seas exist, but unfortunately none of the *J. J. Hathorn* seems to survive. Two written records do, however, describe the vessel: the *J. J. Hathorn's* original registration document, and its entry in the *American Lloyds' Registry.*

As a bark, [60] the *J. J. Hathorn* is a square-rigged vessel with three masts. Carrying conventional square sails on the first two masts, a bark

*The J. J. Hathorn's original permanent enrollment certificate registered the vessel at
Bath, Maine, on November 29, 1848. A vessel's enrollment was the government license
issued by the District Port, naming the owners and first master and certifying the vessel's
capacity (in this case, 398 25/95 tons) and general description. Enrollment papers, or
copies of them, were a required part of the vessel's identification documents carried by the
captain and presented upon arrival in port to the consul or his deputy. If a vessel underwent extensive repairs or alterations, re-enrollment was required.*

carries fore-and-aft rigged sails on its third ("mizzen") mast. Barks were
built not for speed but for their cargo capacity. The racy clipper ships
whose dashes to China for low-volume, high-ticket cargoes such as tea
and opium had by the mid-1850s utterly captured the public imagina-
tion. Clippers were completely square-rigged ships with "sharper," less
capacious hulls, carrying more different kinds of sails than barks. If clippers were the skittish thoroughbreds racing for high stakes, barks were
the draft horses of the merchant fleet—unglamorous but steady in the
harness and capable of carrying the bulky staples of life. And while a
clipper might make a two-week Atlantic crossing, a captain whose bark
crossed in four could say he had had a good run.[61]

Built at the height of the sailing-fleet expansion, the bark *J. J. Hathorn*
was issued its Permanent Enrollment on November 29, 1848, at the
Port of Bath, Maine. Now in the National Archives, this document
shows James Wakefield, deputy surveyor in the Port District of Bath,
certifying that

> said Ship or Vessel has
> Two Decks, and three Masts, and that
> her length is One hundred twenty feet,
> her breadth Twenty seven feet,
> her depth Thirteen feet, six inches,
> and that she measures Three hundred ninety-eight and 25/95 Tons,
> that she is a Bark[,] has a square stern[,] no galleries, and a Billet head.[62]

Having given a sense of the vessel's scale and its masts and decks, the
document tells that the *J. J. Hathorn* had the usual square stern, which
had no windows ("galleries") in it, and did not carry a figurehead, being
instead decorated at the prow with a "billet," an ornamental carved
scroll.[63] The *J. J. Hathorn* may be seen as a utilitarian vessel built with
an eye toward restraint in decoration.

The second source, the *American Lloyds' Registry of American and Foreign Shipping*, adds certain details to the surveyor's enrollment and cor-
roborates its basic facts.[64] *Lloyds'* describes the *J. J. Hathorn* as a "Full"
model—not "medium," "sharp," or "clipper"—which suggests gener-

ous, robust proportions. *Lloyds'* lists the *J. J. Hathorn*'s first master as a Richmond man, Captain J. B. Stuart, who also appears among the seven listed in the "Owner or Consignee" column at the time of registration.

Lloyds' gives further information on the vessel in its rating, which was based on construction materials and worksmanship and was used as a factor in calculating cargo insurance premiums.[65] *Lloyds'* rates the *J. J. Hathorn* a Class A2 vessel, or a vessel of the Second Class. The difference between *Lloyds'* First Class and Second Class has to do with materials and construction, for both categories

> will imply confidence for the transportation of perishable cargoes on long voyages. The degrees of Third Class [A2- and A2½] will not imply confidence for the conveyance of cargoes in their nature subject to sea damage.[66]

The *J. J. Hathorn*'s rating derived chiefly from the fact that it was constructed of "mixed woods" (not "hard" or "hackmatack"), with fastenings of copper and iron.[67]

In many ways the emblem of the Hathorn family, the *J. J. Hathorn* will call Richmond its home port for as long as it sails. The bark is the eponymous pride of the family, carrying the heir to Jefferson and Joseph Hathorn's fledgling shipping dynasty and his bride on a voyage significant to all the Hathorns, especially to Jode and Susan: his first command and their honeymoon.

Cuban Ports

As February begins, Susan and Jode are still in port in Santiago de Cuba, but it is not surprising that they dally there. Winter is not the best time to cross the Atlantic, and most captains considered it the ideal time of year to call in West Indian ports. The Caribbean's long, oppressive, humid summers made many cargoes difficult to deliver in prime condition, and warmer weather brought increased incidence of malaria and yellow fever, both of which frequently proved fatal.

Susan's gastrointestinal infection in Santiago is nothing so serious, and while recuperating she reads the first of the books whose titles she mentions in her diary. Though she calls G. P. R. James's book "a foolish novel," *Agincourt* reveals that Susan has a taste for historical romance.[1] She reads it till her "head aches" on one day, and on the next writes, "Finished 'Agincourt'—read until my head ached again." [2]

But perhaps she is reading assiduously so she will not have to deal with the Cuban customs officer. As the new month begins, a welcome change occurs on the *J. J. Hathorn*: "The Officer from the Custom House left us and rejoiced he was to bid the ship adieu. Another one has come in his place." [3]

Her health improved, Susan goes ashore with Jode and buys towels that caught her eye on an earlier shopping excursion. The Santiagans seem to recognize that the young Hathorns will soon be leaving, and as the social pace is quickened, Susan revels in both the attention and her exotic shopping finds.

Mr. Harvey, from Cobre, came down this morning before we were out of bed. Breakfasted with us, and went to Cuba with Jode. Got me half a dozen beau-

tiful towels for $3.25. and some Guava Jelly — the latter is very cheap —
only $2.00 per doz. boxes. Mr. Harvey did not bring Jane back with him,
as she is not very well, but urged me to go to Cobre, as soon as I shall be able.[4]

The Hathorns' eagerness to get away will preclude additional visits
to Cobre. On Saturday, February 3, Susan writes in her diary:

Very cool indeed and cloudy. About ten o'clock A.M. the last log was taken
out of the ship! Now good bye to Cuba. Jode was ashore this morning —
engaged ballast — if the Custom house will permit him to take it. Is now
ashore to see. Rufus to haul in to the wharf before night — so as to begin
early Monday morning to load.[5]

Since Jode is getting permission to load ballast, the *J. J. Hathorn* will not
take on cargo in Santiago but will call elsewhere for it. Unscrupulous
merchant captains sometimes would use the term *ballast* with great license, but Jode is playing strictly by the rules with the officials.

One interesting feature of nineteenth-century life at sea was the
other-than-human passengers, both authorized and unauthorized. The
J. J. Hathorn did not carry the chickens, ducks, geese, goats, and cows
shipped as provisions by long-haul passenger ships and some whalers,
but Susan discovers they are carrying stowaways. On the first Saturday
morning of February, she comments wryly on the first of her battles with
the interlopers:

Had a regular "bed bug slaughter" this morning. Found the things in the
sofa — under the buttons — a nest under each one. What I shall do with the
cock roaches now, is a question of great moment with me. They are fairly
taking possession of my quarters.[6]

The next week, she continues her exterminating job and puts "more
turpentine about my trunk to keep the cockroaches out. They are very
troublesome indeed." The bedbugs are a tougher problem than she
thought, for she continues to find them infesting the sofa. "Hope I have
the 'last of the Mohigans' now," she says after several skirmishes.[7]

As the *J. J. Hathorn* lingers in Santiago and Susan finishes her in-port
housekeeping chores, she gets to see the city of Santiago by day, for as

she notes, she had previously seen it only by night, during the theater parties. Two friends of Jode's—a Nova Scotian, Captain Holmes, and Captain French of Prospect, Maine—arrive in port, and Susan and Jode visit with them. Ashore, Susan spends a leisurely day with Madame Lavine:

> *A beautiful day — have spent it very happily with Madam Lavine — she has tried, at least, to make me enjoy myself. She delayed breakfast, but had dinner two hours earlier so we could walk out to see the curious flowers. Got a Castor plant (that from which oil is made), a leaf of the tree from which jelly is made, and lots of things. Have worked on my shoe — have got along nicely. Every thing seemed to go right.*[8]

On the same day, Susan indulges herself in one last tropical feast of "water melons & mush melons, as much as I wanted to eat."

Jode has captain's duties to attend to. In addition to arranging for and overseeing the loading of ballast, Jode takes the chronometer to be calibrated before the ocean crossing,[9] for its accuracy is crucial to determining the vessel's navigational position. As she will do several more times during the year, Susan audits the *J. J. Hathorn*'s records while still in Santiago, spending a "whole forenoon over the Account Book— gained nothing only satisfaction as to the accuracy of the work."[10] The amount of customs paperwork created by multiple consignees and importers for a shipload of cargo could be staggering.

The eighth of February, the day following Susan's pleasant visit with Madame Lavine, would have lasting repercussions for the *J. J. Hathorn* on its eastbound Atlantic crossing. The day began pleasantly, as Susan writes,

> *A warm morning but a nice cool day. Went to Cuba in the morning with Jode and spent the day with Mr. Brooks' family — they are very pleasant people. Visited the Cathedral, which is the only thing worth seeing in Cuba. Bought me a linen dress and some worsteds for the shoes.*[11]

The Hathorns find friends waiting at the *J. J. Hathorn* to bid them farewell, but when Jode goes back ashore for the last time to settle their accounts, Susan writes that "Mr. Bell fell from the upper deck clear down to the lower hold. He was very badly hurt. Sent for Jode, but did not get a Physician." [12]

Susan never mentions Mr. Bell's rank, but he is the *J. J. Hathorn's* second mate. (Mates alone are addressed as *Mr.*, and the duties of Mr. Bickford, of whom she wrote, "looked over Mr. Bickford's account of the timber," [13] indicate he was first mate.) Despite her initial alarm, Susan is not urgently concerned about Mr. Bell's injury. The guests stay until 10 P.M. that night. The next day, she reports that Jode got up early to go looking for a doctor, but "found a nobody, who did nothing for Mr. Bell." In the description of the day's subsequent events, getting a doctor is of secondary importance to getting out of the harbor: "After dinner, as we could not sail for want of wind, Jode went after Dr. Forbes, the English Physician. He bled him—took over a quart of blood—he seemed easier, but is very weak and sore." [14] Susan busies herself with her own preparations for the voyage: "I have been cleaning my room. . . . Fixed the fruit to carry to sea—tied it all up & drove nails to hang it on." [15]

At 6 A.M. on Saturday morning, February 10, the *J. J. Hathorn* with its ailing second mate "got under weigh," but gets only as far as the Morro, where Susan recalls their near disaster on the rocks on their way in. That day she writes,

> *I got up early, washed Mr. B. & did all for him I could. Set my room to rights and spent the most of the day looking over accounts, and writing. After completing my book-keeping, worked on the shoe — one back is done, except a little filling in.* [16]

On the same day, she writes, "Jode went out this P.M. to try his chronometer with Capt. Holm[e]s—he supped with us." Over the next weeks Mr. Bell's lingering injury will consume much of Susan's attention, but the Hathorns are not yet away from Santiago harbor and have not even picked up their Cuban cargo.

In the National Archives' repository of consular returns are summary reports submitted quarterly, semiannually, and/or annually by U.S. consuls abroad accounting for the American shipping coming through the consul's port. In 1855 the U.S. consul for Santiago was one Stephen

The Consular Return for January–June 1855 for Santiago de Cuba shows the J. J. Hathorn's arrival and departure on line 5. The entry for the bark Catherine (line 4) bears a striking similarity in captain's name, port of origin, home port, and so on. Consuls were political appointees of the Department of State and, in addition to their stipends, kept fees they collected in the course of overseeing U.S. trade pass through their ports. Most filed "consular returns" reporting this traffic at least semiannually.

Cochran, whose "Consular Return of American Vessels arriving at, and departing from the Port of St. Yago de Cuba, from the first day of January to the 30th day of June 1855 inclusive" lists the *J. J. Hathorn's* January–February call. Cochran's report is both helpful and puzzling.[17]

For January 12, the consul records the arrival of a "Bark Catherine," three hundred tons, hailing from Richmond, Maine, out of Savannah, Georgia. Further, it lists an incoming crew of nine Americans and two "Foreigners," and says that no port was touched between Savannah and Santiago, that the cargo inbound is lumber valued at $3,500, and that the cargo outbound is ballast to be landed in a foreign port. The *Catherine* is listed as departing for "Trinidad de Cuba" on January 27 with a crew of nine Americans and two foreigners. The name of the master is given as "Harthorn."

The next entry in the consul's return is for January 15, four days after Susan's diary says the "barge" of Cuban dignitaries boarded the ship in Santiago harbor. This vessel is also a bark, its name is *Harthorn*, and its master is listed as "S. H. Harthorn." This ship's tonnage is listed as 285, and the value of its lumber cargo is listed as $3,000. All the other particulars listed are identical—crew, nationalities, ports, etc.—except for the departure date, listed as "February 3d." No mention of any of the *J. J. Hathorn*'s misadventures in the harbor appears in the "Remarks" column. Actually, Cochran, the consul, found nothing whatsoever remarkable in his port during the months of January, February, and March 1855, though Santiago saw twenty-five ships totaling 5,747 tons arrive, land cargo valued at nearly $100,000,[18] and ship cargo valued at a total of $126,800.79. Cochran's ledger does not have columns for fees levied (which consuls themselves got to keep) or for noncrew aboard the ship, two categories that many consular returns include. Mr. Cochran, a rather casual consul, makes liberal use of dittos in places where dittos make no sense. This loose record-keeping style among U.S. consuls in Cuba is still prevalent one year later, when the *J. J. Hathorn* will make another important call at Trinidad de Cuba.

In the consular returns, as elsewhere, there is no official record documenting Susan's coming or going in Santiago or any other port. As with almost every other maritime wife who sailed with her husband, Susan's passage through the ports the *J. J. Hathorn* touched is recorded only in her own diary.

🌊

Susan is not a woman often given to emotional displays or even to direct expressions of her feelings, but her feelings about Santiago de Cuba are quite unmistakable as the *J. J. Hathorn* heads seaward toward Trinidad de Cuba, about three hundred miles west on Cuba's southern coast:

> We got out yesterday or just at night rather, from that horrible hole where we had so many misfortunes — the wind was fair until eight or nine o'clock — then calm, but there was a very heavy head sea. The barque plunged into it strangely and sent me to bed in fifteen minutes, sea sick.[19]

Susan's report of seasickness during the first days away from port has many parallels in sea-travelers' journals, particularly those of whaling wives. Women in the whaling fleet were much longer at sea, and even upon landing they experienced nausea until they got their "land legs," while whaling-fleet children who learned to walk on a ship would fail in their first tries at land walking and revert briefly to crawling.[20]

Of course Susan has no way of knowing what awaits her in other ports. The *J. J. Hathorn* heads westward around the point of Cabo Cruz and then northwest past the cays known as Jardines del la Reina. Susan describes the condition of Mr. Bell, who is unable to sleep, with customary understatement, saying he "hardly seems so well."[21] Like the *J. J. Hathorn* in the rough coastal waters, the state of Mr. Bell's health rises and falls through the week.

Susan's thoughts turn homeward, as she observes the February 12 double birthday in the Lennan family: "This is a fine day and Mother fifty-five and Fanny twelve years old tonight. Would much like to take a peep into Mother Lennan's cottage on the post road to see how they are faring through the winter."[22] Along with working on the shoes, Susan is working at becoming a captain's wife, and she records participating in fixing their position:

> *Fine cool day — got up long before sun-rise to get the Lat. and Long. by observing the sun's upper & lower limb. After all, it rose in a cloud. . . . Worked up a sight this morning, which put us out of Jode's reckoning — made a degree to the westward. According to chronometer, our Long. at 8 A.M. is 79"53'. We can get the Long. five times during a day. At Noon, Long. 79"53'. Lat. 20"43'. At 4 P.M. Long. 79"75{,} at sunset 80"01. Have worked on my shoe — got along nicely, although I did not begin to work until late.*[23]

Susan's navigational skills are confounded, as apparently so are Jode's, with conflicting data and an obvious lack of progress. On the next "fine breezy day," Susan says,

> *As nearly as Jode could judge from the looks and from the lay of the land, the ship was this morning, where she was last night, but the chronometer put her to the Westward. Long. by morning sight 80"22'. This hardly seems possible, as she was hove to last night. At light set all sail and made for the land, which proves to be that near Trinidad, so we are a little to the westward of the entrance. Long at Noon — 80"15' Lat. 21"31'. Quietly after dinner steered East, saw white water first a little before two.*

*The city can be seen plainly now — a few hours good breeze would
carry us in. Shall let the Barque drift through the night. Mr. Bell seems
a little better today. I have worked a little, have had a headache.*[24]

"Caught a shark a few minutes past one—a huge fellow more than ten
feet long," she relates, impressed; but she does not mention the common
sailors' superstition that a shark is a harbinger of a shipboard death—
not a happy coincidence, considering Mr. Bell's condition.[25]

The *J. J. Hathorn* experiences the usual delays upon its arrival in Trinidad. Susan reports: "Not getting a Pilot, hove to and threw over ballast
until 3 P.M. Then ran in for the land intending to anchor. When abreast
the Cay, a Pilot came on board. Ran in and brought to for the night."[26]
Susan's entry that day notes the constant tackings of the ship, each of
which would have been a noisy event, but she puts the day to good use.

*I got up very early — did not sleep much, for the ship was tacked so often.
Have spent the day very pleasantly, working on the shoe — have completed the
second back — it will be a most delightful pair — hope the fronts are large
enough for Jode. Mr. Bell is much better today.*[27]

When the *J. J. Hathorn* anchors in Trinidad harbor on Saturday, Feb-
bruary 17, the customs officers board almost immediately, about 11
A.M., which delays Jode's going ashore until after dinner. Then, Jode
immediately takes Mr. Bell to the hospital, and while ashore, "almost
the first person [Jode] met was 'old Bob.' He is going to sea with
us," Susan reports.[28] This encounter illustrates how small and fluid a
community the mid-nineteenth-century worldwide merchant-seafaring
brotherhood is. While ship's articles for U.S. flagged ships obligated
masters to return all U.S.–citizen sailors to a U.S. port, sailors of every
nationality would in fact leave their ships anywhere and everywhere and
sign on with another. A few days later, Susan's diary records such an
event with one of their own men in Trinidad de Cuba: "Our sailor Joe
took his departure today—had a little fuss yesterday with Jode, and
preferred to leave. Have another in his place."[29] Formally recorded as
"desertions," such events made such encounters between an "old Bob"
and a Jode a daily occurrence in the world's ports at midcentury.

Fallings-out with crew members notwithstanding, the brotherhood

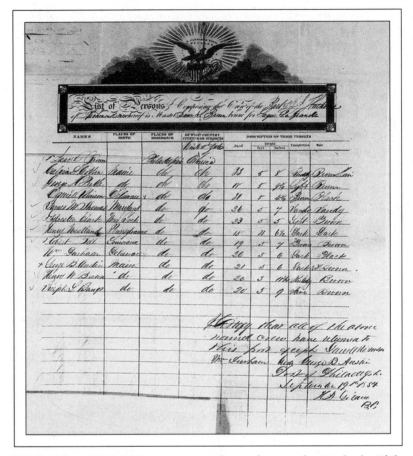

This list of returning J. J. Hathorn *crew members on the voyage from England to Phil-adelphia, September 1854, was filed in accordance with laws requiring masters to ac-count for all who sailed with them. Captain Isaac Brown certified that of the eleven men with whom he left the U.S. for Sagua La Grande (on Cuba's north coast), all returned except Daniel Robinson, William Durham, and George Austin. Crew lists show the captain first, followed by the first and second mates, making thirty-three-year-old Calvin Cotten and eighteen-year-old George Preeble, both of Maine, the vessel's sec-ond and third in command.*

of ships' officers, particularly of captains, formed a kind of superfamily, and it had a further analog among the captains' wives who sailed. This superfamily carried mail and news from port to port to home and back again and looked out for one another, as Susan's diary indicates: "Last evening, Capt. Davidson from New Brunswick called to inquire about Capt. Holmes who was with us at St. Iago. Capt. D. is a right jolly sort."[30] And, later,

> *Capts. Allen & Mann spent the afternoon and evening. . . . Capt. Gibbs of the Franklin spent the evening with us.*

> *Sent the letters today by Capt. Allen of the Brig Princeton, who sails tomorrow for N. York. . . . Capt. Allen with Capt. Mann made a call, and Jode went ashore with them.*[31]

Susan felt the *J. J. Hathorn* had its share of problems in Santiago, but Trinidad de Cuba brings another hazard: "We heard yesterday the yellow fever is here. Capt. Cox from St. Iago had died—his Mate, Barnum takes his place—he has had it too, but has now nearly recovered."[32] The following day, Susan reports the swift transfer of power on Captain Cox's vessel, amid their own work at hand: "Discharged four lighter loads of ballast today. Capt. Barnum left this forenoon."[33] And just a few days later, Susan reports still another death with an astounding juxtaposition: "Jode has been up town—one of his consignees is dead. Got me some cambric for facing at .25 per yard!"[34]

Fortunately the weather in Trinidad turns cooler and cloudy, with occasional rain and heavy winds. Susan has a busy third week of February. She does the washing and ironing. She sews on a green cashmere dress she is making. She mends Jode's shirts and stockings. And with respect to the shoes, apparently at least one pair were not large enough for Jode: "Filled up the odd minutes with putting a few stitches in my shoes, which I think I shall keep for myself."[35]

Susan's entry for February 23 reveals two important facts about their voyage: their destination and their cargo. Susan accepts with equanimity the news that "Our Consignee said today, we are to go to London—not

Hamburg," and she describes the cargo starting to arrive: "Our cargo began to come in today—twenty eight hhds. [hogsheads] of sugar—did not take any more, as after dinner, they took out ballast. Sent one lighter full ashore." [36] And to keep things interesting aboard the *J. J. Hathorn*, the crew is meanwhile up to its old antics. Susan writes, "We had quite a muss—a row between the sailors and the cook."

Fortunately the cooler weather persists through the weekend as Susan uses the opportunity the port presents: "Finished my ironing today—have only been four days doing it. I had very good luck—did up my neck-handkerchief—my wrought pocketh'dkrch'f—a collar for self & three for Jode—beside several other things." [37] Cool weather holds for the next Monday and Tuesday's discharging of ballast and taking on of cargo, about which Susan says,

> *The stevedore came with his crew, to store the cargo — have done a good day's work although the morning seemed to promise but very little. Have taken on board fifty casks of sugar, besides doing a great deal of shovelling {of} the ballast which will be discharged tomorrow.*
>
> *Today, have taken out two lighters of ballast and hoisted in twenty-three casks of sugar, so we have now one hundred and one.* [38]

Susan reports with relief that "Mr. Bell came back from the Hospital after dinner—is quite well," after ten days' recuperation.

Susan's virtual isolation on the *J. J. Hathorn* is implicit in her entries at the end of February. They are not wharf-side in Trinidad de Cuba, and there is no lively social scene to divert her. She guiltily returns to her reading, taking up the first of several Sir Walter Scott novels she will record reading: "For myself, I have lost a day as regards work—have read 'Guy Mannering' instead of making my green dress as I should." [39]

Susan's entry for the last day of February is a model of the material and tone of this diary section, mentioning the weather, matters of the ship's business, wifely chores, her health, a member of the maritime "family," and, not least, the shoes.

The sun shone brightly this morning, but clouded in after dinner and appearances denote a storm. We have not had one for a long while. As there was no sugar coming today, and nobody to be on board but the crew, I thought I could have no better opportunity than this to wash. Had quite a washing for all I did so much last week. Am very tired indeed. Capt. Allen sailed this morning; so we have lost one very pleasant acquaintance. After so long a time, Jode's shoes are really complete, all but the making. Cannot finish mine for lack of one shade, which Jode could not find Sat. when he was up town. This ends February — it has truly been a short month.[40]

Trinidad Sugar

A vessel's time in port loading and discharging cargo can go quickly or slowly, depending on a number of factors, including the nature of the cargo, the weather, the port facilities, and the crew. Almost immediately after the *J. J. Hathorn*'s arrival in the small, crescent-shaped harbor of Trinidad de Cuba, port officials order Jode to reanchor to discharge his ballast onto lighters. Susan, clearly annoyed by the delay, believes this to be an unnecessary inconvenience, and indeed in some ports, ballast is merely heaved overboard at designated places. In Trinidad's relatively shallow port, the *J. J. Hathorn* will always be at anchor and will have to move several times to successively deeper anchorages, away from the main waterfront toward Port Casilda, which is on the arm of land that protects the harbor. Being anchored rather than berthed spells certain isolation for Susan.

Instead of sightseeing and socializing ashore, Susan will spend her days in Trinidad observing and tallying the arrival of the lighters' burdens of casks, hogsheads, barrels, and tierces of sugar, molasses, and rum.[1] Fortunately, Trinidad's weather is kind. In fact, Susan describes March 1 as such a cool day that by evening, "the wind came out of the north, as cold as winter almost." That day, for example, Susan notes that the *J. J. Hathorn* has taken on 111 hogsheads, ten tierces, and twenty-four barrels, which she totals, "in all, one hundred forty-five pieces."[2] They have made an excellent start.

The next morning the loading again is apparently proceeding quite well. ("The lighter came off early, and before dinner,[3] we had in five

tierces, thirty-eight-casks. and 1 Boxes + 3 Barrels.") But at dinner—
actually because of it—there is a crisis:

> *Then the men refused to turn to. Jode went to the Consul, and he came down*
> *to Port Casilda and had them go ashore — upon their promising to work he*
> *did not put them in jail. The reason they gave, for not doing duty, was that*
> *they had nothing fit to eat.* [4]

Susan keeps her distance, not offering an opinion about the crew's com-
plaint, which is the perennial one among seamen, but her sympathies
must be with Jode. This is a mutinous strike, and Jode suffers not only
a personal embarrassment before Susan but also the professional hu-
miliation of appealing to the consul to repair his ship's discipline. [5]

Nevertheless, the incident must have been considered relatively be-
nign or commonplace, at least according to official records. The U.S.
consul at Trinidad de Cuba, a Mississippian named Samuel McLean,
notes it in neither his semiannual consular return to Washington at the
end of June nor any despatch from Trinidad de Cuba for the year 1855. [6]
Susan's entry for the mutiny day concludes with a report not on the
incident but on her sewing: "I have spent the day sewing on my green
dress, and mending a little—Have finished the dress at last." [7] Her comment the next day—"the men are as obedient as you please—their visit
to the Consul did them good"—concludes the matter and shows where
her loyalties are. [8]

On Saturday afternoon, March 3, Jode goes for a pilot to move the *J.
J. Hathorn* to deeper water before Monday, when more cargo will be arriving from their agent, Mr. Fritze. Caribbean lighters do not operate
on Sundays, but the pilot does come aboard to move them. Susan calls
it "the longest day I have seen since I came to sea—was awake early as
the pilot brought us down the harbor, to deeper water." [9] Susan describes
the Trinidad harbor the next day:

> *there are lots of ships coming in — two or three yesterday and as many to-*
> *night. We get along grandly with our loading — were awakened by the*
> *Lighter this morning — Mr. Fritze sent no less than three. They have taken*

*in one hundred thirty boxes, fifty five casks and twenty one barrels — a very
good day's work.* [10]

On Tuesday Mr. Fritze's overseer—a kind of temporary agent's supercargo—comes aboard the *J. J. Hathorn*.[11] In the bark's aftercabin, a surprised Susan puts aside her sewing and plays the captain's wife:

> *Got the Barege skirt ready to begin, when Jode brought in Mr. Fritze{'s}
> Clerk, who spent the afternoon with me. As I had one bare foot, I could not
> get up, but entertained him the best I might with my Cobre minerals.* [12]

That day, the *J. J. Hathorn* loads sixty-six puncheons of rum and thirty-
two hogsheads of sugar (at 70 to 72 gallons per puncheon, the rum
shipped that day comes to nearly 5,000 gallons), so it is not surprising
that Mr. Fritze wants his clerk present. Ships continue to come in, with
"two or three brigs" more arriving that day.

Loading continues so quickly that by the next day, March 8, Susan
describes a chaotic scene aboard the *J. J. Hathorn*:

> *our decks are covered with casks so it is impossible to get along through them.
> We have taken in seventy two hhds. six barrels and six tierces. About as
> much as can be taken unless more tierces and barrels are sent. Hope to get
> away the first of next week.* [13]

Any cargo left on deck is strictly illegal and obviously dangerous.[14]
If cargo is not sorted and secured and the vessel put "in trim" (or bal-
anced), when it encounters heavy seas the cargo comes loose in the hold,
shifts the vessel's center of gravity, and in the worst case causes it to
capsize. Before the *J. J. Hathorn* can safely set to sea, its cargo's many
small components must be properly stowed by the stevedores.[15]

🐚

In port at Trinidad with the *J. J. Hathorn* is another midcoast Maine
vessel, the bark *Archimedes*, under the command of Captain William
Mann. In her diary Susan never mentions Captain Mann's given
name—she is observing Victorian maritime and social formalities—but

the friendship between the Hathorns and William Mann will grow close during their time together in Trinidad.

On that busy Monday, March 5, when the lighters full of cargo arrived at dawn, Captain Mann paid his first call at the *J. J. Hathorn*.[16] Amid this bustling scene, Susan and Jode immediately take to William Mann, who hails from Yarmouth, a Casco Bay port less than twenty-five miles from Richmond. The Hathorns and Captain Mann play the card game "High, Low, Jack" one evening;[17] on another they play the four-handed card game whist, at which Susan excels, with the table's fourth being "Captain Wyman of the *Medora*." So delighted is Susan with the evening that she gives it her highest accolade: "It really seemed like down east times."[18]

Weekends give captains a break from ship's duties, and on Sunday, March 11, Jode and Susan and Captain Mann go to the beach together. One can almost smell the burning sugarcane in the air, as Susan describes the day as

> *Fair, but so smoky it seems like fog. Yesterday more so than today. Went over on the beach with Capt. Mann — had a grand good time. Found about a quart and a half of shells and a beautiful little conch. Got back just in time for a nice dinner.*[19]

These shells become treasured souvenirs of this day in Trinidad de Cuba, and later Susan will write in her diary of placing them on her mantelpiece back in Richmond. Though later still Susan will have sad reasons to recall Trinidad de Cuba, for now she is happy to report, "Captain Mann visits us frequently—it is pleasant to meet a friend among these heathens."[20]

Trinidad itself has not won Susan. In contrast to the polite, hospitable expatriate community she found in Santiago, her diary describes not a single event on the Trinidad social scene. Gone are the theater parties, social events with the U.S. consul, trips to the mountains; absent is the exotic native dancing and visits to the *mercado*. Perhaps most sorely missed of all from Susan's point of view is the company of the worldly, comfortably well-off, socially adept English-speaking women she called

The Hathorns found Trinidad de Cuba quiet, especially compared to Santiago and its social scene. Moreover, an outbreak of yellow fever would claim the Hathorn's cargo agent and one of Jode's fellow captains in port there.

on and did needlework with—the kind of woman Susan might imagine herself to be one day.[21] It would not be impossible to imagine the Hathorns setting up a Caribbean outpost for the family interests, and Jode and Susan living in Cuba.

With the American maritime folk left to their own devices in Trinidad, Susan notes a major drawback to the tropical Cuban wild: "Musquitoes thicker than hoped—we could not sleep a wink if we did not have our bar."[22] To make matters worse, no mail from home reaches the Hathorns in Trinidad, a disappointment that leads Susan to avoid mentioning the port's very name: "If nothing happens, shall go from this place Wed. morning. We have not received a single letter here."[23] To Susan it might seem that the family for whom she and Jode are risking themselves in this wasteland of yellow fever and mosquitoes have forgotten them.

Some of the "heathens" Susan refers to are even closer at hand. In fact, they are under foot. During the week before the loading, when the crew was in port with time on their hands and money in their pockets, she had written, "Old Bob got drunk today. The Cook and his wife are near coming to blows again."[24] To complicate the crew list, one of the sailors decides to go on another vessel ("Our sailor Bill has taken his departure tonight—goes in the Laura. Capt. Weston"), though Susan takes this development in stride.[25] Actually, on the very day when Susan, Jode, and Captain Mann had been enjoying the beach, the crew was having its own party. Susan describes the incident in the next day's entry: "Most of the men went ashore and we had a drunken row in the Forecastle. Today [Monday], they are half corned[,] and the cook and stewardess."[26]

On Tuesday, the thirteenth, Jode goes ashore to settle the *J. J. Hathorn's* accounts so they can leave, but Susan reports that the crew may still be paying the price for their weekend revels ("Bob and Dutch George are sick today").[27] The first mate, Mr. Bickford,[28] is "getting the ship ready for sea tomorrow," and Mr. Bell, seemingly recovered and back on duty, "has been for the water."[29] As it weighs anchor at Trinidad on March 14, the *J. J. Hathorn's* hesitant departure recalls the one from Santiago:

The sun seems scalding hot. We got under weigh about six — not much of a breeze — got a little way from the city — anchored and waited for a land-breeze. Then set sail again, & came a little way farther. Hope to get to sea tomorrow.[30]

To fill the idle time, Jode writes to his father, and Susan to her brother Hosea. "Scaled up Jode's writing this forenoon and began my other sleeve," she adds—an enigmatic notation, since Jode's signature, at least, does not lack for size. This suggests that Susan may be making the fair copy of the ship's log, usually the duty of the first mate. "Our sick seamen are some better," she says, suggesting they may be suffering from something more (or other) than a hangover, perhaps a touch of tropical fever.

"Got underweigh about six," Susan says on March 15, "the breeze very light, but freshened a little, so that the Pilot left us at nine."[31] Using the coordinates Susan records, we find that the *J. J. Hathorn* first heads south into the Caribbean, then turns westward, going south of the Isle of Pines and doubling Cabo San Antonio, Cuba's westernmost point. "Quite a strong head sea right against us," Susan says, again mentioning mild seasickness that makes her feel "dull and sleepy." She sews a little and "works up the sights," but to her diary confesses that the vessel's progress against the oncoming waves is less than encouraging.[32]

Back at sea, the crew cannot satisfy their thirst for liquor as in port, if at all. Many ships' articles prohibited "obscene language" and in bold type proclaimed, "NO GROG ALLOWED—and none to be put on board by the Crew."[33] The Hathorns cannot be against spirits on principle, for the *J. J. Hathorn* carries a cargo of rum. Later, back in Richmond, Susan mentions in her diary that she has installed a bottle of brandy on her mantelpiece, so she distinguishes between the danger of drunken sailors on duty and social or medicinal use of spirits. The abrupt end to the easy availability of liquor in Trinidad may have something to do with surprising news Susan gets from the steward, the first day out of Trinidad: "We had the misfortune to learn this morning, our bonnie barque is haunted—or that it is inhabited by Rats gifted with the power of speech—they disturbed the steward last night—so he told Jode." [34] A mariner's maxim sums up the situation: "Horses at sea, asses on land."

Seafaring life requires an attention to detail and meticulous record keeping, if only to ensure safe arrival at the next port. Everyone has heard of the log, a vessel's official record book, the name of which comes from the means by which vessels' speeds were determined. In the nineteenth century this was done by throwing over the stern the "log chip," a flat, pie-shaped piece of wood attached to a knotted "log-line." As the line would be reeled out, a glass timer with sand would be turned; when the sand was out, the knots (speed) would be counted and noted in the log book. [35]

In the days of sail, a ship's log noted, in addition to speed, its position; the compass headings; the weather, wind, and state of the sea; the sails set; any soundings taken; any vessels "spoke" or sighted; and landfalls. By listing a vessel's successive positions, its progress or lack of it became a matter of permanent record. [36] No logs for the *J. J. Hathorn* appear to have survived, and while Susan's diary often records information of the kind found in the ship's log, hers is a personal diary, not an official navigational record. However, Susan values record keeping. Her eye for business is demonstrated in her auditing the vessel's accounts after the lumber was landed at Santiago and in her keeping a personal record of the cargo shipped in Trinidad, possibly to check against the ship's (and the agent's) records.

In addition, Susan also kept a detailed list of personal expenditures in the account-book section at the back of her diary. Here the diary's printed format provides separate pages for each month's "Cash Account" and "Bills Payable/Receivable." [37] The expenditures Susan lists throughout 1855 and into 1856 shed important light on her passage through foreign ports and on her life in Richmond.

During 1855 Susan accounts for a total of $151.66 in "personal expenses," of which she spends exactly $15.22 in Cuba. What were these expenses? The first was on January 17, when she went to the Harveys'

Santiago home for a stay ashore: "Paid negro for carrying budgets [suit-cases], 20 cents."[38] Susan's January 19 shopping expedition is a virtual splurge by thrifty New England standards. She buys a hair comb for thirty cents, and spends fifteen cents on a doll for "Sis Ring"—her five-year-old neice, Lucy Ellen Ring, Lucy's daughter. Susan buys clothing, probably for herself: eight pairs of cotton stockings at twenty-five cents each. The "Loose Wrapper or Blouse" she buys for $1.50 would be for herself, perhaps in imitation of the Santiago ladies' negligee attire. Comparing the account ledger and the diary's version of this shopping trip reveals a few minor differences:

> *After dinner, all the family took a walk — we went down to the shops — purchased a couple of handkerchiefs, and a hair comb. Things are not so expensive here as I expected. Saw some beautiful towels — shall get them if possible before we leave Cuba.*[39]

The handkerchiefs do not appear in the account book, but on February 2 Susan does enter the purchase of "6 Towels at $7 per Dozen . . . $3.50."

Remarkably, Susan's accounts do not specify any purchases she made for Jode. She says in her diary she has bought a handkerchief for him, and hems it, but her accounts do not itemize it. In viewing her "personal" accounts as personal, independent, and individual, Susan's accounting system does not reflect the financial dependency one might expect. In a sense, however, she is keeping the Victorian spheres—his and hers—properly separate.[40] Towels could have been considered a household expense, and therefore in Susan's sphere.

Susan's personal accounts in Cuba do not list any foods, such as the delicious melons that she says she and Jode enjoyed on February 7. Foods would likely have been charged to the ship's provisions, or since Jode bought them, he may have paid for them from his own petty cash. While Susan's diary mentions the purchase of "some Guava Jelly—the latter is very cheap—only $2.00 per doz. boxes," the guava jelly is missing from the accounts.[41] Perhaps a quantity was purchased for the ship's provisions, for gifts, or as an unofficial export, a common way for ships' captains to augment their incomes. Why Susan pays the "Negro

Wench" forty cents on February 8—twice what the first luggage carrier got—her diary does not explain. Since February 8 marks the end of her stay ashore at the Harveys' Santiago home, Susan may be tipping Mrs. Harvey's maid for services rendered during the visit, as well as for carrying her things. And February 8 is also the day of Mr. Bell's accident, which may help explain Susan's inattention or inaccuracy.

Both Susan's diary and the accounts mention her purchase while still in Santiago of a "Linen Lawn Dress . . . $4.45" that February 8; "Bought me a linen dress," Susan writes in her diary that day, "and some worsteds for the shoes." Moreover, the accounts show that on January 25, Susan had purchased a "Fan . . . $2.12½," which she does not mention in the diary. This must have been an extraordinary fan, judging from its cost compared to what she pays for the "loose wrapper" and to the "paper fan" she buys later that costs only eight cents. Perhaps the fancy fan was less important to report than that day's fumigation of the cabin for cockroaches and noting that cook, mate, and steward were at war.[42]

Susan's expenditures of $15.22 in Cuba and what they reveal about her possessions and her situation place her relatively high on the economic scale. The Hathorns are not extravagantly wealthy or ostentatious people, but Susan has, besides fans and furs, a cashmere dress and the cashmere scarf that was stolen from the boat. Susan keeps a careful count of her pennies and halfpennies, but she has the luxury of buying worsteds for needlepoint without thinking twice about the expense. During the Atlantic crossing she will find more than enough time for her fancy sewing—so much time, in fact, that she runs out of fancy work. And when Susan reaches London to shop, her shopping will be of a different kind, for she will be buying material to sew a baby's layette.

Of the 365 days during 1855, Susan Hathorn has marked two entries with small, inked asterisks just after the printed day of the week and month—Tuesday, January 23, and Saturday, February 24. As one reads through the diary for the first time, those two marks—and an occasionally appearing odd glyph that resembles an ampersand—stand out, for

TUESDAY, 23.

A pleasant day— not quite so hot as we have had it— Spent the morning cleaning up the cabin and cleaning it. After dinner set ward. robe in order a little, but it needs a great deal more of righting. Hemmed a handkerchief that I got at Cobee. for Jode. Capt Jyan engaged a box at the theater— So about six, Mons. & Madame Lavine, Capt. Jyan, Jane & Josiah, Jode & myself set out for St. Jayo— the first time I have been there. Was introduced to the Consul. Sent out, & had a nice new fan bought. The plays were beautiful. The first act or whatever it may be called), was of tableaux— representing the gods & goddesses. The 2nd rope dancing— third stand-ing on one another's shoulders & heads. 4th Dances— 5th & Pantomime.

SATURDAY, 24.

A most beautiful day— no breeze but just enough for coolness. Finished my ironing today— have only been four days doing it. I had very good luck— did up my neck handkerchief— my wrought pocket handkerchief— a collar for self & three for Jode— beside several other things. Jode has been up town— one of his consignees is dead. Got me some cambric for facing at 25 per yard!

MARCH.   MONDAY, 12.   1855.

Fair, but so smoky it seems like fog. Yesterday more so than today. Went over on the beach with Capt. Mann— had a grand good time. Found about a quart and a half of shells and a beautiful little Conch. Got back just in time for a nice dinner. Most of the men went ashore and we had a drunken row in the Forecastle. Today, they are half round and the cook and stewardess. I have managed to do quite a washing— besides picking over the shells. If nothing happens, shall go from this place Wed. morning. We have not received a single letter here. Have taken on board nine hhds. today— The stevedore finished stowing this afternoon & barrel of Flour found today

These entries from Susan Hathorn's diary for January 23, February 24, and March 12 include her coded record. In the first, Susan describes her port-housekeeping and the theater party in Santiago. In the second, Susan reports on domestic duties and that a Trinidad business associate has died of yellow fever there. These two entries are marked with asterisks. The last describes the Hathorns' beach party with Captain Mann and the "row in the Forecastle," and includes Susan's glyph.

nothing about Susan's diary appears casual or haphazard. The diary's appearance makes clear that Susan is not a doodler, and any marks she makes in this book have a meaning.

Female readers may quickly guess the meaning of Susan's asterisks, since many women keep a menstrual calendar in a similar way. Since February 24 is thirty-two days after January 23, a reader's next reaction may be to question this theory. But given the unusual climate and diet Susan is experiencing, plus the hormonal upset travel commonly creates, a four-day variance from the theoretical twenty-eight-day cycle is really no deviation. It is also possible that Susan's normal cycle was slightly longer than average. In her list of items laundered on February 22, Susan mentions, "my under handkerchief among the rest," which, given Susan's constitutional preparedness, suggests she does not expect the beginning of a period before then.

One of Susan's ampersand glyphs appears on March 12, the day of the beach trip about which Susan has already written glowingly. Though in her diary Susan never breathes a word of sexual activity, this would be the fifteenth day after February 24, when it is highly likely that a child could be conceived. The fact is, Susan never even mentions the word *pregnancy*, nor does she ever directly express her feelings about becoming a mother. As we read on in the diary realizing that she is pregnant, we wonder at first *if* and then *at what point* Jode learns about the baby, for Susan never mentions sharing the news with him or what his reaction is. But there seems little doubt that Susan has put a tiny, encrypted record of her reproductive life—fastidiously inked in nonwords—in her diary. On November 20, a reasonably normal 254 days after March 12, the birth of Jode and Susan's baby clearly decodes her ampersand glyphs.

During the second half of March, the *J. J. Hathorn* rounds the western end of Cuba, leaves the Caribbean, and heads north to catch the strong easterly current of the Gulf Stream. Determined to be a good captain's wife, Susan fills her diary for these weeks with matters of navigation. She is intellectually stimulated by the challenge of getting the coordinates and learning variant methods for determining their vessel's position. Here her formal education stands her in good stead, for she easily does the requisite trigonometry and occasionally good-naturedly differs with Jode on the correct calculations.

Their luck with good weather in Trinidad runs out practically the minute they clear the harbor. "The current is against us," she writes on the first day out,

> *for all she was steered the whole night S.W. and all day today WSW we have made very little Southern. Nothing has disturbed the day's monotony, but Jode's prophecies of a long voyage. . . . Saw a Ship or Barque, this afternoon walking up towards us strangely.*[43]

Susan decides to fill the dead time with a useful job, and after she finishes her sewing, braids rags. "Have almost completed the pile," she says, as she thinks of home: "It reminded me of the dull spring days at home to be braiding rags, and seemed very homelike to Jode too. This has been a very long week indeed—it seems a month since I went shelling on the beach."[44] During those long days, we see a new side to Jode, revealing an interest he shares with Susan: "He has read, and slept alternately—has resumed the perusal of Guy Mannering, one of the Waverly Novels."[45]

As the weekend comes, Susan frets about the weather ("the clouds look wild and threatening"[46]) and seems uncertain about their position. The clouds make good, and during the next two days, the *J. J. Hathorn* runs into heavy weather. The bark is having to do a lot of tacking, not Susan's idea of a pleasant sail:

> *Pleasant today, but a head wind — tonight seems rather wild. The ship lays over a great deal and makes it worse than it is. Our Long. at 8 A.M. was 85"59. At noon, {by} double altitudes 85"49. At 4 P.M. 85"39. Latitude at noon 23"07. We tacked ship at 4 this morning and stood off — at 12 and stood on until 8. P.M. when we tacked again and stood off — this wind is dead against us.*

> *Last night was somewhat rough — reminded me of the night in the gulf, when we were coming out to Savanah {sic}. Tacked Ship at 12 and again*

at 4. She plunged strangely a part of the time — there being a heavy head
sea. This morning, got the Lat. and Long. by Sumner's Method — found
we were in 22"56 Lat and 85"28 Long. — have not gained ground remark-
ably fast.[47]

In the midst of the stormy weather, Susan proclaims on Tuesday,
March 20, "Just six months today since we were married."[48]

Susan takes clear pleasure in surveying the sea scene, mentioning
landmarks and vessels in sight.

Today has been pleasant. This morning there were five sails in sight — a
ship, a barque, two brigs and a schooner. . . . The hills of Cuba can be seen.
The vessels we saw this morning are quite near us — one is the Clarissa from
Trinidad.

Blows fresh this morning. Land of Cuba can be seen but very indistinctly.
Our yesterday's company still in sight, except the large ship.

{T}he wind continued through the night, and we made a great run for this
place. Long. 80"56; — Lat. by Sumner's method, 23"30' at 8 A.M.
At eleven o'clock, could see land — at 12, made Salt Cay, and took our de-
parture therefrom, tacking ship, and steering to the westward.[49]

Susan's entries for the remaining days in March undoubtedly mirror
Jode's concern with getting the *J. J. Hathorn* into the Gulf Stream as soon
as possible, for riding the stream's current east- and northward will
shorten the trip to England. The Gulf Stream flows eastward from the
Gulf of Mexico between Cuba and Florida, then turns north along the
eastern coast of Florida, separating the cold water on the continental
slope and the warm Sargasso Sea. Off Florida the current is about fifty
miles wide, and its surface velocity often exceeds 5.5 mph. Finally, the
Gulf Stream flows eastward into the North Atlantic Current, a less pow-
erful and more diffuse stream heading toward England, the Hathorns'
destination.[50]

One might think it would be difficult to miss a current of this size,
but the ocean is a large expanse, and time wasted finding the Gulf
Stream would be precious. Too much time wasted could even be a matter

of life and death. Susan describes the process of finding the stream in a
series of successive entries at the end of March:

> *The sea is pretty high. The water occasionally dashes over the decks from the
> weather side. Are not in the stream, for the water is Cold, although there
> must be some current. . . . Winds still fair, but has changed from the N. to
> North West. Put two reefs in the topsail and one in the mainsail — glass
> going down. Sea quite rough. Cloudy and signs of rain — could get no after-
> noon observation.*

> *Fair today, with very little wind but a heavy sea, so we spank at a great
> rate. Have made but little progress — we are out of the stream, although by
> the chart we should be in its strength. . . . One sail in sight today, going on
> an opposite course to ours.*

> *Last night was very rough indeed. The glass kept going up, and the wind
> blew all the harder. It came in gusts. Furled the Mainsail and close reefed
> the Topsails, stowed Foresail, jib and spanker. There was a tremendous sea,
> and we nearly thumped to pieces. This morning cloudy and did not get an
> observation of the sun. At noon, our latitude was 31"55'. Rather slower
> getting along than some days since. It is as cold as Greenland — was yester-
> day. Long. at 4 P.M. was 77" Lat 32"00. It is quite calm, but the sea is
> still rough.*

> *The sea is as smooth as glass. It was nearly calm for the most part of last
> night — a little breeze for a while. . . . It seems fated we shall not get into
> the current. . . . The air feels like snow — the glass is going down and it
> seems as if we should have a blow. At six tonight we are going along at three
> or four knots. . . . Are not in the edge of the stream.*[51]

The last day of March is a Saturday, and though Susan often reviews the
week in her Saturday entries, this week she is intent on the immediate
situation. Susan's entry for that day makes clear that she is aware of the
dangers of the Carolina Banks and of their reputation as the "graveyard
of the Atlantic."

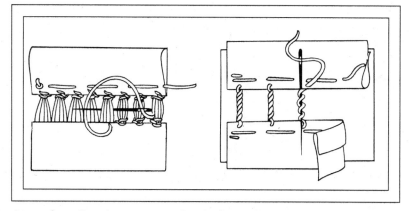

Among the needlework projects Susan describes during the year, she mentions doing hem-stitching (left) on handkerchiefs and embellishing another project with fagoting (right). Her real forte was wool embroidery, particularly needlepoint.

A damp, dark, cloudy morning, and rainy afternoon. Could neither get our Latitude or longitude today. The glass keeps going down and seems to threaten a heavy storm. We are not far off the Carolinian Capes, but are steering away from them as fast as possible. Hope we shall keep clear of them. Now at half past one, are reefing the sails. The wind comes in heavy gusts. There is very little sea, and that right after us. The gale comes on harder and harder — the sea is very high now at five — almost all the sails are taken in, the glass continues to go down. We shall have a wild night. Do not know our Lat. or longitude as we could get no observation.[52]

Susan does not make much of her needlework in the midst of all the seamanship, but she is working at it. The *J. J. Hathorn*'s progress is of great concern to her, but since there is little she can do to help, she turns to her needlework for solace:

I have spent today and yesterday in sewing on my patch work — putting the white into my "orange peel" quilt.

I have finished putting the white into my "orange peel" quilt — it is very pretty. Have also worked a little on the back to my sleeve.

Have worked on my shoe today.

I have well nigh completed the second pair of shoes which have been on the carpet so long. Jode has made a cover for his octant, and read "Old Mortality" — finished it sabbath day.

I finished my last pair of shoes today — also mended purse fringe.

Have sewed patchwork today — that Ann & Lucy gave me.[53]

Wide Blue Atlantic

A month is a long time at sea, and the *J. J. Hathorn's* eastbound crossing from Trinidad de Cuba to London in the spring of 1855 will take nearly twice that. The Hathorns disembarked their Trinidad pilot on March 15 and will not make their landfall, Beachy Head Light, on the south coast of England, until May 8. At Beachy Head, the *J. J. Hathorn* will take on a pilot and proceed northeast past Dover and Deal, making their pilot-to-pilot passage fifty-four days. Two more days will pass before the *J. J. Hathorn* makes her way upriver to London and St. Katherine's Dock, adjacent to the Tower of London.[1]

As April begins, however, Susan is far from London. In fact, April 1 finds the *J. J. Hathorn* in nasty weather:

> *Last night was wild enough. The sea was very high and short and it really seemed as if we should lose the <u>after</u> part of the bark. The wind continues blowing and at 4.A.M. — well nigh blew us out of the sea — furled the topsail and went under bare poled. The sea came in on deck in torrents, at every plunge we made. Lat. at 12, 34"48. One ship in sight on an opposite course. Long. at 4.P.M. 75"13'.*

> *Spoke a Brig, one mast gone, the "Mary Perkins,{"} of Dennis.*[2]

Storms continue through April's first week, giving Susan a strong taste of life at sea, but on board the *J. J. Hathorn*, a human drama continues. Through kindheartedness or adherence to the letter of maritime law, or for want of a suitable replacement, Jode has kept Mr. Bell on. The second mate had not completely recovered from his fall into the hold in Santiago and may have also contracted a tropical fever in Cuba. With each day, Mr. Bell's condition seems to deteriorate.

To Susan falls the task of caring for him. On the first Monday in April, Susan reports, "Mr. Bell is sick again—had not been able to do his duty since Sat. afternoon."[3] The next day she reiterates: Mr. Bell is "still unable to do duty and Jode has to take his place, which comes rather hard for him."[4] On Wednesday she writes, "Mr. Bell does not seem to recover any—but rather goes back."[5] The rest of that week, Susan makes no mention of him, and on the following Wednesday she says, "Mr. Bell has not been able to do anything yet—is very poorly indeed."[6] In the second Saturday of April's summing-up entry, Susan concludes: "Mr. Bell does not seem to recover—remains about the same. Unable to do any thing except braid ropes for some fancy work or other."[7] Coming from Susan, who spends so much of her own time on fancy work, the tone of "some fancy work or other" is noteworthy. While it need not suggest that "fancy work" only properly belongs to the woman's sphere, it is clear that to Susan fancy work—done by whomever— should not take the place of plain. It is one thing for Susan to nurse a desperately sick man at sea, but it is another for an inexperienced captain to lose one of his two officers. Susan, seeing that Mr. Bell's disability has doubled Jode's workload, recognizes that on a ship, as at Mount Holyoke, a requisite amount of work has to be done by a finite number of human hands. She unburdens Jode in whatever way she can, such as when she writes, "As Jode was sleeping, did not wake him to take an afternoon observation."[8] But of course the situation continues.

"Mr. Bell is some worse today—he is miserable enough," she reports the following Thursday, and then on the next day, refers to the *J. J. Hathorn*'s dwindling provisions: "Mr. Bell continues about the same. Hope we shall arrive soon on his account—as well as on account of our provisions. We shall be fairly 'eaten out.' Hope we shall not be put upon allowance."[9] Then there is no mention of Mr. Bell until twelve days later, by which time the *J. J. Hathorn* has reached the English Channel shipping lanes:

A great many vessels pass us going West—four or five last night and two steamers—one bound in and one out. It was very rough and there was such a

clatter — everything shaking. I scarce slept a wink. Mr. Bell coughed until
twelve as an accompaniment.[10]

The closer they get to London, the more alarming grow Susan's reports
about Mr. Bell. On successive days, Susan writes:

Mr. Bell is quite sick — a constant cough and tickling in his throat. Has
very little appetite indeed. We live on scouse, hasty pudding, and salt beef.
But as long as we have enough we will not complain.

Mr. Bell is quite sick — vomitted {sic} blood this morning — is feeble
enough.

Mr. Bell is very sick indeed today — coughs almost constantly — his throat is
so sore, he can eat no solid food.[11]

As April turns to May, Mr. Bell is barely clinging to life.

❧

What kind of woman is this who finds herself in this sad, almost des-
perate situation? What had Susan's life been like before she picked up
her pen on that first day of 1855? Where had she been, what had she
done, who had her friends been? What experiences had formed her values, her hopes, her dreams? And is it possible to know?

We do know that she taught school, that she lived in and around
Richmond, and that she attended Mount Holyoke, where she mentions
and describes her roommates; we know she was very close to her sister
Lucy and had a good relationship with Jode's parents; we know she was
quiet but outgoing enough to make friends easily; we know she enjoyed
reading, but wore her learning lightly. Most clues beyond her own writings have disappeared with time. A first reading of Susan's 1855 diary
weaves a slight, mysterious story of a few slim threads, yet the simple
surface is deceptive, and beneath its web lie complex behaviors and relationships. Apart from the events the diary relates, it tells us a great
deal about Susan from the simple fact that it came into being and has
survived. Susan not only could write, she wanted to write, she felt compelled to write, and she did write. She seems never to have even briefly
entertained the idea of throwing the idea of writing and this diary over-

board—she was saving something important to herself and perhaps to others. And in light of events after December 31, 1855, it is all the more significant that she chose to let this diary survive.

Susan's diary holds countless examples of her impatience (particularly about finishing tasks), but hers was an impatience yoked not to capitulation but to stubborn persistence. Once Susan undertook a quilt-top, a bed-bug fumigation, or a baby's layette, she saw it through, tedious though the task might become, with practically a desperation to see it completed. In a diary overflowing with over three hundred references to work (tabulated in appendix E) on specific sewing, embroidering, knitting, crocheting, and other domestic projects, Susan does not report abandoning a single one. Susan's drive to complete her work speedily comes close to compulsion. This Susan is the Susan she tells herself about, in her diary, and thus shares with her latter-day readers.

Susan's omissions are also worth considering. Though she frequently reports on many domestic activities and accomplishments, she seldom mentions cooking and eating. This omission may be partly because Susan spent so much of the year at sea, where the food was less than wonderful and the cooking done for her.[12] Nevertheless, even on dry land and freed of constraints on her movements and the lack of a kitchen, Susan reports little about food and cooking, her interests remaining with needlework. If she does cook during the three and a half months in Richmond at the end of the year, she never deems it worth mentioning. Susan's two recorded cooking exploits are worth noting: the first takes place on January 16, when she makes cupcakes and ginger crackers while in port at Santiago, probably as a special treat for visitors calling at the *J. J. Hathorn.* The next cooking spree takes place at the end of April, when she spends the morning cooking "—made some Ginger Snaps and Sugar Cakes—" as the ship nears its landing in London.[13]

The enterprises of cooking and needlework differ in fundamental and significant ways. Cooking, in both the doing and the enjoying of its result, is a more sensually complex affair, involving touch, sight, smell, and taste. Cooking can hold intellectual gratifications, but in its usual applications it is an activity tied more to the present and to the senses. Its products are necessary on a regular basis to sustain life; its products are consumed and in essence disappear. It is interesting to note that the other allusions to food in the diary (the guava jelly, the watermelon and mangoes that Jode buys, and the fruit that Susan dries by hanging on nails in the *J. J. Hathorn*'s cabin) generally involve foods that do not need cooking.

In contrast, Susan's handwork encompasses both necessary "plain" sewing and aesthetic "fancy" and operates in an intellectual as well as a physical space. The products of Susan's needles function in the realm of only two senses, touch and sight. Almost all of Susan's sewing and needlework projects are not projects "of the moment," such as sewing on a button might be, but involve planning strategies and often long-term work. Paradoxically, difficult as these longer-duration projects might seem for impatient Susan to tolerate, the gratifications of almost all of her needlework must be deferred, so the satisfactions take on sublimated, intellectual qualities that amplify the immediate and sensual. Nearly all of Susan's handwork products can be said to have some utilitarian function, but constructing the plainest, most strictly utilitarian garment possible, for either herself or anyone else, does not seem to appeal to her. Through sewing, embroidery, and other needlework, Susan makes the world a more comfortable, beautiful, civilized place for herself and those she loves.

Susan is almost compulsively neat in keeping her diary, not only by today's standards of penmanship but also when viewed alongside the diaries of contemporaneous captains' wives. Almost without exception she conscientiously and completely fills each day's space. Certain exceptions are noteworthy and understandable: the briefest of Susan's entries, for example, will be on the day of her baby's birth, lending authenticity to the fact that she wrote the entry on or soon after that day.

Susan's diary writing is only one of several forms of self-discipline to which she subjects herself, but it is that which can be observed firsthand.[14] There are days when the diary's entries become so perfunctory it seems she does not completely enjoy the task she has set for herself. The year-long story of Susan's affection for Jode, her enthusiasm for encountering new people and places, the evidences of her caring nature, even Susan's most mechanical, lackluster entries, speak to the diary's genuineness and its writer's humanness.

Susan's April 10 entry, when the *J. J. Hathorn* is nearly four weeks out of Trinidad, reveals that she knows she needs something to do with her mind. Having compulsively exhausted her sewing supplies, she is forced to improvise and turns to a new kind of project, producing results that do not completely satisfy her. Finally, she recognizes that even her beloved fancy sewing and diversionary knitting go only so far, and she reveals that her husband shares her interest in books and poetry:

> *I have well nigh consumed my entire stock of work which I brought. This forenoon, I worked the purple rose from the shoe pattern on a piece of my cashmere dress, for a Pin Cushion. This afternoon knit me a cappiola*[15] *— my first was so very homely I though best to improve upon it. We should die of the dumps if it were not for books — we are reading Byron's Poems. It is so cold, I cannot stay out on deck at all.*[16]

The next day, Susan reports again that "Jode kills time by reading Byron—he has become great admirer of his Lordship." The affinity is an understandable one for the young captain, considering Byron's strong identification with the sea.

Through the isolation of the long Atlantic passage, Susan and Jode test and deepen their relationship. We have no record of their first meeting, their courtship. We have a public record of their marriage, but no daguerreotype taken on the wedding day and no photos of them in 1855. No diary of Susan's from the period before her marriage survives—just the letter and essay in her college's archives. To be sure, Susan's is more of a record of herself than most women of the time left. On the subject of their marriage, Susan's diary is our only source, and during that month of April, Susan's reticence begins to yield, and she speaks more openly of matters of feeling.

She has expressed her concern that Jode's health will be sapped by doing Mr. Bell's work as well as his own, letting him sleep through a 4 P.M. observation of the sun.[17] On the previous day, she reported, "while Jode took his afternoon nap, I bound his General Chart."[18] On the same day, she reports cryptically, "I have finished one blue stocking and begun the other." That Friday she is again at work on her "blue stocking." Considering Susan's training at Mount Holyoke, she would know what a bluestocking is, and given her penchant for mockery, she may be commenting on the intellectual life at sea.[19]

As Susan's affection and concern for Jode becomes more and more evident, her affection is reciprocated in small and touching ways. She has found still another use for her needle skills in binding Jode's general chart, and despite his general exhaustion, Jode fashions for Susan "a pair of tidy needles. They are of hickory with mangrove heads!"[20] One can almost see Jode painstakingly carving these knitting needles for his bride. In this perfect gift, he incorporates Susan's passion for needlework and the exotic materials provided by his nomadic occupation.

℔

The North Atlantic is a formidable body of water whose vastness, icebergs, and gales properly give voyagers pause. In 1855 such a voyage in the *J. J. Hathorn*, a 398-ton wooden sailing ship with crude navigational tools, an untried captain, and communications limited to chance sightings of other vessels in the sea lane, took courage, especially for one as unaccustomed as Susan to such voyages. Historical data on frequency of gales, wave heights, and visibility make clear that February is a terrible month to cross the North Atlantic, and March is only marginally better. By April, however, ocean conditions are much different.

Using the coordinates Susan gives in her diary, the Hathorns' day-by-day, sometimes hour-by-hour, course can be plotted from their departure from Trinidad de Cuba till their vessel's docking in London. The *Atlas of Pilot Charts: North Atlantic Ocean* gives historical and statistical weather observations that corroborate Susan's observations and notes the mileage on the great circle routes, which gives one an appreciation for the scale of the Hathorns' voyage.[21] The hypothetical great circle route is the shortest distance between any two points on the earth's surface. Examples, in terms of the earth, would be the equator and meridians of longitude. The pilot's *Atlas* shows great circle routes between typical points, and using these distances the Hathorns' crossing would have totalled 3,487 miles on the great circle.[22] To this distance would be added the approximately seven hundred miles from Trinidad around the western end of Cuba and into the Florida Straits, plus roughly another five hundred for the English Channel and Thames Estuary leg. Therefore, the *J. J. Hathorn*'s course covered at the very least 4,687 nautical miles, or (at 6,080 feet per nautical mile) at least 5,300 land miles. Figuring

This map shows the J. J. Hathorn*'s eastbound Atlantic crossing, March 14–May 7, 1855. Roughly weekly progress marks illustrate the coordinates that Susan recorded in her diary. As the* J. J. Hathorn *neared England and the Gulf Stream's flow diminished, the vessel's progress slowed perceptibly, heightening Susan's impatience and concern for their injured mate's safe arrival.*

that the *J. J. Hathorn* was at sea for fifty-five days, or 1,320 hours, its average speed was slightly over 3.55 knots. However, one must always keep in mind that the great circle is an *ideal* and not a realizable, actual course. Thus, despite Susan's expectations and impatience, the *J. J. Hathorn*'s average speed would actually have been somewhat greater than 3.55 knots, quite good for a vessel of its size and type.[23]

Ocean currents played such an important role in the days of sail, though catching the right current often meant sailing in what might initially appear to be the wrong direction. Currents and winds explain why the *J. J. Hathorn* could not retrace its course and leave Cuba via the Windward Passage. The Hathorns had to travel some distance directly south from Trinidad to get into the current to take them around the west end of Cuba. Once past Cabo San Antonio, the *J. J. Hathorn* caught the minor current taking it along the northwest coast of Cuba and into the Gulf Stream's Florida Current, which could give as much as a 2.8-knot advantage. And as Susan's coordinates confirm, the *J. J. Hathorn* had caught the right currents.

Historical weather data show that during April, a 10 percent frequency of wave heights of twelve feet or more appears over about three fourths of the *J. J. Hathorn*'s route; a 20 percent frequency covers about one half of the route; and a 30 percent frequency covers about one tenth of the route, almost exactly in midocean.[24] As the Hathorns reach this potential trouble zone, Susan's record of one week's conditions shows that they were in fact favored with reasonably good weather:

Sunday, 8th   Last night was not so bad after all. Calm a part of the time. This morning the seas were very bad — cross seas — they thumped us at a terrible rate. The wind suddenly changed about half past ten from NE to SW which favors us again — it had been ahead ever since some time early in the morning.

We have had a fine run for four days — the wind has blown steadily for ever since yesterday — a great rest of the time, we had made 8 knots.

It is so cold, I cannot stay out on deck at all.

The glass is very high, and the wind is hauling around to the eastward. We are now steering south east by east (by compass.)

So cloudy before 4 P.M. could not take an observation. Seems to be preparing for another storm. The glass has not gone down much as yet. Our Long. this morning was 46" 13. Had head winds through the past night — it changed however, at 4 A.M. so we steered our course again.

*Last night was dark but not at all storm{y?}. A fine wind carried us along
all night at the rate of eight knots per hour.*

*Our fine breeze continued through the night but almost became a gale —
however did not take in any of the sails. Today the wind still continues to
blow, and the glass going down, indicates a storm brewing. There was a
circle around the sun at noon. The seas are high but very long. They look
majestic enough. We are making northern much faster than we wish, but it
cannot be helped.*[25]

However, in the next entry, the Trinidad stevedores' work proves
sorely lacking:

*Sunday. April 15th 1855.   Last night was one of the most uncomfortable
nights I ever passed. It blew very hard through the first watch. At 11, took
in all sail & hove to. A little pas{t} 12, the wind changed, and such cross
seas were never seen. The Barque thumped until pas{t} six this morning, and
it seemed as if at every thump, she would loose her counter. Then half the
cargo was flying about between decks, and everything in the cabin rattling —
one might as well sleep in Bedlam.*

*Monday   It was calm nearly all night, and this morning until eleven —
then a light breeze sprang up, but the wind has been very variable all day. It
is calm again tonight. There is a long, heavy swell, the effects of the past
blow.*[26]

Susan reports something that is more likely the onset of morning
sickness than seasickness, as she continues describing midatlantic
conditions:

*We have had a fine breeze ever since yesterday afternoon. Our Latitude at
4 P.M. is 48"07. Longitude by "dead Reckoning" 28"41. so at this rate we
shall soon be in the Channel. . . . I have been sick today and have spent the
time moping.*

*We had a fine breeze through the night but the water was so smooth I though
it calm. At five this morning passed a full rigged Brig, bound Statesward.
A few days more of favorable winds would be very acceptable to us.*

*Clouded up last night — rained a little and the wind came around ahead.
Has continued cloudy all day and some showery — almost as if undecided in
what quarter to settle. The glass is high but moves down a little then up. We
have made but slight progress.*

*Another calm day — no wind last night, except a slight breeze through
one watch. At four this morning, passed a large ship quite near us, but
did not speak her. It is a shame we do not have a breeze, now we are so near
our port.*[27]

With Susan giving the *J. J. Hathorn*'s coordinates at latitude 48°09′
and longitude 24°46′, her estimate of their arrival is more hopeful than
correct. The Hathorns will not reach London itself for another nineteen
days. Has Jode misled Susan to soothe her anxieties? Could he have con-
vinced her they are closer than they really are, given Susan's curiosity
and the fact that she is probably reading the charts for herself? Or is it
more likely that Susan's comment bespeaks her eagerness for their arrival
for other reasons?

On April 2 when the *J. J. Hathorn* was at 35°48′N, 73°13′W (about 175
miles directly east of Cape Hatteras, North Carolina), Susan had given
the good news, "Are in the Gulf"—exactly where Jode Hathorn wanted
to be.[28] The Gulf Stream would help account for some spectacular daily
runs the *J. J. Hathorn* would have on its eastbound Atlantic crossing. But
as they near England and the current dissipates, the London destination—like others—eludes them.

Mr. Bell has become desperately ill. With the combination of morning sickness and high seas, Susan herself is not as well as she might be.
Jode is overworked and neglecting his own health. And ironically,
though Susan herself never evinces great interest in food or cooking,
when the *J. J. Hathorn* enters the sea lanes into the English Channel she
fixes on the subject of food and records her fears about the low supply
of their provisions:

*Our beef is all gone, except a barrel that is so tough one needs steel teeth to
masticate it — Pork all gone — fish was all eaten today — one hhd. of water*

*left, that smells so no mortal can drink it with a good stomach — one pup
{?} and meat all gone, but one solitary box — the flour is so musty, it is next
to impossible to get it down your throat without vomiting — a part of one
ham only left, which we are keeping in case we should ever get a pilot. So
here we are, Longitude at 4 P.M. 13"20. Lat. 49"53. There are fifteen sail
in sight — if a breeze would only spring up, so we could reach one, we would
beg or borrow some provisions.*

*Sunday April 29th   Last night at 7 P.M. spoke the Barque Athena from
the coast of Africa — for Liverpool — 61 days out. Short of provisions. Long.
he gave. 13"50 — a degree and a half different from ours. Lat. at 4 P.M.
48"03 Longitude 12"09. Today our <u>tea</u> has given out, and the beans
nearly so.*

*There are several sail in sight bound our way. A great many vessels pass us
going West — four or five last night and two steamers — one bound in and
one out. It was very rough and there was such a clatter — everything shaking. I scarce slept a wink.*

*We live on scouse, hasty pudding, and salt beef. But as long as we have
enough we will not complain.*

*Our provisions are getting very low — can last but a few days longer. Our
water is all gone but about a fourth of a cask.*[29]

Food is so prominent in Susan's mind that she even substitutes writing
about food for cooking and eating it, as she reports an uncharacteristic
activity:

*I wrote receipts for cooking all this forenoon and this afternoon, have read the
Tragedy "Werner" in Byron. I manage to pass away the time although it
hangs rather heavy. If I had any work, should do better.*[30]

And two days later, still enjoying her food in the abstract, she writes, "I
have spent the day copying Mrs. Hale's recipes for cooking."[31]

Finally on May 8, one week short of two months since setting out
from Trinidad de Cuba, Susan jubilantly writes,

*We passed Dover — a beautiful place, with its old Roman fort and tower —
its high cliffs are white enough. A boat came off to us and has got us some
provisions, for we had literally eaten the last — all the flour and bread gone,
and but a bit of beef. Mr. Bell is very feeble. I have copied from Mrs. Hale's
Cook Book today.*[32]

Susan, reassured by the sight of the cliffs and the emergency provisions,
finally knows they will not starve within sight of land.

The Port of London

Full of expectations about the British capital of which she has read much, Susan sets foot on English soil for the first time on the afternoon of Thursday, May 10, 1855. Though her excitement is tempered by exhaustion, she is relieved to be on any land. In reporting her arrival in ebullient style, Susan brings the saga of Mr. Bell to a happy close:

> This morning by one or two o'clock, we were underweigh and got up towards the dock — got Mr. Bell dressed and he was far better than we had anticipated. The poor fellow was rejoiced to think he was going to the Hospital. Expected the searchers on board and waited from one until four when the ship was towed into the berth. [1]

Susan's diary never specifies the exact location of their berth, but it seems likely that the Hathorns used St. Katherine's Dock, the most proximate to their lodgings and to the sugar and spirits warehouses.

Docks on shallow tidal estuaries like the Thames are large-scale engineering projects, and early-nineteenth-century docks routinely used locks at their entrances to maintain high-tide water levels within the dock. Begun in 1802, St. Katherine's Dock was a project planned by the most celebrated engineer of his time, Thomas Telford, and after twenty-six years of construction and much public debate, it finally opened in 1828. The controversy arose because construction required razing some 1,250 dwellings and displacing more than eleven thousand residents from its twenty-three-acre site. The lure of economic gains anticipated from the exponentially expanding overseas trade finally won out, and Telford's dock was built. Since St. Katherine's accommodated

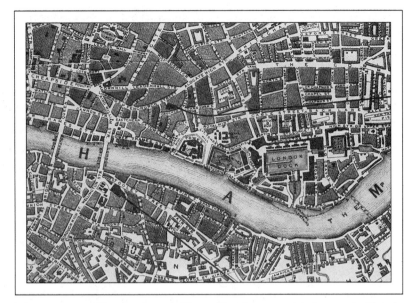

This 1851 map of London shows the Tower of London area, with the tower itself at the center. To the right of the tower, three docks are visible: St. Katherine's Dock, London Dock, and East London Dock, each with locks opening onto the Thames. Crossing the Thames in this part of London was possible via London or Southwark Bridges, or the Thames Tunnel, at the right. Extending north from the tower is the street called The Minories, and just to the west of The Minories lies the three-part George Dance architectural project that included America Square. The dark line running parallel to Cable Street and terminating west of the tower at Fenchurch Street is the Blackwall Railway. America Square, where the Hathorns stayed, lies just south of John Street, between John and the Blackwall Railway.

vessels up to 250 feet long and 24 feet of draft, the *J. J. Hathorn*—at 120 feet long and 13 feet of draft—could easily use that dock.[2]

What did Susan Hathorn do when she reached London? Where did the Hathorns stay, and how did she spend her time while Jode attended to the vessel's business? Susan immediately names their lodging—a sizeable boardinghouse frequented by ships' officers and run by "the Misses Bragge"—which suggests the place was a destination known to them before they arrived.

The Bragge house is situated in tiny America Square,[3] on John Street near its intersection with The Minories, and near the western terminus of the Blackwall Railway.[4] The square runs north-south with John Street passing through it, and its center stands about 275 yards from the northern edge of the Tower of London. First developed in the eighteenth century, the area's street names suggest its history: Blue Anchor Yard, Cooper's Row, Ensign Street, India Street, Lloyds Street. The ambitious project of which America Square was a part was designed by the celebrated architect, George Dance the Younger, and it included, in tandem, a square, a crescent, and a circle.[5]

Within a quarter-mile of America Square, just upstream from the Tower of London, is the port of London's Custom House, from where the "searchers" Susan mentioned would come. Within the same quarter-mile radius lay the enormous East and West India Dock Company Warehouses, the Internal Revenue Office, the Corn Exchange and Commercial Sale Rooms, the Royal Mint, the Victoria Royal Railway Depot, Fenchurch Street Railway Station, the Northwest Railway Goods Depot, and of course St. Katherine's Dock.

In the nineteenth century, seafaring people, even ships' masters, were not always welcome at respectable boardinghouses, since the ill-repute of sailors' in-port behavior placed maritime folk at a social disadvantage.[6] Docks' environs have never been considered safe neighborhoods, but the Hathorns' proceeding to the Bragge house without hesitation suggests that Jode knows the place either personally or through the recommendation of other captains as a place both hospitable to their kind and safe and comfortable for his wife.

Susan reports on the household at once, giving it a good initial review:

> *we took a cab for Miss Bragg{e}'s. Found any quantity of Capts, and three or four Ladies. The place is very good indeed — spent a pleasant evening, playing whist with Capt. House {Howes} and Lady and Capt. Rowe. There is a Mrs. Cle{a}veland here from Martha's Vineyard for her health — and the wife of Capt. Crocker of the new Clipper Ship Edwin Forrest. These are the only ladies at present. Miss Bragge is very kind.*[7]

Street directories such as *Watkins's* give a sense of the neighborhood in which Susan finds herself. In 1855 America Square is almost completely given over to boardinghouses, wine merchants, and shipping-related interests. Of America Square's sixteen numbered addresses, the Bragge house has two (8 and 9), and five other boardinghouses are listed. In addition, three merchants deal in wine and spirits, and there are two general merchants, two agents, a shipowner, a solicitor, a china dealer, and a builder.[8] Comparison of earlier nineteenth-century directories with those of midcentury clearly indicates the changes brought to the area by St. Katherine's Dock and the increased maritime activity.

Susan's reports of the milieu of the Misses Bragge's rooming house is substantiated by the London census of 1851, which lists all individuals under the roof on the night of April 1, 1851, including those only temporarily in residence. First enumerated is Elizabeth Bragge, an unmarried 41-year-old female, listed as the head of the house, her occupation given as "Lodging House Keeper," and her place of birth, Winchester, Suffolk. Four captains, all American, are in residence: Joseph Alexander, age 47, and William Hull, age 40, listed as "Lodgers"; George E. Patten, age 28 (shown as "unmarried"), and John Lillinghurst, age 38, are called "Visitors." George Alexander, age 41 (another "Lodger"), lists his birthplace as Jersey.[9] The three others listed are the servants: a 24-year-old widow named Eliza Wiggins, a 14-year-old unmarried male named Richard Carter, and a 26-year-old unmarried female named Elizabeth Gaffney, all of whose birthplaces are listed as "St. Lukes Middx" (Middlesex). Patten and Alexander are names that appear elsewhere in Susan's diary, for there were Pattens and Alexanders in Richmond. The census shows that America Square's boardinghouses have distinctly national characters; the Bragge house catered to Americans, while the boardinghouse at Number 9, which in 1851 was run by a Scots widow named Elizabeth Reed, had all Scots boarders.[10]

The area's other streets are full of boardinghouses, merchants, shipping agents, manufacturers, and some professionals. In the nineteenth century, John Street, the neighborhood shopping thoroughfare, was called Crosswall,[11] and since mariners traveled light and needed to replace their clothing when they arrived in port, the two tailors and two

This undated sketch of America Square shows it as the widened area that it was, for it did not include a green or park as many London squares did. The George Dance buildings were buff brick, four-story structures with Georgian porticos. This view is looking toward the west and the intersection with John Street.

boot and shoe makers there are not surprising. The Angel, a public house at the northeast corner of Crosswall/John and Vine, does not figure in Susan's diary.[12] The other intersecting street, Vine, had miscellaneous residents: a dairyman, a gun maker, a seed merchant, wine coopers and merchants, a tea dealer, a ship and insurance agent, a stationer, a "carpenter &c," an export pickle warehouse, a hemp and flax merchant, an optician. In the Crescent Mews, Charles Dillimore kept a livery stable, and at the intersection, Number 8, was "Mrs. Elizabeth Bragge" and her boardinghouse.[13] The Bragge establishment appears to be among the largest in the area, having addresses on Vine and America Square. The numbers of people Susan writes of there involve more than a spare room or two let out to visiting captains and their wives and confirm the Bragge enterprise as a commercial and not a casual one.

✌

Like most visitors, Susan finds London's weather a puzzle. As she begins the London portion of her diary, it is May 11, but to her, she says, it seems "A sort of April day—sunny and showery by turns—quite cool—cannot think of sitting without a fire any more than in winter time." [14] She reports a day-long stint of letter writing, to her sisters, Molly and Lucy, possibly to share the news of the baby, and to Captain Hathorn. She at the very least will confirm the *J. J. Hathorn*'s safe arrival, posting her letters via the mail-packet steamer to the United States. The Hathorns and the Lennans should have mail from Susan and Jode within two weeks.

When a vessel comes into port, there are business matters to attend to, and Susan increasingly takes an active role in the partnership with Jode, helping him with clerical tasks. And she freely expresses her views on a few members of the crew with whom she shared two months at sea.

> {H}elped Jode this afternoon, making out the sailors' bills. Was glad when it was done — they all left the ninth or tenth rather — the day we hauled into dock — the Cook and stewardess are going too — so we shall be rid of the whole kit. [15]

Seamen's "bills" must be tallied at the end of each voyage. They are accountings of wages due, against which are levied certain charges. Many vessels charged for medical supplies issued from the ship's medicine chest. In addition, pay could be docked for any number of reasons, including disciplinary causes. Since life at sea is hard on clothing, the sailors' bills could include deductions for items taken from the ship's "slop chest"—the supply of clothing and other personal items carried by the vessel and often sold at outrageous markups. On some vessels the captain's wife maintained the slop chest, but Susan makes no mention of assuming this role. [16]

As the weather that first Saturday in London turns more agreeable, Susan works on two sure cures for her aftercabin fever: shopping and sightseeing:

> {W}ent shopping and purchased a lot of things and spent a heap of money. Shall be poorer than Job's turkeys before we go away. Made the acquaintance

*of Mrs. Soule, an acquaintance of Mrs. Howes. In the evening, we went to
Madame Tussaud's or some such name to see wax figures — they were most
beautiful. I was so tired when I got back, I did not know what to do with
myself. Mrs. Cle{a}veland, and Capt. and Mrs. Howes accompanied us.* [17]

But her protestations aside, Susan does know what to do with herself:
she writes in her diary, concluding her first day in London with "Have
filled up the odd minutes today writing." [18]

On the cold and rainy Sunday that follows, Susan remarks "not much
church-going" among the boarders at the Misses Bragge's. She spends
her Sabbath writing a few letters, but has come down with a cold,

*one of the very worst ones a body could be blest with — head ache, eyes ache —
back ache and legs ache. Nose running, sneezing, throat sore, and <u>raw</u> all the
way up and down. Am always blest in one way or another, so sure as I set
my foot on shore.*

*. . . have played "Old Mother Midnight" with my night cap on — just able
to sit up and mope.* [19]

Susan can still write, however: "I have written to the folks at home and
to Mrs. Hathorn," [20] and she finishes what she refers to as her "'Journal'
to Amasa." Susan never explains her choice of Amasa Ring, her sister
Lucy's husband, as the first recipient of the one letter of this kind Susan
mentions writing on this trip. An epistolary form used by many sea
travelers, both male and female, and in the overland American westward
migration in the 1800s, a journal-letter is added to throughout the journey and sent home for the whole family to share. [21]

Having filed her reports with the family, Susan feels free to socialize,
though she is still convalescing: "Mrs. Howes came up to see me after
tea, & Capt Howes came in with Jode soon after and we had three or
four games of 'High low Jack' and a game of whist. Went to bed tired
enough." [22]

On Wednesday, five days after arriving in London, Susan remains con-
fined to the Misses Bragge's, though she tries to minimize the problem
by saying she is "much better today, although hoarse and plenty of business to attend to my nose. I spent this morning in the Parlor—had a

pleasant chat with a Miss Henderson of Canada. Also with Mrs. Howes
& Cle[a]veland." Susan makes herself two calico aprons while visiting
with "Mrs. C.," and because it is "so cold and chilly," the ladies of the
Bragges' boardinghouse take Susan's care into their own hands. Susan
reports, "They would not allow me to go shopping, and we were going
to the Crystal Palace but deferred it till tomorrow, hoping it would be
more favorable for me." [23]

Finally on Thursday Susan's cold and the weather are both improved:
"have not seen so much of the sun, a day since we arrived here," she says.
It will be a remarkable day for another reason: Susan, Jode, and a party
of captains and their wives will take a train trip to the famous Crystal
Palace. Built as a temporary structure in London's Hyde Park to house
the "first world's fair," the 1851 Great Exhibition of the Works of Industry of All Nations, the iron and glass Crystal Palace was dis-
assembled, moved about eight miles south, and reerected in a somewhat
enlarged version in the south-central London suburb of Sydenham in
1853. Susan is clearly beside herself with excitement as she writes,

> *Capt & Mrs. Howes, Capt Forrest & Miss Henderson, Jode & myself made a*
> *visit to the Crystal Palace — spent the day there. It is impossible to describe*
> *it — I can only say it is a wilderness of beauty. The statuary — the flowers*
> *and fountains — the music — every thing is beautiful and so tastefully ar-*
> *ranged. I could have spent pounds there — but was not very prodigal. We*
> *dined out there and came back in the five o'clock train, almost tired to death.* [24]

While Susan may have been enthralled with the personal shopping pos-
sibilities, statuary, and music, visiting the Crystal Palace had professional implications for sea captains looking out for cargo ideas. The
1850s saw the pace of shipbuilding, maritime trade, and merchant sail
reach a fever pitch. As the Crystal Palace exhibit whetted and reinforced
the public appetite for exotic goods, this appetite created the need for a
fast, economical means of getting the goods to the consumer. The enormous popularity of the Crystal Palace—some six million visitors entered this prototype world trade show during the six months it stood in
Hyde Park—may have been in effect the first mass-marketing cam-
paign. Leigh Hunt pronounced the exposition "neither crystal nor a

palace. . . . It was a bazaar."[25] Queen Victoria herself, a frequent visitor to the exposition, wrote in her own diary, "Some of the inventions were very ingenious, many of them quite Utopian."[26]

One English nursery rhyme begins, "Pussy cat, pussy cat, where have you been? I've been to London to look at the queen." On the day following her Crystal Palace visit, Susan lives the nursery rhyme, after chiding herself for her habit of getting her nose stuck in a book: "I ought to have been gadding about to see the sights as it is almost my last chance, but I got interested in a novel "The Lofty and the Lowly" and could not leave it until finished."[27] Late that morning, however, she does tear herself away. She accompanies Jode and Captain and Mrs. Howes and "a Mr. Shields"

> *to see the good Queen distribute medals to the soldiers who had been wounded while at the Crimea — we were late and could not get near enough to see the ceremony. Only saw the Queen's Carriage — but had a capital view of the Dutchess [sic] of Kent, of the Lord Cardigan (very popular) of the Dukes of Sutherland and Cambridge. The companies on horse were perfectly splendid — I never saw anything equal to their uniforms.*[28]

The medal-ceremony account is one of the rare allusions Susan makes to political matters, though she does not discuss the implications of the Crimean war, perhaps being unaware of the extent of the Crimean conflict and the Royal Navy's pivotal role in it. At stake, after all, was Britain's maritime dominance of the eastern Mediterranean. Believing that her strategic and economic interests would be compromised by Russian control of Constantinople and the Straits, Britain had mounted an all-out effort to prevent this by supporting the Ottoman Empire. To Susan, however, the medal ceremony is a spectator event promising a glimpse of royalty and peers of the realm, a sight of London to be seen; without further reflection, she describes the end of her day: "About five went out & shopped a little with Mrs. Cleaveland. Played a game of whist in the evening, with Mr. Weeks and Mrs. Cleaveland."[29]

On May 13, 1842, the *Illustrated London News (ILN)* had revolutionized the news media by publishing engravings depicting news events, and the *ILN* is a valuable resource in reconstructing the scene that Su-

The May 18, 1855, Crimean War medal ceremony, at which Susan was a spectator, was depicted in the Illustrated London News. *The lengthy account there includes mention of dignitaries whom Susan reports seeing, though from her vantage point she could not herself see Queen Victoria.*

san witnessed. The *ILN*'s fortnightly coverage was not generally "hard news" but personality-centered and human-interest journalism. Along with stories devoted to royalty and nobility, it offered sensational accounts of murders and other crimes in a style prefiguring later "tabloid" journalism.[30] The *ILN* covered certain cultural events as well, such as the story in the issue of May 12, 1855, which would have been on the stands during Susan's visit, on the opening of a controversial exhibit of paintings at the Royal Academy in Trafalgar Square the previous week, which Susan does not mention visiting.[31] The *ILN* reviewed theater offerings,[32] horticultural "fetes," and the latest in Paris bustles, shawls, and parasols. It recorded the tides and the daily temperatures and weather conditions, and stories on various maritime subjects appear frequently in the *ILN*'s pages. The May 12 issue carried a story on the departure of the Royal Navy's Baltic fleet only days before the *J. J. Hathorn* arrived, on which Susan does not remark. Nor does she note the story of the May 3rd loss of the bark *John* and its 282 passengers.[33] The May 12 issue also quotes the *New York Herald* on a matter of interest to mariners: "the renowned sea-serpent, after an absence of several years, has turned up, off the Capes of Delaware. He is reported to be 100 feet in length."[34]

The *ILN* was not all sensationalism or celebrity puff: a May 19 story discusses U.S. President Pierce's embarrassment over the slavery question, something the British government would be pleased to point out. As the summer of 1855 wears on, Lord Raglan (posted back to the Crimea and acting as the *ILN*'s war correspondent) will send his dispatches via the latest in news technology, the telegraph. The May 26 issue, which carried the medals-ceremony story, is full of war news, including an account of shot and shell casings being loaded into Royal Navy vessels at Woolwich.[35] It is hard to imagine that Susan could not have noticed so much military activity on the Thames.

🦢

*I thought as I was so soon to leave I must go shopping and get the girls' dresses, so Mrs. Howes and myself posted away up to Tottingham Square —
would not go there again, for what is saved on {that} which {is} bought is lost in cab hire and sheer bother.*[36]

Still suffering from her cold, Susan says she "could just crawl back" from Tottingham Square. But then after dinner (and hemming two silk handkerchiefs for Jode), Susan joins Jode, Captain and Mrs. Howes, and Mrs. Cleaveland to form a party to visit another of London's tourist attractions, the Thames Tunnel.

Begun in 1825 and opened March 25, 1843,[37] the first Thames tunnel was still, in 1855, considered a must for tourists and included a variety of amusements that Susan reports as she writes,

{I}t is a curious place — went into the lunching room & took a glass of lemonade. It was hung with spangles and ornaments with tissue paper. And

the farther end is a saloon for taking profiles, dageurrotypes {sic}, & Drawings {&}c.[38]

Susan gives few details about most guests at the Misses Bragge's, but her entry of Monday, May 21, raises some interesting questions. She writes of the rainy weather that forces her to spend her time with Mrs. Crocker and Mrs. Howes "in the house, quite profitably," making a brown muslin skirt, sewing "the breadths of my blue all wool de Laine," and running "the breadths of the flounces—shall have two." It is a busy day at the Bragge house: "Mrs. Ainsworth had company and Mrs. Cleaveland went out to get her hair dressed—then departed with Mr. Weeks for the Doctor's where she will remain for a week, when she expects to return to New York."[39] One wonders why Mrs. Cleaveland, traveling without a husband and in the company of Mr. Weeks, is spending a week at a doctor's prior to her return to New York. She seems to have been a favorite of Susan's, who may have taken pity on Mrs. Cleaveland's solitary state. Was Mrs. Cleaveland, like Susan, pregnant? Mrs. Cleaveland's first name is never given, but she was among those in residence when the Hathorns arrived, first appearing in Susan's diary on May 10 ("There is a Mrs. Cle[a]veland here from Martha's Vineyard for her health"). Her health was not all that poor, however, for on May 12 she was among those who went to Madame Tussaud's. On the sixteenth, when Susan was ill, "Mrs. C. came to my room after dinner and spent this afternoon." And on the eighteenth, "About five went out & shopped a little with Mrs. Cleaveland. Played a game of whist in the evening, with Mr. Weeks and Mrs. Cleaveland"; on the nineteenth, Mrs. Cleaveland went to the Thames Tunnel with Susan and Jode.[40]

Eager as they had been to get to London, both Hathorns find themselves looking forward to the *J. J. Hathorn's* departure. "Jode was out of sorts today," she writes on Monday, May 21, and gives as the reason, "—nothing doing—will not get away until the middle or last of the week."[41] "Hope to get to sea Thursday if nothing happens," she says on Tuesday.[42]

Susan's predictions of departure prove more optimistic than accurate. She fills the days while waiting with her sewing ("my blue plaid dress . . . my reddish pink lawn . . . my green dress") and visits St. Paul's

and a picture frame shop in nearby Houndsditch Lane, though the diary
never says what picture she had framed there:

> {T}he sun came out finally and we have had a fine day. I went shopping this
> morning in Aldgate Street, also this afternoon.

> The most pleasant day I have seen in London and the most nearly approach-
> ing summer. Mrs. Ainsworth, Mrs. Howes and myself went to St. Paul's
> Cathedral after breakfast. It is the most truly grand structure I ever beheld.
> Grandness is the only word that applies to it. . . . After resting a little
> while, went all alone down to the end of Houndsditch and found a store
> where picture frames were kept, and my picture is to be framed tomorrow by
> 10 A.M.[43]

Unfortunately, on the Thursday when Jode had hoped to leave, the *J. J.
Hathorn* is not ready to sail. For Susan this is a piece of good luck, for
she has not yet visited the Tower of London, the landmark closest to
America Square:

> A fine day today and quite moderate, almost like summer. . . . Went to the
> Tower at half past twelve with Capt. Forrest as Jode was busy. Have not
> been to a place in London which interested me so much. There is everything to
> remind you of the past, armors and trophies from the time of Wm., the Con-
> queror to the present time. Elizabeth in full dress on horseback — her favorite
> Essex in complete Armor — many of the kings of England — the place where
> the unfortunate princes were smothered — when first-buried, and where after-
> wards interred was shown us — the ax that beheaded Essex & probably Lady
> Jane Grey, also the place where she was executed — I enjoyed it much.[44]

After the tower, the following day—"A sort of a lost day—have done
nothing, been no where and seen nothing"—is a featureless day of
waiting.

> We expected to go today. My trunk is packed, so I could get at no work, and
> I have loitered away the day. Wrote to Sarah Remington, and then walked
> down the street, and got some apples, nuts & oranges to eat of an old Market
> woman.[45]

That evening she stays in, reading "nearly through" a travel book, " 'Six
Months in Italy' by Hillard," while

all the rest went to the theater or some other place of amusement. Miss
Bragge, Capt. & Mrs. Ainsworth went to see Charlotte Cushman, as Miz
Mirilies in Guy Mannering. Capt & Mrs. Crocker to the Polytechnic, &
Capt. & Mrs. Erskine to Madame Tussaud's. So Mrs. Howes & myself were
left alone in our glory.[46]

Saturday morning bright and early, Susan is more than ready to sail.
She is clearly annoyed by but probably not surprised to learn of a personnel problem on the *J. J. Hathorn*:

Packed my things this morning for a start, expecting to go away to Dover, by
the rail road, when lo: Jode had a telegraphic despatch from the mate that
the Pilot had left drunk, and the Barque was still at Gravesend.[47]

This entry reveals several things, most important that the *J. J. Hathorn*,
having discharged its cargo, had been towed down the Thames; simple
economics would urge this, for the expense of a berth had to be kept to
a minimum. The entry also shows that Susan will take the train to meet
the *J. J. Hathorn* at Gravesend, rather than Dover, which means that
Susan will be aboard as the bark leaves the Thames Estuary.

After sixteen days in London, when the Hathorns get away on the
twenty-sixth, Susan expresses regret at leaving new friends at the Misses
Bragge's. She also makes explicit her feeling that the *J. J. Hathorn* is now
"home."

So {Jode} settled his business, remitted what money he could spare, and by
four o'clock, we bade adieu to dear good Mrs. Howes, to Mrs. Ainsworth,
Mrs. Crocker, & the Misses Bragge, and were on our winding way. I was
rejoiced to think of getting <u>home</u> to the ship again. I had been ready so long,
and feeling as if one foot was on shore, and the other on the water, it was
a pleasure to be sure of something. The Barque lay a long way up from the
station, and a boatman took us up to her — arrived at about half past six.
Found every thing in nice order. Tired enough. (Warm day.)[48]

Light to Cardiff

If we were only out, we should have got to Cardiff by this time—the wind has blown a smashing breeze," Susan writes aboard the *J. J. Hathorn* on the last Sunday of May 1855.[1] But the *J. J. Hathorn* is still at anchor at Gravesend with the wind "against us," and Jode has not succeeded in replacing the drunken pilot. Susan writes that the cool weather is "not at all like the last of May," and though her own cold is better, Jode's is "very bad." Not an auspicious departure. Yet she is happy to be back aboard the *J. J. Hathorn*, virtually in the sole company of her husband. She says, "Have not felt a bit lonely, although we just left such a house full."[2]

Finally on a rainy, cool Monday, May 28, Susan reports,

> *Jode got up real early and went ashore for a Pilot — finally succeeded in obtaining one — the wind was fair until noon, when it changed against us. So shall have to anchor before long, as the tide will be against us too.*[3]

On that day she plays two roles: the house/ship wife and Jode's business partner. With her usual phrase for housekeeping, she says she puts "things a little to rights this morning," and reports she "then sat down to settle accounts—have put our own and the ship's to rights."[4]

The next day, however, the *J. J. Hathorn* is truly under way, for Susan reports that the "pilot left us about half past seven" in the morning, and that afternoon they make good progress: "The wind was tolerably fair, and we went along finely until nearly dinner time—then died away—was calm until six—then came round ahead. We are tonight off Beachy Head."[5]

Susan has set to work on still *another* pair of shoes: she has a new pattern that she describes as "the oak leaves and coral," has already made five of the leaves on the front, and says she has spent the day working very happily. But Jode's health troubles her: "My cold is better, but Jode is downright sick with his—he looks as pale as if he had a month's sickness." As Susan finishes her long May 29 entry, she describes the way the bark is handling, confirming that the *J. J. Hathorn* is going "light"—without cargo or much ballast—to Cardiff: "Just after writing this, the wind changed in a minute in our favor and a good stiff breeze it is—things went flying over the cabin strangely as the vessel is so light, she laid over a good deal." [6] A light vessel is a top-heavy one, and with the wind behind them and the prevailing current against them, they do not find smooth sailing. Susan, about four months pregnant, has a mishap that may have concerned her, though she minimizes the accident in the way she characterizes it:

> *The fine breeze has continued all day, but it has been as cold as Greenland. We could have no fire, it smoked so. I got out of bed this morning, and took a hasty roll down against my trunk. I never saw the barque lay over so bad. You walk up hill at an angle of full forty-five degrees. But we are getting along finely.* [7]

And she has started recording coordinates again. "Our Lat is 49"50 Long. 4"35," at 4 P.M. on the afternoon of the thirtieth, which puts the *J. J. Hathorn* approximately twenty miles off the coast of Cornwall, about midway between Plymouth and the island's southernmost point, "The Lizard."

🐚

Susan, for once, says she is tired of "working." Instead, she starts reading a book by Harriet Beecher Stowe, *Sunny Memories of Foreign Lands.* "Like it better than I thought I should on first opening it." [8] *Sunny Memories* is an appropriate choice for Susan, as it is an account of Mrs. Stowe's 1853 trip to Liverpool. [9] In addition, Harriet Beecher Stowe has midcoast Maine ties, having written *Uncle Tom's Cabin* while a faculty wife at Bowdoin College in Brunswick, Maine, some fifteen miles from Susan's girl-

This map shows the J. J. Hathorn's calls in British ports, May 10–June 30, 1855. During the week between May 3 and the J. J. Hathorn's landing in London, Susan reported rough sailing in the English Channel. On the eighth, the Hathorns took on a pilot due south of London, at Beachy Head. Leaving London, the Hathorns would sail without cargo to Cardiff to load iron rails.

hood home. *Uncle Tom's Cabin* had been first published serially in 1851–52, and even if apolitical Susan had no particular feelings about the abolitionist cause, she might have been curious about her neighbor's celebrity. Jode's feelings about Mrs. Stowe turn out to be another matter.

Written in the form of letters home to her children during her voyage, Mrs. Stowe's *Sunny Memories* was first published in New York and

Boston in 1854, and Susan may well have identified with the author on its very first page: "You know how often we have longed for a sea voyage, as the fulfilment of all our dreams of poetry and romance, the realization of our highest conceptions of free, joyous existence." But, as Mrs. Stowe adds and Susan knows, "Let me assure you, my dears, . . . that going to sea is not at all the thing that we have taken it to be." [10]

In Richmond, Susan would have witnessed ship launchings, including that of the *J. J. Hathorn* itself, and Mrs. Stowe's florid description is reminiscent of Susan's "Ship Graduate" essay:

> You remember our ship-launching parties in Maine, when we used to ride to the seaside through dark pine forests, lighted up with the gold, scarlet, and orange tints of autumn . . . how all our sympathies went forth with the grand new ship about to be launched. How graceful and noble a thing she looked, as she sprang from the shore to the blue waters, like a human soul springing from life into immortality! How all our feelings went with her! how we longed to be with her, and a part of her—to go with her to India, China, or any where, so that we might rise and fall on the bosom of that magnificent ocean, and share a part of that glorified existence. [11]

Like Susan, Mrs. Stowe finds that *real* life at sea held less exalted moments. While Susan is part of the ship's company on a sailing vessel and Mrs. Stowe is a passenger on a steamer, their realizations seem to have come with similar shock. "Alas! what a contrast between all this poetry and the real prose fact of going to sea!" Mrs. Stowe proclaims, as she sets about demystifying life at sea. "The one step from the sublime to the ridiculous is never taken with such alacrity as in a sea voyage." [12]

The fact that "ship life is not at all that fragrant" leads Mrs. Stowe to that topic irresistible to all who write about the sea—seasickness:

> that disgust of existence, which, in half an hour after sailing, begins to come upon you; that strange, mysterious ineffable sensation which steals slowly and inexplicably upon you; which makes every heaving billow, every white-capped wave, the ship, the people, the sight,

taste, sound, and smell of every thing a matter of inexpressible loathing! Man cannot utter it.[13]

Mrs. Stowe writes of scenes she, like Susan, had imagined: sitting in her stateroom, passing the time by reading, sewing, sketching, and chatting, and

> accordingly I laid in a magnificent provision in the way of literature and divers matters of fancy work with which to pass the time. Some last, airy touches, in the way of making up bows, disposing ribbons, and binding collarets, had been left to these long, leisure hours, as matters of amusement.[14]

Instead, real life at sea gets her worst recommendation: "I wonder that people who wanted to break the souls of heroes and martyrs never thought of sending them to sea and keeping them a little seasick."[15] Susan's rapture over the moon in Cuban waters contrasts sharply with Mrs. Stowe's view of the nocturnal seascape:

> the beauties of night on shipboard!—down in your berth, with the sea hissing and fizzing, gurgling and booming, within an inch of your ear; and then the steward comes along at twelve o'clock and puts out your light, and there you are! Jonah in the whale was not darker or more dismal. There, in proud ignorance and blindness, you lie, and feel yourself rolled upwards, and downwards, and sidewise, and all ways, like a cork in a tub of water. . . .
>   . . . the old blue-haired Ocean whispers through the planks, "Here you are; I've got you. Your grand ship is my plaything. I can do what I like with it."[16]

But Harriet Beecher Stowe does arrive in England safely, and as she does, she expresses feelings other American travelers, including Susan, might have:

> Say what we will, an American, particularly a New Englander, can never approach the old country without a kind of thrill and pulsation of kindred. Its history for two centuries was our history. . . . Our very life-blood is English life-blood.[17]

On its way to Cardiff, the *J. J. Hathorn* finds cold Channel weather. In her entry for May 30, Susan is still concerned about Jode's health ("Jode's cold is still bad"), and she observes that he does not take care of himself properly: "He is so careless of himself he keeps constantly adding to it. He went to bed to get warm this afternoon." [18] With a fire going in the aftercabin, Susan notes that this is "The last day of spring and it is cold enough to be the first." [19]

The "fine breeze" of which Susan spoke a day earlier has become a "double-reefed topsail head wind today—can do nothing at all in the way of beating, it blows so hard." The *J. J. Hathorn* has its sails furled except for the topsails, and those are double-reefed (twice-shortened) to reduce the area exposed to the wind. "Reefing" is necessary when a vessel encounters headwinds or begins to labor because of the wind's strength. [20] "Beating" is the trick of sailing to windward through a series of alternate tacks, or turnings of the vessel across the wind, to bring the wind onto the vessel's opposite side. [21] Of course, when the wind is too high or changeable, as Susan notes, beating is not possible.

"We passed the Scilly Islands about twelve last night," Susan writes on May 31. Rough seas and pregnancy, she finds, are not such a good combination: "I have been most comfortably sick—have been such a glutton, I can now eat nothing—vomit it up, so soon as I get it down. Hope to be better tomorrow." [22] Throughout Susan's diary, calendar milestones serve to turn her thoughts homeward. As June arrives and Susan observes "the first day of summer," she writes, "wish I were home to see how things look." [23] The sun shines and the weather is warmer along the Cornish coast, and she writes, "I got up a little before dinner, complaining of feeling much better, although so weak I can hardly step." She reports eating "some nice roasted potatoes" for dinner.

Susan has finished with Mrs. Stowe's book and passed it on to her husband. As *Sunny Memories of Foreign Lands* progresses, Mrs. Stowe drops the device of letters-to-the-children and her message becomes pointedly abolitionist. Susan expresses surprise at Jode's reaction to Mrs. Stowe's book, reporting, "Jode has commenced reading 'Sunny Memo-

Reefing a sail on a square-rigged vessel involved sending crew members aloft to gather and tie the canvas, thereby decreasing its surface area.

ries'! for all he is so prejudiced against Mrs. Stowe—he likes it too." [24] Jode's view of Mrs. Stowe raises the question as to whether the Hathorns were involved in the African slave trade. That a maritime family's fortunes rise in times when fortunes could have been made in the slave trade proves nothing. [25] Though trafficking in slaves and profiting from slave labor are two different matters, they are related. Surely Jode Hathorn realizes that the sugar, molasses, and rum they load in Cuba are produced through the labors of Cuban slaves, and that without the Caribbean leg of their trade voyages, the profits would plummet.

Jode's positive response to Mrs. Stowe's latest book may have been in response to the seagoing subject matter. As the *J. J. Hathorn* draws near the Bristol Channel, Jode "finishes" Mrs. Stowe's book in a day—perhaps by not bothering with the latter chapters. For all the charm with which it begins, *Sunny Memories* develops into a long, dense, polemical book.

Susan says they are "close to the Fundy Islands," by which she means Lundy Island, the largest in the Bristol Channel.[26] Once again the Hathorns wait for a pilot. "If one does not come off to us tonight, shall anchor, Susan says, and she looks back over the week: "it seems hardly possible, it is a week today since we bid adieu to all the good folks of America Square. Hope all the weeks will glide by as swiftly until we reach home."[27] She reports that not only is she "nicely today" but she has made five leaves on the front of her second shoe: "it seems so good to feel like working, and feel able to work."[28]

As Susan's entry for a cloudy and pleasant June 3 reveals, she has visited New York harbor, most likely en route to meet the *J. J. Hathorn* at Philadelphia. The hills of Exmoor are a welcome sight, as Susan looks forward to seeing other Maine captains in Cardiff:

> *The wind was ahead, but finally came round fair, so we got up finely to the anchoring ground. There are <u>hosts</u> of ships here. — the harbor presents almost as much of a forest of masts as N.Y. We saw the "Waltham." Capt. Wheeler, among the number. The view in many places was beautiful — the green fields looked so refreshing, & sloped so prettily, it did one's eyes good to look on them. I have written Fannie & Hosea today.*[29]

With a "beautiful mild morning like spring," Susan reports a storm during the night and lingering showers, after which "the face of nature looks as if it had had a good washing." Susan has the day to herself; with the *J. J. Hathorn* riding at anchor, Jode disembarks after breakfast to go to town and will spend the night there. She is back at work on her shoes and making good progress, and then "Just at dark, took me up a cotton stocking."[30]

🌊

Jode has chosen a poor time to be away, as Susan's entry for the next day reports,

Last night was quite wild, and what made it still more so, a little French
Barque came down upon us, and we had a real collision. The Frenchman
sustained little injury apparently, but we had the main yard carried
away — bulwarks stove in several places, and chain plates torn up. All were
asleep on board the other Barque and the accident happened while the vessels
were swinging.[31]

Without a U.S. consul in Cardiff, no consular posts document this incident. The *J. J. Hathorn*'s damages sound not exactly minor, but in the
close quarters of anchoring grounds, incidents of this type were not unusual. It has upset Susan, however, and she again seems impatient with
the men around her. She makes great strides with her alpaca skirt until
they return:

Jode came back about eleven — Capt. Wheeler with him. Had a very sociable
time, talking over home affairs and people. Jode carried him to his ship, to see
the Major, who is still with him. I began to quilt my alpacca [sic] skirt —
got along famously until they came, then knit.[32]

The next morning just before 10 A.M., Susan says the sun disappeared
and "the rain poured down in torrents." When the rain lets up about
11 A.M. Jode and Captain Wheeler go ashore to arrange docking for the
J. J. Hathorn, leaving Susan aboard the bark, quilting, through another
torrential rain and continuing showers the rest of the day. Then we learn
that Jode has a musical talent: "Capt. Wheeler & Jode came back about
four o'clock—Capt. W. spent the evening with us. Jode bought him an
accordian [*sic*] and entertained us with a little music. I knit all the
evening."[33]

Securing immediate docking was not easy in a time when port construction could not keep pace with maritime activity. The seventh of
June finds the Hathorn bark still at anchor in the roads off Cardiff. Built
around a Norman fortress that became Cardiff Castle, the city was en-
ergized in the 1830s by the completion of the Bute Dock:

[B]egun and completed by the nobleman whose name they bear, at
the enormous outlay of £300,000, these docks have proved a source
of vast emoluments to the town, as before their construction great

impediments were found to exist of a character detrimental to the commercial interests of Cardiff and the mining districts generally. These colossal docks, which were opened on the 9th of October, 1839, embrace a wide extent being 1450 yards in length, and 200 in width, with an area of 200 acres of water, the basin is of sufficient depth to float vessels of 1000 tons burthen.[34]

Port facilities at Cardiff are comparable to London's, though on a much smaller scale. On a cloudy June 7,

> *Jode went ashore about half past ten with Capt. Wheeler, but {they} were not more successful about getting the ships into dock than the day before. They returned about half past four. Capt. W. took supper with us and spent the evening.*[35]

While the men visit, Susan knits. She has finished quilting her alpaca skirt and bound it around the bottom with velvet she salvages from another piece of clothing. The weekend is fast approaching, and they are "still out in the stream." Jode takes this opportunity to see that the *J. J. Hathorn* gets its repairs: "Capt. W. went ashore again today to make a last effort, but Jode staid on board, fitting the main yard, which was carried away the other night."[36] Susan incidentally provides a glimpse of the *J. J. Hathorn*'s captain's quarters and still embroidering, she passes the time writing to her family:

> *took up the carpet and John washed it — the steward cleaned the most of the cabin for me, and I cleaned the state-room. It is a decided improvement. After I got dressed, worked a little on the slippers, but was too tired to do much. My letter home goes today{;} intended writing to Pap, but thought I would wait until we got into dock, and found when we were to do any thing.*[37]

Frustrated by the wait, Susan offers a June 9 critique of the British summer—hardly that different from Maine's—as she notes more rain: "that is too common an occurrence to be noticed in England."[38] Jode and Captain Wheeler return that afternoon, bringing "a Capt. Bird with them." Jode seems to sense Susan's growing restlessness:

> *I had so pressing an invitation from Capt. W. seconded by Jode, to go on board his ship and spend the night and Sabbath that I concluded to go.*

This 1850s lithograph depicts the entrance to Cardiff's Bute Dock at high tide, with a steam towboat taking a full-rigged ship out through the open gates. In the foreground, next to the buoy, a couple is being rowed ashore; the vessel from which they have apparently come is anchored outside the dock, as the J. J. Hathorn *was for some days.*

> *So rigged up and off we set. Capt. Bird also took tea with us. He is a Thomaston man.*[39]

And Susan admits her opinion of Captain Wheeler's passenger, "Major Witham," was mistaken: " . . . never got acquainted with him before— like him very much indeed."[40]

❦

Back at work on her shoes, Susan goes aboard the *Waltham.* Captain Wheeler's ship, having reached Cardiff before the *J. J. Hathorn*, is in line to dock first, and Susan is clearly eager to see what Cardiff holds in store. During Sunday noon dinner aboard the *Waltham,* Susan gets herself stranded:

> *the steamboat came to take Capt. Wheeler's ship into dock — so I had to be taken in too, and as our ship will probably come in tomorrow, I am*

going to stay on board the Waltham — it is a nice ship — every thing is so neat, and convenient.[41]

Susan makes herself useful aboard the *Waltham*, acting as hostess for Captain Wheeler: "Capt. Jones from Maryland called after we got in, and Capt. Hinkley of Blue-hill, Me.," she says. "They are both very pleasant men."[42] The visit to the *Waltham* turns out to be longer than Susan expects. On Monday, June 11, she writes, "A fair day—the Waltham has hauled up the dock to her berth, but the 'J.J.' has no prospect of getting in, so I am still a visitor with Capt. W. Have spent the day pleasantly, reading Byron."[43]

She also tells us, "Jode made me a present of 'Moore's Poems'" and reports that the Hathorns have "an invitation to go out to Mr. Brown's about two miles in the country tomorrow."[44]

Who is Mr. Brown, and where "in the country" does he live? The *Hunt and Co. Directory* lists "Joseph Brown & Co. Bute Street" in its business section under two categories: Ship Brokers and Ship Chandlers.[45] Susan tells us later that the Brown home is located in the then-suburb of Roath, only about a mile and a quarter from the center of Cardiff, on the South Wales Railway. The new railroad, which increased the population of Roath nearly eightfold in the years 1851–61 (394 to 3,044),[46] provided the "cars" Susan and Jode used on one trip between Bute Dock and the Brown residence.

Finally, on June 12, the *J. J. Hathorn* is "hauled up above the Waltham." A party of sea captains and Susan—the only wife present—set out for Roath. Susan's long, eventful day includes a visit to an ancient cathedral and finding a new friend in Mr. Brown's sister:

Started about three — Capt.s Wheeler, Jones, Hinkley, York, Thorndike, and Hathorn — such a fine time as we had. Mr. Brown has a most beautiful house — splendidly furnished — his sister keeps it for him, Mrs. Parry. She is a pleasant Lady — a widow. We had a grand dinner — every thing nice, among other things, cucumbers. After dinner, the gents went on a ride — Mrs. P. and self took a walk — visited one of the oldest Cathedrals in England — it is in ruins and over-run with ivy. The scenery is as beautiful and

romantic as can be imagined. Had supper & got back to the ship at half past
twelve.[47]

But life for a captain's wife cannot be all country house parties; for the
next few days Susan is busy with washing and ironing her own and Jode's
clothing, and housekeeping in the captain's quarters.

Jode, too, has work to do. One issue he must deal with, now that the
vessel is in port, is his labor force for the crossing. Susan offers her ironic
opinion (possibly reflecting Jode's) on the nameless mate who came on
at London to replace the disabled Mr. Bell: "Our <u>Fish</u> mate left today,
and we have a new man in his place."[48] Changes of mates were one
matter; of the changes in crew, Susan writes,

> *Our sailors left today — all except John and old Charley, and John wants*
> *to go, but Jode thinks he shall keep him until he gets to Savannah. Old Bob*
> *and Irish Jack are in town — think they will come back again to the ship.*[49]

Since the vessel is empty, cargo can be taken on immediately. "We
have had a lighter of iron! Are coming on famously," Susan reports on
June 13. She does not describe the iron or say where it is going. Since
the destination of the *J. J. Hathorn* will be Savannah (and since Savannah
is at this time busily building its railways), the iron can be presumed to
be railroad rails.[50]

In Cardiff Susan seems content on board attending to her domestic
duties as the cargo comes on: "I set things to rights this morning and
after Jode went up town, got my wash tub out once more. Washed the
stockings, hand kerchiefs, collars, &c. It really seemed good to get into
the suds again."[51] Other captains continue calling on the Hathorns,
though not always to Susan's delight:

> *Capt. W. and Capt. Laurence called, the latter has just arrived from Havre.*
> *Capt. Dinsmore also came in today. Their call spoiled my afternoon for*
> *work, so I mended my undersleeves, and a few other things. Felt tired enough*
> *at night, for all I washed so little. Went to bed at eight.*

> *Jode got some cloth for shirts yesterday, so I shall now have enough to do.*
> *Have hemmed three table cloths for the ship, and sewed a little on my linen*

chemise I cut out so long ago, at sea. Have also done my ironing and starch-
ing — had quite a little heap.[52]

Though still impatient with interruptions, Susan truly seems to have
found her métier as captain's wife.

On the weekend, Susan will go visiting. "Got up quite early and
dressed my hair," Susan writes on Saturday, June 16. Captain Wheeler
takes her "to call on the Misses Brown, who are to teach me to do leather
work." At 10 P.M. that night she reports the day's events:

*At two o'clock, we set out — found a carriage at the ship chandler's and had
a fine drive to "Elm Place, Roath." Just one of the neatest little cottages,
shaded by trees, that one need see. Miss Brown was very much pleased to see
me — Capt. Wheeler & Jode left me there, and I got along considerably in
the work. Mr. Brown came with them, about six and we drove out to his
place — saw Mrs. Parry and Miss Jane Brown. Had a fine drive home, and
Capt. W. spent the evening with us.*[53]

But upon her return to the *J. J. Hathorn*, Susan finds that "The washer-
woman brought my clothes and they were lying in heaps on the sofa,
writing desk and trunk."[54] Into this messy scene ("The bed was not
made, and everything was in magnificent confusion") come visitors—
Captains Wheeler and Jones. Jode comes to Susan's social rescue, taking
the company "for a walk when I improved this time setting things to
rights. They came in again after dinner—Capt. Bird with them—took
tea, and spent the evening."[55]

The workaday week begins with a cool, rainy Monday, June 18, and
Susan mending "my stockings and the flannels this forenoon." It has
turned so cold that Susan says "it takes me half the time to rub my
fingers to keep them from stiffening." The stalwart Major Witham
spends the evening with the Hathorns, with Susan reporting "we had a
nice sociable time."[56]

❧

The biweekly *Shipping and Commercial List* for June 20 details the activity in Cardiff, showing vessel, captain, and the port arriving from or
departing for:

CARDIFF—Arr. June 10, Waltham, Wheeler, Havre (to load for Mobile); 12th, J. J. Hathorn, Hathorn, London (to load for Savannah); 12th, Clarissa Bird, Bird, Havre; 14th, Ella Reed, King, London; Sentinel, Soule, Havre.[57]

This makes clear that the *J. J. Hathorn* carried no cargo to Cardiff, and that Captain Wheeler's *Waltham* also arrived empty. In fact, British law allowed coastwise cargoes (between two British ports) to be carried only by British-flagged ships. The *Shipping and Commercial List* for June 16 confirms the names of other captains and vessels Susan mentions in her diary:

CARDIFF—Arr. May 30, General Cobb, Haskell, Antwerp; 28, Jos. Jones, Hosmer [Osman]; H. Purrington, Hinkley, Havre. Sld. [Sailed] 26th, Lydia, Jones, Charleston; Lotus, Vickery, City Point, Va.[58]

These brief listings for Cardiff do not capture the real romance of maritime life conveyed in the *List*'s prose-poems. Names of vessels drawn from mythology, literature, and history are juxtaposed with names of storied Yankee captains and those of their exotic destinations, from Apalachicola to Zanzibar, and through this remarkable publication runs the trail of the *J. J. Hathorn* and Susan's husband, Jode, shuttling back and forth between Europe and the Caribbean, paralleling Susan's diary.

With the new week in Cardiff, there is business to attend to on the *J. J. Hathorn*. On Tuesday morning the bark is hauled farther down the dock "as the place where we were lying was too shallow for us to load there."[59] Susan might well be recalling the several moves the *J. J. Hathorn* had to make in Trinidad de Cuba, for she grumbles: "It takes half the time to move the ship about. The stevedore thinks we shall be loaded by Thursday night—over a third is now in the hold."

Then Susan records an interesting scene that takes place during the moving of the *J. J. Hathorn*:

As we came near the "Waltham," Mr. Bickford told me to hurry and go on board, else I might not be able to get on shore — so without combing my head,

*or waiting to half dress, I scrambled up one ladder and down another, and
landed safely on deck, {and} found the cabin full.*[60]

The *J. J. Hathorn*'s first mate, Mr. Bickford, is looking out for Jode's
bride, for the Bickfords and Hathorns, besides being kin, have a long
shared history at sea.

Among the National Archives maritime records are the applications
for the rudimentary form of passport for seamen called Seamen's Protection Papers, intended to protect them from impressment in foreign
navies or merchant services, particularly the British, who made a practice of manning ships in this way. These applications describe the
individual in general terms, and on January 29, 1831, heading the list
of four young mariners who presented themselves to the collector of the
Customs District of Plymouth, North Carolina, was "Jefferson Hathorn,
age 22, 5'11", light complexion, born Dresden Maine." Following him
was his relative "Edward Bickford, age 22, 5'5–3/4," light complexion,
born Dresden Maine."[61] As already noted, the Richmond Hathorns descended from a John Hathorn who settled in the Dresden community in
the early eighteenth century. His son John Jr. had two wives and thirteen children—six by Esther Gray, and seven by Elizabeth Bickford.
Jefferson Hathorn, Jode's father, was the first of John Jr. and Elizabeth
Bickford's four sons, and J. J. Hathorn was their youngest child. Their
relative George Bickford would be the *J. J. Hathorn*'s first mate on her
final voyage.[62]

⚓

The loading of the iron continues through the week of June 18. Susan
reports, "We are progressing finely with our loading business" and on
Friday can say, "Our ship is all loaded."[63] She expects the *J. J. Hathorn*
to sail for Savannah early the following week. During loading, Susan has
immersed herself in the port's social life and become adept at jumping
between ships, as she returns that night to the *J. J. Hathorn*:

*Dined with {Captain and Mrs. Barnes, Captain Laurence, and Captain
Dinsmore}, and then went to Miss Brown's — had a nice time — Got back
without any trouble by climbing over the Clarissa Bird — Capt.s Wheeler &
Dinsmore spent the evening with us.*[64]

The Hathorns take their turn hosting the group: "Capt.s Wheeler and Hinkley took dinner with us," Susan says, describing an aftercabin full of captains and their pipes relaxing in port:

> *Capt. Wheeler came in with Jode and spent the evening — also Capt.s. Bird, and Millikin of the Anna Smidt. I was so sleepy, I thought I should give up the ghost. And they well nigh smoked & talked me to death. Did not go until about eleven — then I was not long in popping into bed.*[65]

In these comments of Susan's, ostensibly about Captains Dinsmore and Wheeler, Cardiff's less-than-perfect environmental conditions become evident, perhaps a sailing captain's wife's derogations of the steamships' soot and smoke:

> *Capt. Dinsmore . . . has gone out to his ship, still in the roads, as in a place of refuge from the coal dust and dirt.*

> *Capt. Wheeler was acquainted with {some visitors named Walts} and as Capt. Barnes was gone, and {as} his own ship in a sad plight with the coal dust, he asked them in to see us.*[66]

Mr. and Mrs. Walts, from Bristol, who were friends of Captain Barnes's wife, spent the afternoon of Friday, June 22, with Susan on the *J. J. Hathorn*. There she entertained them at tea, despite the report that

> *I was sick this morning. . . . Capt. Wheeler came in just after he got back from Bristol, and found me with the room in disorder — bed not made, head uncombed, and my dressing gown on. After he went out, I put things to right, but I have felt miserably all day.*[67]

Nevertheless, Susan reports that day, "[The Waltses] are very pleasant people," and the feeling appears to have been mutual. The following day, she receives a get well gift: "Old Mr. Walts sent me some curious specimens of iron ore—I shall have quite a cabinet by the time I get home—if he can, he will send me on Monday some curious rocks and stones from Bristol."[68]

The visit to Cardiff has given Susan a new form of handwork to add to her accomplishments:

{M}y head was so full of leather work and wax flowers. I woke up making them long before sun rise — could not get asleep again, although my eyes ached so I could hardly get them open. Got up early and cut out all my patterns for flowers and leaves. Also the Card rack.

I have been very busy in the leather work — have tried my hand at leaves today — had <u>extra</u> good luck with them.[69]

And not least, Susan shares glimpses of tenderness between herself and Jode:

Capt. Osman of the J. Jones spent the evening with us and a fine man he is — he is from Camden{,} Me. Capt. Bird also came in. I was not quite so sleepy as the night before. They left quite early, and Jode and I promenaded the deck as the evening was most beautiful.

This has been a very pleasant day. After dinner, Jode went shopping with me. I had quite a little walk — went into a fruit store — got some white cherries, some cucumbers, and nuts. In the evening, Capt.s Wheeler, and Dinsmore went over with us, to the "Clarissa Bird" — Capt. Osman was there, we had a game of Whist and a very pleasant evening. The night was beautiful — got back about half past ten.[70]

Just when Susan grows despondent about her in-port ironing ("had such bad luck, it would have made Job swear at his unlucky stars. Every thing I starched is just fit to go in the wash-tub again"[71]), Jode goes shopping and brings Susan "a beautiful little present . . . a china tea-pot and stand to heat it on." She mentions that he has also bought "a Concertina today." Susan seems pleased with the prospect of music during the Atlantic crossing, venturing the opinion that the concertina "is better than an accordion."[72]

By the last week of June, the *J. J. Hathorn* is ready to sail, but the weather is uncooperative; Susan reports strong, unfavorable winds. The Hathorns spend their last Sunday in Cardiff entertaining ("Capt.s Bird, Dinsmore and Wheeler took dinner with us—they soon left"), resting up for the trip ("Jode took a nap"), and writing some last-minute letters ("I wrote a letter to Mary Pollard") to send by mail-steamer.[73]

Then a mishap in the Bute Dock strands the Hathorn vessel high and dry: "We expected to go out into the roads—everything in readiness, when some part of the dock gave way & they were obliged to let off the water, so here we are still." [74] Resourceful to the core, Susan "improves the time," making use of the last fresh water she will have for some time: "I have done our washing and glad enough of the chance— it is so much better to start with all things clean. Capt. Houstin arrived today from London. Capt. Foster yesterday." [75] Tuesday finds the Hathorns "still in the docks, and are not sure of getting out tomorrow," [76] but by Wednesday, the *J. J. Hathorn* is

> *anchored once more out in the Roads! ready for sea. This morning we did not expect to get out of Dock, but something lucky happened, and this afternoon, we made out to get through. Capt.s Bird, Wheeler, Houstin, and Dinsmore came in to bid us good bye and see us off. Capt. Wheeler expected to come out too, but they would not let him — he will get away tomorrow if nothing happens. Mr. Brown, the Broker, also dropped in to wish us a speedy & pleasant passage.* [77]

As Susan knows by now, persuading sailors to leave the pleasures of port is not always easy. Jode is forced to take the towboat back to shore, leaving Susan alone on the *J. J. Hathorn*:

> *Jode went back with the steamer after three men — all the rest are on board as sober as judges. I have sewed on a shirt today, but the time has been so broken, have not accomplished much. Also wrote to "Sister Mine" and Amasa.* [78]

The now all-too-familiar scene plays itself out again.

> *Last night Jode came back to the ship, with the promise of having the men on board at three this morning — they did not come until five o'clock — then of the six shipped, not one could speak English. So Jode went back to get them changed — finally succeeded, and at three P.M. they made their appearance.* [79]

Other ships are leaving Cardiff with the *J. J. Hathorn*—two English ships and those commanded by the Yankee ship-masters Wheeler, Os-

man, and Thorndike. Susan writes that "Jode came off with Capt. Osman, who is also coming out of the Channel with us." She proudly reports, "We are having a fine breeze and shall be down to Fundy before
we know it. Are beating all the rest."[80] In the middle of the Bristol
Channel, changes in personnel had taken place, for Jode was not the only
captain with crew troubles: "Capt. Wheeler came out this morning—
was obliged to anchor as 'Old Bob' was missing. He came on board to
breakfast, and staid until past ten. One of our foreigners went with him
in Bob's place."[81]

Susan sews shirts and reports wildly variable weather: a "fine sunny
forenoon and a brisk breeze," but then a cloudy day that ends with rain,
"heavy thunder and quite sharp lightning." Their pilot leaves them on
Friday, June 29, "about half past four A.M." Captain Osman's ship, the
J. Jones, Susan says,

> was a little ahead of us and has kept so all day, but we have left the others
> far behind. We have made about a Westerly course by Compass. I have not
> been sea sick — felt a little squalmish, but it passed off. Have finished one
> shirt and made the bosom & sleeves of the second.

> All our company have left us — the "J. Jones" was in sight all day yesterday,
> but we lost her last night. Cape Clear was visible tonight.[82]

As Susan accepts the isolation of life at sea, she resumes her reports of
the J. J. Hathorn's coordinates:

> We got an observation of the Sun this morning and at noon — so cloudy at
> four was unable to get one. By "Dead reckoning," we were in Latitude
> 50"36' and Longitude 6"34'. Probably a little farther south, if anything.

> Showery today and dark and cloudy, although the sun came out just long
> enough this morning for Jode to get an observation — also got the latitude at
> noon. The wind has been ahead until about eight tonight, — it came round
> a little more favorable. Our Latitude at four P.M. was 50"08' Longitude
> 9"14.[83]

Susan's "Ship Graduate"

I gazed upon the noble barque that was to be my home. She was the largest I had ever seen, and for thirteen years had gallantly braved the storms. As I first saw her by the silvery moonlight, no stars or stripes were streaming from her topmast, nor crescent flaunted in the breeze; but on a field of blue gleamed a snowy cross, encircled by a halo of light. And methought we might look up to this, when warm and weary with the toilsome cares of life, and it would cheer us onward in the rugged way.[1]

In her first imagined glimpse of "The Ship Graduate," Susan may well have been recalling the bark *J. J. Hathorn*, which she had seen rise from the ways in Richmond about four years before she wrote the essay. As Susan's "rugged way" following 1855 would unfold, she would again have good reason to yoke together matters of seafaring and faith.

Susan's metaphorical account of her departure from England in "The Ship Graduate" and the real-life one in her diary present striking contrasts. The essay is full of extravagant language and playful allusions to mathematical studies, which would play a role in her real-life navigational calculations:

We were scarcely off the coast of England; when a dense fog completely enveloped us, and here our troubles began. Starless night succeeded sunless days, and as our ship drove onward; we lost our reckoning, and our where-a-bouts was [a] problem we could not solve. Sailors are generally superstitious, and we began carefully to notice every sign; but this only

involved us the more deeply in trouble. Our situation was truly critical—the sharp and jagged rocks; that surround the barren desert isle
of . . . equations kept us in terrible suspense, and I tremble even now at
the thoughts of those fathomless depths. . . . But another drop was added
to our cup of sorrow, as the phantom, shadowy forms of a Binomial
Theorem presented itself to view. Steadily on it came, through the misty
darkness, but it met strong hearts and ready hands, and like the ghosts of
old, it vanished like a passing dream. Only those who have experienced
the terrible dangers of the ocean, can appreciate our feelings, as at length
the misty shroud rolled slowly away, and the cheering beams of the sun
gladdened our hearts.[2]

Three years later, on Sunday, July 1, 1855, Susan writes tersely of the
practical, nonpoetic matters of weather and navigation: "Rained hard
this morning, and has been dark and foggy all day. Also head wind or
calm. Tonight the wind is a little more favorable, but flies about. No
observation at all today."[3] Susan is experiencing the reality of not knowing, exactly, the *J. J. Hathorn*'s whereabouts, just as she imagined in her
essay. But the real sun that will eventually come out will do more than
gladden their hearts. They will get their coordinates and apply their
math, and Susan will proceed cheerily with the work of her hands,
though not her leather work:

> *Monday. July 2d.   Today has been calm or but a very light breeze — The*
> *sun has shone and it has been warm and pleasant. . . . Our Longitude at*
> *4 P.M. was 11"05 Latitude 50"08 — rather slow getting along. I have*
> *sewed on the shirts — have made one all but the sleeves. Jode has varnished*
> *my leather work and I have not done so much as I might. I was fussing*
> *over them.*[4]

Work—Susan's, Jode's, and their collaboration, both in the enterprise
of marriage and that of the *J. J. Hathorn*—becomes the dominant theme
of the westward Atlantic crossing. They will spend the entire month of
July at sea. Susan's account of herself for the rest of the week shows her
industriously, incessantly sewing:

This morning I got up bright and early, intending to finish my shirt in a hurry. Got one sleeve done before breakfast. . . . the shirt is minus one sleeve tonight. The wristband is sewed on, and stitched and the gusset in.

I have sewed all day finished the third shirt and began the fourth — got the body pretty nearly completed.

I have finished my fourth shirt and cut out the fifth — ready to begin upon tomorrow. I cannot sew so steadily as if at home — there are many little interruptions that use up the time.

I have done famously sewing — have made the body and a sleeve of the fifth shirt — also sewed in the sleeve. Am tired enough tonight.

I finished my shirt and cut out nine more. Then tried to do a little at the leather work, but it was so rough did not succeed.[5]

On the following Saturday, Susan totals up her work, and instead of resting on her accomplishment, she sets an even higher goal: "I have finished my eighth shirt today, and done a little at the 'Leather business.' Think I must be smarter next week and make four instead of three."[6] Indefatigable Susan plunges on during the week of what is unmistakably the prettiest sailing weather of the crossing: "I have finished the body of the eleventh shirt—and partly did one sleeve—hope to complete it with another one this week."[7]

By July's third Saturday, the weather has turned hot and Susan cheerfully sardonic:

This week ends with a fine day and a fair but light wind. The sun is very hot, and the cabin warm and uncomfortable, but we manage nicely. There is an awning outside, so I sit under it and sew. I have finished my twelfth shirt — have made four this week. But I have had to sew pretty hard. Should have thought a body was working me pretty sharp, if any body had made me do so much.[8]

With that, Susan is done with the shirt making for Jode and on to perfecting the leather crafting learned from Miss Brown in Roath. Susan's June accounts show expenditures for leather work and sewing supplies in Cardiff:[9]

June 19	Leather for Leather work	1.92
"	Shoe maker's Punch	.60
"	Naptha and Gum Shellac	.24
23	Round Pounce for Leather work	.24
"	Inserting and Edge for Chemisette	.42
"	Edging and inserting for Linen Chemises	1.12
"	Postage	.26
"	Oranges	.24
"	Gum Shellac	.12

Cardiff shopping opportunities would have been nothing like London's, and indeed Susan's expenditures in Cardiff are modest by comparison. Nearly a third of Susan's London expenditures went toward materials for her Atlantic sewing marathon, and about half went for ready-to-wear clothing. Notably extravagant were a $14.00 cashmere shawl (perhaps to replace the shawl stolen in Santiago) and the $6.50 mantilla (a belated Cuban souvenir?); there are also such frou-frous as the "Frizettes" (hair curlers). Susan had the embroidered slippers on which she was working in January made up in London at a cost of $1.12. Her accounts do not show an expenditure for the picture framing she mentions at the end of her stay in London, but her exclamation point shows what she thought of the cost of board:

May 1st	Amount brought over	$15.22
2	1 Pr Gaiter Boots & 2 prs Slippers	3.75
"	Cashmere Shawl	14.00
"	Mantilla	6.50
"	Undersleeves	.75
"	Four Collars	3.55
"	2 Pairs of Gloves	1.00
"	2 Calico Aprons	.28
"	24 yds. Lawn	2.88
"	20 yds. Blue Plaid	5.50
"	15 yds. Blue All wool de Laine	5.55
17	1 Crochet Collar	.33
"	2 Pocket. handkerh'f's for girls & 1 vase for Lucy	.75

"	Toys for Sis Ring & Fanny	.36
"	1 Box of Thread	.40
"	"Sunny Memories" and "Fashion & Famine"	.75
18	Making Embroidered Slippers	1.12
"	Crochet Hooks, Books, Patterns, &c., Pins	1.08
"	Velvet trimming for Green dress	.37
"	2 Pairs Black Cashmere stockings	.81
"	4 Rolls wadding	.41
"	1 Bunch knitting cotton	.31
19	oz. Sewing Silk	.37
"	2 Prs. Scissors	.87
"	5 yds. Lining for Blue de Laine	.45
23	Sewing silk for " " "	.03
24	Visit to Tower with Book	.43
"	Gloves, Piping, Fruit &c	.63
26	Hair Band .75 Frizettes .50 Velvet Ribbon	1.87
"	Board 2 weeks and 2 days	17.00 !
"	Fare to Gravesend	.37

Altogether Susan spent over half of her expenses for 1855 during that one month in London, and this amount does not include the special segregated account of London expenditures for the baby-sewing frenzy that will take place in Richmond that fall.

🐦

July's weather is generally the best for an Atlantic crossing under sail between England and a southern U.S. port. Once the *J. J. Hathorn* leaves the misty rain off Wales and reaches open water, the Hathorns find the best sailing of the entire year. But early on they encounter head seas and head winds that, despite the heavy iron cargo that would stabilize the vessel, make for an uncomfortable ride.

Susan resumes her tracking of the *J. J. Hathorn*'s position, but she has streamlined her methodology. No longer does she bother with multiple readings of position for a day, unless there is some relevant discrepancy.

The sun has shone and it has been warm and pleasant. There are several sail in sight — one we take for the "J. Jones." Our Longitude at 4 P.M. was 11"05 Latitude 50"08 — rather slow getting along. . . . Saw a steamer bound home this morning.

The memorable Fourth today — wonder where they are celebrating it at home. It is cold as April and dark and cloudy. No observation. About twelve, {we} spoke the American Brig, "James Caskie" forty six days from Pensacola — bound to Hull with cotton. Wished to know his longitude — we have not kept much sure of our whereabouts — as nearly as we could judge Long. was 14"04 Lat 49"00. We had a fine breeze all night — and it still continues fair, but there is a heavy head sea.

It was raining in torrents this morning when I awoke but it cleared away before breakfast and has been quite pleasant. But such a sea! Every thing has jumped and rattled all day long. After dinner the wind hauled round fair and we pray it may continue so for at least twenty four hours. But to-night, we are diving terribly.[10]

On July 8 the weather changes dramatically. The wind comes around, and Susan quotes Jode's phrase—"chalk ginger blue"—describing the *J. J. Hathorn*'s exhilarating speed as they make a tremendous day's run to the south:

Sunday. July 8th 1855.   A fine breezy day, but still rough. We have walked Jode says "chalk ginger blue." We have done pretty well. Our Latitude at 4.P.M. was 44"18 Long. 18"47. It has been so sunny and pleasant. I have thought I'd like to be at home to go out on the hill, and see how pretty it would look.[11]

Jode's phrase appears to be his own poetic invention: maritime lexicons, mariners, maritime history experts, and maritime archivists all fail to recognize the phrase as a common one. But the context makes clear and logical the meaning of Jode's rough, beautifully evocative language:

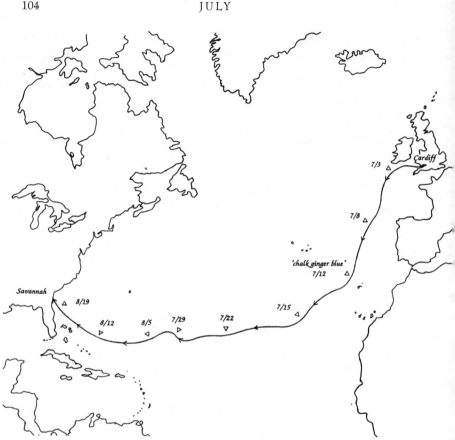

This map approximates the J. J. Hathorn's *westbound Atlantic crossing, June 27–August 19, 1855. Based on Susan's coordinates, the progress during the week of July 8–15, during which she records Jode's phrase "chalk ginger blue," was a phenomenal run. The* J. J. Hathorn *was riding a strong southerly current and favored by good weather; by comparison, the* J. J. Hathorn's *meandering course in the "horse latitudes" (July 29–August 5) explains Susan's impatience with their progress then.*

The *J. J. Hathorn* was tearing through the water like a blue streak, taking a course—straight as a blue chalk line snapped on a piece of wood—that took one's breath away, as with the zip of ginger, as it rushed on. These are the only words of Jode's that Susan ever quotes directly, and in recording them Susan seems to recognize and appreciate the image's complex power.

Susan finds in the routine of shipboard life not boredom but a great serenity and happiness, as in this series of entries:

Today has been cloudy, dark, and rough but so long as we have a fair wind that sends us nine knots an hour, we will not complain. Tonight it blows very hard, although the glass is very high. The spray flies up over the side and keeps up a constant shower bath for some poor body.

A most beautiful day — fine fun going to sea, if every thing was as pleasant as today — a brisk breeze carrying us along at the rate of seven knots per hour, a bright sun and a blue sea and sky. The water has been the deepest blue all day, I ever saw it.

A most glorious day — a bright sun, a blue sky and a fine breeze. The air just warm enough to seem pleasant. One could not but be happy {with} such weather. Through the night, there was very little wind, — went two, three and four knots, but it breeze{d} up towards morning, and through the day, and at night we went eight. . . . We get to the west but slowly. Are steering more towards that point now.

Through last night had a smashing breeze, which has continued through the day. We are having a fine run these six days past.

Another most beautiful day and a fine breeze through out. One could not ask for things more pleasant than we have had through the whole week. We are speeding home fast and if nothing happens, it will not be many weeks before we are there.

July. Sunday 15th   Most beautiful day. The wind continues fair and is stronger than yesterday. We have sped along at a fine rate.

Still pleasant weather and a prosperous breeze. This is the ninth day we have had a fair wind — a body cannot surely complain at that usage. Our Latitude at 4 P.M. was 27"50 Longitude 28"43 — almost three degrees of west{ward} since yesterday.

A good breeze today, but not quite so strong as some days past. Our Latitude at 4 P.M. was 27"21 Longitude 34"25. We have fine weather. This is the eleventh day we have had a fair wind. — still it will take us a long while to get in.

A warm sunny day — not a great deal of wind but what there has been was
favorable. Our Latitude at 4 P.M. 27"19 Longitude 37"00 We saw three
sail during the day — two bound north. [12]

A vessel under sail could not follow a great circle route to get across
the Atlantic; winds and currents drive the *J. J. Hathorn*, and Jode must
use what the sea and the sky give him. The *Pilot's Atlas* July chart, showing the prevailing currents and winds and marked with the course Susan's diary records, shows their route takes them much farther south
than might seem necessary. However, during Jode's extraordinary "chalk
ginger blue" days, the *J. J. Hathorn* has caught the clockwise Canaries
Current running southward along the west coast of Europe. This current
runs as far south as the central African coast, then turns west toward
the Caribbean. If one envisions the Atlantic as the face of a clock,
its currents generally flow in a clockwise manner, and at the center is
the more or less "dead" area of unpredictable or nonexistent currents
known as the Sargasso Sea. Thus it is reasonable for Susan to suppose
that vessels sighted are traveling between Africa and South America. In
1855 maritime trade in African slaves still existed, despite its long being prohibited by law and treaty, but Susan's diary never mentions the
slave trade:

Less wind today than we have had for some time — what there has been,
has been favorable. Last night it was calm for several hours. . . . Latitude
at 4 P.M. 27"24. Long. 39"14 . . . Two or three ships in sight today —
all bound to the north — think they must be from the coast of Africa or
S. America. [13]

By the middle of the third week in July, the *J. J. Hathorn* has reached
a point due west of the Canaries and due south of Greenland. Their "fine
run" is at an end, and they are approaching the southeastern edge of the
Sargasso Sea. Between now and their arrival in Savannah, Susan's impatience will get ample exercise, but she can manage a wry comment on
their unofficial passengers and the bark's laying over:

A warm day — the weather is fine — most of the time a fine cool breeze, but
the cabin is as hot as an oven, although we keep doors and window open.

*Last night I could not sleep half the time, the heat was so stifling. Then the
barque rolls a great deal and half the time, we were on our heads. The rats
too, keep up a constant din. They have well nigh taken possession. The same
wind still favors us although for the last eight days, it has been rather light.*

*A sultry day — the wind light, but favorable, so we make but slow progress.
We seem destined to have a long passage. Roll and tumble about as if we
cost nothing. There has been for several days, a terrible heavy swell from the
south, which has kept us rolling, ever since it began.*[14]

On this same day, July 25, Susan discovers that their westbound crossing will not be without medical problems, for a crew member named
Jack has become ill: "The second mate had quite a time with sick Jack—
he made him <u>come to</u> though. This is the first trouble we have had this
passage."

Surely Susan sees Jode's chart, and this direct woman, to whom effi-
ciency is paramount, might not be pleased with the *J. J. Hathorn's*
meandering:

*Showery today but the heat has been oppressive. This morning considerable
rain fell. After dinner the wind changed and came round ahead, but finally
settled down fair, and is rather stronger than it has been for two days past.
The sky looks dark and threatening tonight and seems to betoken a storm.*

*Very warm indeed, and either calm or the wind light and so variable that
we have steered every point in the compass half a dozen times over.*

*Very warm — wind light and tonight is dead ahead. Our Latitude at 4 P.M.
was 26"30 — Longitude 62"49. This is the thirty seventh day we have been
out, and still eighteen degrees lie between us and Savannah.*[15]

🍂

Susan's account book lists her London "board"—$17.00 for sixteen days
(about $1.06 per day)—and it is worth noting that she pays for her
board, or at least accounts for it, possibly to Jode's father and certainly
to herself. On board the *J. J. Hathorn*, Susan is the captain's unofficial,
unpaid administrative assistant. She has bound Jode's charts for him,

and three days out of Cardiff, she had written: "Then sat down to settle up accounts, which took until dinner. After dinner took a nap—slept until almost three." [17]

Increasingly the shared, cooperative quality of the Hathorns' marriage grows and strengthens. It is manifest not just in the many shirts Susan makes for her husband, but in the increasingly reciprocal, complementary nature of their relationship. Susan makes explicit her perception of this new dimension of their marriage; several times she expresses her appreciation for Jode's help and thoughtfulness, and her understanding and approval of his sense of responsibility in, as she says, being a "good fellow" in working for the *J. J. Hathorn*:

Jode has varnished my leather work and I have not done so much as I might. I was fussing over them.

Jode has been painting his capstan cover yesterday and today has succeeded nicely. Did not think he could do so well.

Jode has worked all day — fixing his boat.

Jode has been working for the benefit of the "J.J." all day, like a good fellow.

Jode has made me a card case frame — it is quite pretty — also the bottom for my vase.

With a great deal of Jode's help have made the Card Case — should have given it up for a bad bargain, if he had not come to my assistance. As it is, quite pretty — I give him all the praise of it.

Jode has made me a spool stand.

Jode is making his fancy Capstan cover. [18]

Life is not all work, though. These days of light winds make for a lull in the kind of work with sails and tackle known as "working ship." During these lulls, aside from making his bride useful gifts for her needlework and making ornamentations for his ship, Jode again reveals his interest in literature:

Jode has been reading "Ivanhoe" — he is very much interested in it. I think it one of Scott{'s} very best stories.

A warm sunny day, and a very pleasant one to me. Did not get up till breakfast — then had a good bath and drest. Jode read Moore and Byron meanwhile. Then I took them and read aloud for his benefit. So the day has passed very happily.[19]

Now Jode has time to play the concertina, and Susan reviews Jode's musical offerings. In these July entries, one can almost see Susan gritting her teeth:

Jode has played on the Concertina almost ever since he got out of bed this morning.

Jode has finished his painting, and returned to his beloved "Concertina." Thus ends a very pleasant week.[20]

Awful as the concertina music may be, Susan must realize that after the next few months, when she is alone in Richmond awaiting the birth of the baby, she will long to hear it.

Merchant captains' wives—unlike whaling captains' wives—sailed with their husbands less frequently, and fewer still would be with their husbands when a birth was imminent. In the Jefferson Hathorn family, the men generally go to sea, and the women stay home and rear the children. Sally Hathorn Brown, Jode's sister, may have provided a family precedent for Susan to stay with Jode on the *J. J. Hathorn*, or it may be that Sally's experience argued against it. Sally's first child, Benicia, was born when Sally was with Lemuel in California waters, and they named their daughter, as maritime parents often did, for the place where the child was born.[21] But Sally had since returned to Richmond with the baby, and Lemuel Brown had gone back to sea without them, as Jefferson Hathorn had without his family.

Knowing that Susan and Jode's time together is growing short lends a poignancy to Susan's preparations for their arrival in Savannah, and her ambivalence is perfectly understandable. Eager for the passage to be finished and to see loved ones back in Richmond, she must feel sadness as she cleans the cabin, packs away handwork, and sets Jode's sea clothing, including underwear, in order. She writes during the last week of July:

"I have been mending all day—putting Jode's clothing in order—mended his singlets—Drawers, shirts &c. After breakfast I put away my leather work most sorrowfully, and cleaned out the cabin." [22]

The Atlantic off the southern United States can be torrid in July. As the *J. J. Hathorn* approaches, Jode has the men stretch a sail as a deck awning to give protection from the sun's blazing heat. On that month's last night, Susan writes,

> *The cabin is suffocatingly hot. So I stay out on deck — take a chair and sit in the Shade. I am getting "black as Toby."* [23]

And the next night,

> *Jode took the sofa cushion and slept out on deck. I was reading "Fashion and Famine" until twelve — after that slept soundly until nearly six this morning. Finished enlarging the slippers — then mended Jode's coats.* [24]

Increasingly Susan seems occupied with thoughts of Richmond and family members there, and her diary confirms that the *J. J. Hathorn* will not be going to Maine:

> *I have begun to quilt my skirt — of which Mrs. Hathorn gave me the outside. It will be a very pretty one indeed.*

> *They are painting the ship — it looks nice as can be — everything so new and clean. Would like to go north with the barque to show her, she looks so well.* [25]

Since Jode will oversee unloading at Savannah and then accompany Susan to Maine, they cannot just leave as soon as the *J. J. Hathorn* reaches port. Recalling her stop in Savannah in the fall of 1854, Susan is dreading the Low Country's mosquitoes: "This is the thirty seventh day we have been out, and still eighteen degrees lie between us and Savannah—but there are no musquitoes here, so we are better of[f] than if there." [26] Illness and contagion remain a worry for Susan, now in her sixth month of pregnancy. As she finishes work on the quilted skirt, she looks back over the swiftly moving year since a day she spent with Mrs. Hathorn in Richmond:

Today I have finished quilting my skirt — it looks quite as well as if it had been done in the frames. A year ago, I was at Mrs. Hathorn's and spent this week quilting — What a little year ago! It was very warm indeed I remember and there was a great deal of sickness at the village.[27]

Jode's Slippers

The August 1854 "sickness" in Richmond that Susan is remembering a year later was an unprecedented epidemic of cholera.[1] Dr. Abial Libby, one of the town's two physicians, filed the official report to the State Medical Society, noting that the incidence had begun around June 1 and claimed about forty lives. "It was very fatal," he wrote; "not more than one in ten recovered. . . . Those attacked usually died within 24 hours." Describing "a complete panic among the people," he reported that all work stopped and "the inhabitants left the town by the hundreds."

> The first cases occurred after eating baked pigs (young pigs baked whole) and left over night after a celebration for which they had been prepared. I state this fact but cannot say as this was the origin of cholera in our place. . . . The sickness prevailed for six weeks then subsided as suddenly as it came. We have had nothing of the kind since.[2]

Dr. Libby found the incidence particularly high "among the Irish, some of whom had lately arrived in our place," but allowed that some of "our best citizens in the best localities died" as well. Dr. Libby's report suggested no connection between immigrants' crowded living conditions and the high incidence of cholera in their households.

Another contemporaneous theory speculated that "some sailor coming from foreign waters brought [the cholera] to the town." Captain Levi Howe, returning to Richmond in June, "reached home for a visit between voyages, contracted the disease at once, and died within a few hours."[3] However the disease reached Richmond, Dr. Libby's observations during the epidemic of 1854 resonate with Susan's recollections of her early-August quilting session with Mrs. Hathorn, and their quilting together provides insight into Susan's relationship with Jode's parents. The cholera epidemic may well have spurred the decision for Susan to go to sea with Jode in September 1854.

Cholera, which claimed many sailors' lives, was not a particular worry in the ports Susan and Jode were visiting. There were, however, the Caribbean and American South health hazards of malaria and yellow fever, two distinct, often fatal tropical illnesses transmitted by mosquito bites.[4] In Trinidad de Cuba Susan's diary had already recorded that yellow fever caused the deaths of one of their consignees and of "Capt. Cox from St. Iago."[5] As the *J. J. Hathorn* again nears Savannah, Susan, being constitutionally given to worry, knows they are returning to a port that lies some distance up the serpentine Savannah River, and that the *J. J. Hathorn* will be slowly towed up that estuary bordered by low-lying, mosquito-infested marshes. It will not be temperate autumn, but steamy August.

Susan's diary refers in only two places to the *J. J. Hathorn*'s pre–January 1 itinerary during the early days of the Hathorn marriage. Using these, the succession of ports the *J. J. Hathorn* visited during 1854–56 can be reconstructed by searching the departures and arrivals lists in the *Shipping and Commercial List and New York Prices Current*. One can then turn to the maritime records of the National Archives for additional details of the Hathorns' time at sea.

Susan's diary tells on the anniversary of the event that the newlyweds departed Richmond on October 2, 1854, shortly after their September wedding, to meet the *J. J. Hathorn* in Philadelphia.[6] The Hathorns then took the vessel to Savannah,[7] as arrivals and departures lists in the *Shipping and Commercial List* confirm. Reported dates in that publication should be viewed with some skepticism, however, for the exact dates appear to have depended on whether a port's correspondent reported the vessel's actual arrival or its clearance through customs. For example, there is a two-day discrepancy (April 24 and April 26) between the *Shipping and Commercial List*'s date and Susan's diary date for the *J. J. Hathorn*'s

```
SAVANNAH, Geo.————————Arrived
Aug. 16.—Schr. Wm. Totten, Thompson,
                                   New-York
Aug. 18.—Steamer Augusta, Lyon...New-York
Steamer State of Georgia,Garvin..Philadelphia
Schr. L. S. Davis, Davis............New-York
Aug. 19.—Barque M. H. Kendall, Brex,
                                   Philadelphia
Schr. Woodbridge, White............Baltimore
Aug. 20.—Steamer Alabama, Schenck,
                                   New-York
Barque Exact, Saunders.............New-York
Barque Nagitta, Maker..............New-York
Barque B. Hallett, Little..........Philadelphia
Brig Matilda, Percy,...............Charleston
Aug. 21.—Barque Hathorn, Hathorn....Cardiff
Barque Saboois, M'Neil..................Boston
Schr. John Boston, Lingo............New-York
Schr. Sheet Anchor, Orcutt...........Camden
Aug. 22.—Schr. Enchantress, Simpson,
                                   New-York
————————————————————Cleared
Aug. 16.—Schr. Chas. Pennine, Hoffman,
                                   Baltimore
Schr. J. W. Anderson, Watson,......Baltimore
Aug. 18.—Steamer Florida, Woodhull,
                                   New-York
Aug. 19.—Schr. Jonas Smith, Smith.New-York
Aug. 20.—Brig Macon, Watkins.....New-York
Aug. 22.—Steamer State of Georgia, Garvin,
                                   Philadelphia
Steamer Augusta, Lyon.............New-York
```

This detail of the Savannah report in the Shipping and Commercial List and New York Prices Current *for August 29, 1855, shows the* J. J. Hathorn's *arrival from Cardiff listed first among the four August 21 arrivals in that port.*

departure from London. A minor discrepancy also appears on the *J. J. Hathorn*'s arrival in Savannah, though here Susan is reckoning the arrival by their entering the Savannah River and taking a pilot, not by landing and clearing customs. Since the *Shipping and Commercial List* gives the port arriving from and departing for, a vessel's trail can be reconstructed.

If the listing one finds is of an arrival, one searches the lists of the origi-
nating port for the approximate likely date of departure; if the listing
is of a departure, obviously one searches the lists of the destination.
Once a vessel is found entering a port, one can continue to scan the
lists until the vessel leaves, and then see where it is bound. In this way
the *J. J. Hathorn*'s itinerary may be reconstructed from the time of its
arrival in Philadelphia, just prior to Susan's joining it, up to its Savannah
arrival.

Date	Ar/Dep	Port	From/To	Master
09/19/54	A	Philadelphia	Newcastle	Brown
10/20/54	D	Philadelphia	Savannah	Hathorn
10/30/54	A	Savannah	Philadelphia	Hathorn
12/15/54	D	Savannah	St. Jago	Hathorn
1/03/55	A	St. Jago	Savannah	Hathorn
2/10/55	D	St. Jago	Trinidad/Cuba	Hathorn
2/16/55	A	Trinidad/Cuba	St. Jago	Hathorn
3/14/55	D	Trinidad/Cuba	London	Hathorn
5/09/55	A	London	Trinidad/Cuba	Hathorn
5/10/55	D	London	Cardiff	Hathorn
6/12/55	A	Cardiff	London	Hathorn
6/27/55	D	Cardiff	Savannah	Hathorn
8/21/55	A	Savannah	Cardiff	Hathorn

Source: Shipping and Commercial List[8]

🐚

On August 3, the *J. J. Hathorn*'s thirty-seventh day out of Cardiff, when
"Jode is making his fancy Capstan cover" and Susan "prospers famously"
at her quilting, she rationalizes the considerable distance remaining to
Savannah by pointing out that "there are no musquitoes here, so we are
better of[f] than if there." The wind is against them. Susan comments
on the bark's progress that day:

> {T}here is a good breeze from the <u>West</u> — favorable for us. Our Latitude at
> 4 P.M. was 26"05 Longitude 63"15, so we have made the amazing dis-
> tance of twenty-six miles in twenty four hours. The wind was ahead all
> last night.[9]

Susan cannot know a full two weeks will pass before the *J. J. Hathorn* reaches Savannah, giving her ample opportunity to exercise her characteristic impatience. Still, these are two eventful weeks, a time when Susan must set her possessions "to rights," as she always says, to leave the bark and return to Richmond. Soon the Hathorns' private time will be at an end. She eagerly writes of seeing family and friends back home, but with the birth of her baby, this segment of her life is nearly over.

On board the *J. J. Hathorn* it is hot. Any progress Susan would have observed on Jode's chart for the first week of August could only have been disheartening. But by the second week in August, the bark has rounded the southwestern edge of the Sargasso Sea and caught the northerly flow of the Gulf Stream once again. Susan observes:

> *The wind is rather light but the heat of the water seems to show that we are in the Gulf Stream. The thermometer was up to 85°. At 4 P.M. the Latitude was 28"35 and Longitude 78"52.*

> *Calm and oh! so hot! the sun perfectly <u>broils</u> one.* [10]

At this reading the *J. J. Hathorn* is about one hundred miles due east of Cape Canaveral.

Besides its current and warmth, the Gulf Stream, being a shipping lane, brings sightings of other vessels:

> *This morning a schooner was in sight — yesterday three sail could be seen, but very distant.*

> *We have made the astonishing distance of 22 miles in the last twenty four hours. . . . Tonight the wind is a little more favorable. A brig was quite near us all the morning, but not within hailing distance.*

> *This is the third day we have been in 70 {degrees longitude}. There are several sail in sight — so we are not the only people in the world waiting for a breath of air. The glass is going down, so I hope we shall be favored with a breeze.* [11]

The waters in which the *J. J. Hathorn* is sailing teem with sea life, and Susan describes with clear enjoyment several days' encounters with various sea creatures. She juxtaposes these observations with a playful allusion to her reading and with her seemingly endless work on slippers:

The mates caught a dolphin this morning which we had for breakfast and we have caught little fish enough for tea. I have read the "Epicurean" in Moore today.

Last night, three whales came close to the ship — so near you could have struck them from the deck. Lots of dolphins & fish. Have worked on the slippers.

We caught a Dolphin this forenoon — one of the largest kind — also more than a dozen nice little fish, and we have seen a sword fish, lots of flying fish and "bonitas." There have been gulls and petrels without number. So this has been quite a day of adventures notwithstanding the calm & heat. After dinner, had a little shower of rain.[12]

Susan spends her time out on deck, under the awning, sewing and reading, enjoying the book of Moore's poems that Jode presented to her in Cardiff. "I have spent [Sunday] quite pleasantly, reading 'Lalla Rookh,' "[13] she writes. She has developed a pattern of reading on Sunday—often out loud to Jode, or he to her—foregoing her usual "work" on the Sabbath.[14] With the *J. J. Hathorn* practically racing along at five knots, Susan has other duties to attend to: "The breeze is cool & refreshing this morning. At 4 P.M. Lat. 26"40 Long. 66"22—have made two degrees today. I have cleaned out our state-room and got some of my rubbish together."[15] For four successive days this hot week at sea, the slippers consume her and things are going beautifully, until one windy Friday morning disaster strikes!

I have worked on the slippers — the oak leaf & coral — have had real good luck and have done lots.

. . . very little breeze stirring — it has seemed a part of the time, as if I should melt down to a grease spot. I have spent these last two days under the awning, on the top of the house. Have freckled as bad as if out in the sun &

Embroidering slipper-tops was a popular Victorian needlework project, and Susan began a new pair for Jode on the first day of 1855. She made several pair during her time at sea and had two pair made up in London, probably by one of the shoemakers near the Misses Bragge's boardinghouse.

> *tanned as "black as Toby" but cannot help it, for I cannot stay in the cabin, it is so close. Have worked on the slippers — have not been so smart as yesterday, or I should have completed one.*
>
> *I have worked on the slippers — finished one and have done a lot on the other.*
>
> *I have done a little on the slippers — have had a head ache, and have not felt much like working today. Lost my pattern <u>overboard</u> this morning.*[16]

Undaunted, Susan apparently has the pattern memorized by now, for she continues to report work on the slippers the next day, Saturday, August 11. "Very warm indeed again today and calm," she says. In the lull she and Jode "again read aloud from 'Lalla Rookh.' "[17] Susan suffers from a guilty conscience about letting her housekeeping slide while she finishes the slippers. The day before she completes them she writes: "I have worked on the slippers. Hope to complete it tomorrow, unless I clean house—the steward's part shames mine. I never let it go so sluttishly as I have this passage."[18]

Persistence personified, Susan writes triumphantly on Wednesday, August 15:

> *I have finished the slippers. They are very pretty indeed, and quite large enough for Jode. As it was afternoon before I completed them, thought I*

*would not clean until tomorrow, so put my trunk and the drawers to rights
and put things away ready for tomorrow.*[19]

So with Jode's slippers finished, Susan resumes her more mundane duties
and tries out the new set of crochet hooks she bought in London ("Like
my hooks very much"[20]) on some edgings as the *J. J. Hathorn* nears Savannah: "I cleaned up a little this morning—got through at dinner
time—have knit a little and lazed a good deal. It is so warm I have no
appetite or strength. Am glad we are drawing near the end of our long
passage."[21]

Jode's slippers have, of course, become more than slippers. First, Susan
has not made just one pair of slippers, but has had to make several,
trying out and adjusting them so they will fit. They have become em-
blematic of voyage and marriage; Susan's evolving perception of her husband and their relationship, like any close relationship, is subject to
revision and growth. What was once unfamiliar and she "needed in-
structions" for, now comes as second nature to her. The slippers have
come through some unpleasant, uncomfortable, and dangerous times,
but also some elevated circumstances. As Susan has fashioned the slippers, Jode has helped her make her leather work. She has helped him
with his books and charts; he has played the concertina until she was
ready to throw him and it overboard; they have spent lazy Sundays at
sea reading Scott and Moore and Byron to each other. By the time the
pattern for the slippers falls overboard, Susan no longer needs instruc-
tions. And in her own way and following her own curriculum, she has
fulfilled the vision of "The Ship Graduate."

As the Hathorns near Savannah, the "company" of other vessels in the
Gulf Stream become competitors for a pilot boat to tow them upriver.
Susan describes their wait within sight of Tybee Lighthouse, the land-
mark for Savannah, as a storm approaches:

*The breeze continued and at five P.M. made Tybee light — stood in until the
water shallowed to 3 1/2 fathoms, then fearful of getting aground, tacked
ship, and stood off South — then SE{;} not a sign of a Pilot boat. There is a
schooner lying of{f}, also waiting a Pilot. At seven tonight the lights were*

lit in the light house & at the beacon. It looks a little wild tonight —
lightens, & thunder distant.[22]

The *J. J. Hathorn*'s hold is listed in its registration papers as "13 feet,
6 inches," but this is not the same as a vessel's "deep load draught"—
the necessary depth of water to keep the fully loaded vessel afloat; with
the load of iron from Cardiff, the Hathorns would be at maximum draft
coming into Savannah. With the heavily loaded vessel in shallow water
and a bad storm coming, Susan has a right to be worried. As the storm
approaches, the *J. J. Hathorn* goes back to sea to ride it out:

Sunday, Aug. 19. 1855.   Last night was very squally. About 7½ a very
heavy squall of wind struck us — the next squall, little wind but sharp
lightning and a few claps of heavy thunder. The third squall, the rain came
in torrents and continued at intervals through the night. Showery all
day — sometimes heavy winds. Too bad to be drifting about in the storm, just
through the pilots' laziness.

Monday 20th   Still at sea, and still stormy. The sun has not been out
clear — just discern him a little before noon — find we must be to the south of
Savannah, and the wind is dead ahead. Must spend another night thump-
ing about.[23]

By Tuesday morning, Susan can write, "The wind came around a little
so we made sail and once more turned our prow toward Savannah." After
the noon "dinner," the wind increases, but by 4:30 P.M., the *J. J. Hathorn*
had its pilot on board. Finally Susan articulates the real cause of her
eagerness:

{A}s it is low water, we cannot get inside tonight, so here we are banging
about yet. Fate seems against us. If we had the letters that probably are at
the office for us, I would not care so much. I am impatient to hear from home.[24]

With assurances from the pilot that "it is very healthy at the city," Susan
notes, "The musquitoes are not so plenty as I expected." Yet the *J. J.*
Hathorn is not home free:

Last night about ten, we had quite a heavy squall of wind and rain — it looked very bad, and we thought the night would be rough. It was dark and rainy, but nothing bad. We beat back and forth for a while — then hove to. This morning were six or eight miles from Tybee.[25]

As the tide comes in, the *J. J. Hathorn* is towed up the marshy Savannah River estuary. Susan continues fretting, this time worrying that they may not get far enough to anchor. At last with relief she reports that "at a little past two P.M. [we] dropped our anchor once more on the bottom of the Savannah."[26]

Jode disembarks and spends the night in Savannah, leaving Susan aboard the *J. J. Hathorn*. At 8:30 the next morning, the customs house officer arrives at the bark. Jode does not return until that evening, but he has engaged a lighter to remove some of the iron cargo, lessening the vessel's draft, so, as Susan says, "we hope to get the ship up Sat. or Sunday."

At 7 P.M. that night, Jode returns bringing the long-anticipated letters from home. And there is an important change of plans. Whether prompted by letters from the family or by his concern to see Susan home safely, Jode has decided he too will go north to Richmond, rather than take the bark back out immediately on another voyage. This means that they cannot leave until the cargo is discharged, so Jode has made arrangements for Susan to stay ashore while he oversees the operation:

He brought lots of such good letters — they made me impatient to get home. Jode thinks he shall go home too. We are going out to Mr. Dickinson's Saturday — I am to remain there, and Jode will come out when convenient. Would prefer a room all to ourselves, but it cannot be obtained.[27]

The intervening Friday is a busy day, with Susan preparing to be installed at "Mr. Dickerson's Country seat" (Susan corrects her earlier version of his name), and the iron being unloaded so quickly that Susan anticipates being able to "go up tomorrow with the ship, they have taken out so much today."[28]

The J. J. Hathorn's *outgoing coastwise manifest itemizes the cargo the vessel carried between Philadelphia and Savannah in October–November 1854. Of particular interest are Item 29, "1 Locomotive & Tender Complete in 24 ps.," and Item 41, "192 RR Wheels on 96 Axles." While these extremely heavy items must have taken up a good part of the vessel's weight capacity, the rest, mainly household items and construction materials, served to fill out the hold and increase the voyage's profitability. At the document's bottom right, Jode signed off a cargo for the first time as the vessel's master.*

Susan's ink changes color as her entry for Saturday, August 25, is written from "Montgomery," where Captain Dickerson has a country house. In one of her more breathless entries, she describes the climactic trip into the country, including another moonlit scene:

> *Got up bright and early, and the sailors rowed us up the river. Got to Capt. Dickerson's house a little after eight. It was quite warm, but I passed the day very comfortably. Dined at Capt. D{'}s and about six, he took me in his buggy and drove out to Montgomery, his summer resort 12 miles from the city. The ride was glorious through the pine woods hanging with long moss. The moon was nearly full so it was beautiful. Jode came out with Wm. D. Two other gents also. Capt. D. has a fine family — his eldest daughter is quite pretty, and a very pleasant girl. We supped at nine and retired at eleven. I was pretty tired.*

Galloway's *Directory of the City of Savannah* for 1850 lists one "Dickerson, J. H. [*sic*] r[esidence] 67 York street." [29] The Savannah city directory for 1858 lists "Dickerson, Henry J. r 67 York St, cor Abercorn," [30] and by 1859, the Dickerson listings include the following members of the household of "Capt. Dickerson" whom Susan mentions in her diary:

Dickerson, Gorge [*sic*] W. machinist at R & J Laehlison & Co. foundry,
  bds cor of York and Abercorn.
Dickerson, Capt. H. J., h S E cor York and Abercorn.
Dickerson, H.J & Son, stevedores, 120 Bay cor Bull.
Dickerson, Wm H. h cor Abercorn and York. [31]

Lost during the Civil War along with the Savannah port records for this period are many details about Captain Dickerson's maritime activities. From the information Susan provides, H. J. Dickerson appears to be roughly a Savannah counterpart, perhaps slightly more prosperous, of Jefferson Hathorn. [32] With the Hathorns in shipowning and international trade, and the Dickersons in Savannah piloting, towing, and agenting, their activities were complementary but different, and the communities in which they flourished could not have been more dissimilar.

For a young woman who grew up in a rural setting, Susan seems

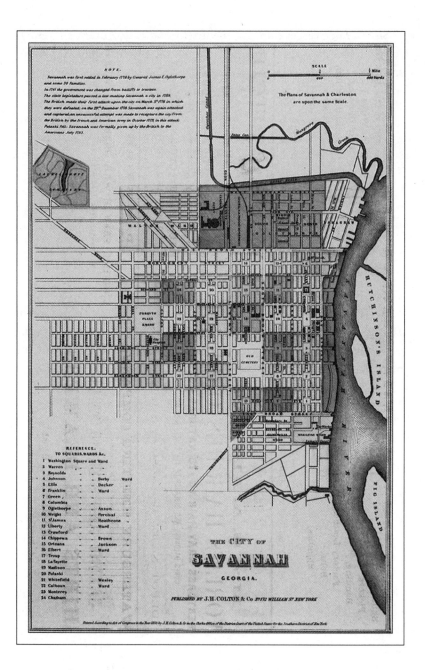

THE CITY OF
SAVANNAH
GEORGIA.

PUBLISHED BY J.H. COLTON & Co. No 172 WILLIAM ST NEW YORK

wildly taken with the romance of a country residence; it must be the number of residences, not simply their settings, that Susan finds attractive, for she seems impressed that the Cardiff Browns and the Savannah Dickersons both have a town and a country place. Susan writes about her first day in Montgomery: "Sunday. Aug. 26th   A fine day—it is most delightful here so nice and cool. The scenery beautiful. Never saw a more delightful place for summer. Jode went back to the city tonight. Capt. D. goes tomorrow morning."[33] With Jode absent and the cool spell ending, the enchantment of Montgomery begins to pale by Monday, and the equestrian activities of the comely Miss Dickerson and friends produce an emergency:

> *The musquitoes troubled me so I did not get to sleep until late, so woke up late. — heard the girls going to ride horseback. Miss Dickerson was thrown and severely injured. Her father had set off for the city. George went for him & the Doctor. Found she was badly bruised but had no bones broken. Tonight she is quite bright. . . . Tonight had a capital bath in the salt water.*[34]

The salt bath improves Susan's spirits. She reports the following day as "A fair day, but very warm," and notes that "The evening was glorious—a full moon, and cool breeze." Nevertheless, the "musquitoes" trouble Susan greatly and in fact threaten the aura of the Dickersons' country house: "in the house, the musquitoes were too numerous to be quite agreeable." Susan reports on Miss Dickerson's halting recovery:

> *Miss Dickerson is quite smart today, although her head is very sore. She is beginning to feel the effects of the fall. After dinner, did not seem so bright as in the morning.*

◀ *This 1855 Savannah map shows the city's important cotton factors' (agents')
warehouse-wharves on the Savannah River, at the right. The townhouse of Captain
Dickerson was at the corner of Abercorn and York, on Oglethorpe Square (9) in the
sixteen-square-block "ward" just to the right of the "Old Cemetery." The Dickerson
business was well situated at the corner of Bay and Bull, at the very center of the cotton
factors' row. The boardinghouse where Susan and Jode stayed briefly before returning to
Maine was on Broughton Street between Oglethorpe Square and Wright Square (10);
Broughton Street is the first main through street parallel to the river after Bay. At the
top of the map, a navigable creek and a canal connect the Central Rail Road Depot to
the Savannah River.*

Miss Dickerson is not so well — feels the effects of her fall far more than at first. [35]

Persistent "musquitoes" make life miserable for Susan the rest of August's last week, as she writes:

Did not sleep two hours last night, with the musquitoes and heat. Mr. Wm. D came out last eve — returned this morning. The musquitoes are not satisfied with tormenting one's life out by night but they bite all day. I have scarce sewed a stitch, for them.

. . . so hot and close I never did feel so uncomfortable in all my life — I thought I should die before morning. The musquitoes were thicker than hops — and no bar — so I lay all night and fanned myself to keep the "bref {sic} of life" in me.

Heavy showers of rain accompanied with thunder. The air is much cooler — musquitoes still abundant. But I slept last night so soundly — did not wake at all. I had slept so little the two or three nights past, I was nearly sick.

This is the first day of fall — rather cooler than the three or four days past. The musquitoes however are still abundant. Took another bath today — I think I feel better for it. The salt water kills the heat and burning in the musquito bites. [36]

By now it is clear: Susan has had enough of Captain Dickerson's "summer resort." Without Jode, she has only her diary to confide in, and she tells it, "Would give anything if I were in town." She worries about Jode's health, writing, "Hear Jode has a nice sore under his arm." She misses him, and their time together is growing short. When Jode comes out to Montgomery on Saturday night, Susan's spirits lift perceptibly, for she now can write, "I am to go to town with Capt. D. on Tuesday or Wednesday." [37] With the end of this exile to Montgomery in sight, Susan stops complaining about mosquitoes, and her remaining entries from the Dickersons' home are the equable reports of an even-tempered houseguest relishing the rusticated life:

Tonight Mr. W. D. and Mr. Wade came out. The boat race is deferred.

Towards noon cleared up and the boats raced a little. Dr. Banks brought Miss Olmsted and Miss Meredith over here, and they spent the day.

The house is full of company. Last night Capt. D. brought down a Mr. Taylor. Jode came down with Wm. D. and a Mr. Golding. Today, Messrs. Gay & Brigham arrived, so there is no lack of company.

Capt. D. took the young ladies & children out sailing. . . . At night Mrs. Bulard & Mrs. Epping called & with Miss Fanning, planned a fishing excursion for tomorrow morning early.

Before 7, Mrs. E. & Miss Fanning came to go fishing. Miss D & Miss Lizzy accompanied them, but I staid at home with Mrs. D.[38]

From Susan's account of it, the Dickersons' life seems a little decadent and silly, though Susan never offers any such judgment of her hosts. Curiously, she never describes Mrs. Dickerson (one almost thinks the captain is a widower for a while, since she is so absent), only mentioning that she stays home with her the morning the girls go fishing. Susan's reports quite naturally deal with the generation nearer her own, and the comings and goings of the menfolk, in particular Jode. Susan's entries from Montgomery make it difficult to imagine that she would let herself in for this scene twice, so it appears that Susan and Jode probably stayed at a "public convenience," as hotels and boardinghouses were known, when they stopped in Savannah for their load of Georgia timber in the fall of 1854.

On Tuesday Susan has her "budgets" packed "to be ready," since the plan calls for her "going to town tomorrow if nothing happens, with Capt. D. . . . We shall take the steamer for the North Sat. if Jode can finish his business to suit him, and neither of us is sick."[39] So on Wednesday, after a stay of eleven days and without a hint of the regret she expressed on leaving London, Susan reports tersely, "Got up bright and early and came out to the city with Capt. Dickerson. Breakfasted there, and then Jode came for me."[40]

☙

Just as Susan gets back to Savannah, there is a heavy thunderstorm, and after waiting it out, Jode takes her down to the *J. J. Hathorn*, where she "commenced packing." Finally she adjudges the situation "in readiness for a start." But they must await the steamer for New York, and since the mosquitoes are "so plenty" on the bark as well, she and Jode take a room at a Mrs. McNelty's boardinghouse. Susan's Maine constitution rebels against the southern heat: "The day has been very sultry—the heat oppressive," she says. "There is not a breath of air stirring."[41] On Thursday, September 6, Susan and Jode take their room, though clearly no place but home will satisfy Susan at this point:

> *After tea last night we walked up to the famous boarding house of Savannah, Mrs. McNelty's — in Boston or any northern state, it would not be a third rate house. But I am to stay so short a time I do not mind it.*[42]

Earlier that day, Jode finishes up business necessary to leave the *J. J. Hathorn*, settling up accounts with the customs officials and consignees. In his absence Susan again busies herself: "I have spent the day, which has been cloudy, showery and very sultry, in my room. Jode came up quite early, and will spend the night as the musquitoes are intolerable down on board the Barque."[43] She is sewing for Jode: "Have sewed on the shirts—made one, and hem stitched it." Hand-hemstitching is not a trivial accomplishment, but to Susan, hemstitching is a norm. In fact she goes one better, saying she "must '<u>maggot</u> stitch' the next." The next day, however, she revises this plan, saying, "Have sewed and made another shirt—hem stitched that too, as I could not remember the 'maggot stitch.'[44]

Susan celebrates her birthday in Savannah, and on that day, September 7, she writes:

> *This is my birth day — am twenty five today! Thought to have spent it at home, but know they did not forget me. . . . It has been very much cooler than yesterday and the good wholesome air has seemed to brace me up. I have felt better than for some time. . . . Jode came up quite late and we had part of a game of whist — Mrs & Miss McNelty, Jode and myself.*

Whether a reflection on the company at whist, her weariness with the Savannah heat and mosquitoes, the fatigue normal for a woman in her third trimester of pregnancy, the apparent omission of a birthday gift from Jode, disappointment that he is late on the night of her birthday, or simply Susan's eagerness to get home to Maine, she concludes her birthday entry by saying, "Am thankful we go tomorrow." [45]

In Savannah Susan's account book continues to provide a parallel account of her activities. The fourth of September, Susan's last day at the Dickerson house in Montgomery, she notes an expenditure of twenty-five cents to a "Negro wench," presumably a servant who attended to Susan while she was there. That same day, Susan manages to spend twenty cents for "Cloth & needles," though her diary does not mention going shopping. Back in Savannah, she makes three purchases on the sixth totaling nineteen cents: a paper fan for eight cents, apples for eight cents, and a "Palmetto Fan" for three cents. The remainder of Susan's expenditures before returning to Richmond appear on September 8:

Fare from Savannah to N. York... 20.00
Board at Mrs. Mc.Nelty's 2 days 4.00
Apples .14, 1 Trunk 3.00 ....3.14
Fare from NY to Richmond... 13.25

The $2.00-per-day tariff at Mrs. McNelty's was probably for Susan only. The 1850 Galloway's city directory lists "terms" for "Transient Boarders, per day—$1.50." [46] Although Susan herself does not give a location for "Mrs. McNelty's," the 1858 directory shows "McNulty [sic], Wm capt stm" at 177 Broughton Street; the following year Mrs. Jane McNelty herself appears in the directory at the same address, with "McNelty, Capt Wm." [47] Whether the *J. J. Hathorn* was berthed at Savannah's main landing or had been towed up the canal to the railroad terminus, Broughton Street would have been an easy walk.

At last the day Susan both longs for and dreads arrives. She and Jode go to the *J. J. Hathorn* and put their overnight things from McNelty's into their luggage:

It was nice and cool all last night, and I slept soundly without waking; until four or five this morning. Took my leave of Mrs. McNelty just after

breakfast and came down on board. Packed up the few things I had with me,
and prepared to take the steamer at 4 P.M.

Susan writes the remainder of this day's entry in pencil, and later inks it
over in uncharacteristic blue ink. This artifact, and the content, suggests
Susan wrote the first part on board the *J. J. Hathorn*, and the rest on board
the *Alabama*, after its departure.

Bidding farewell to her honeymoon "barque," Susan shares a tender,
wistful moment:

Was all ready by three — took a last look of the "J.J." — the good old steward
and John — and went on board the "Alabama" en route for home. Almost a
year since we left the loved ones there. Hope no one will be wanting. Am not
at all sea sick but very tired.[48]

Homeward

The Hathorns' decision to make the trip north in the steamship *Alabama* would have been made with an eye to saving time. Susan was seven months pregnant and eager to get home; Jode, who would soon take the *J. J. Hathorn* from Savannah to Liverpool, was equally pressed for time. Travel by steamship would shrink the trip, which would take weeks under sail, to a matter of days. Though the Hathorns' cargo attests to the expanding railroads in Georgia in 1855, no through-route from Savannah north existed; in fact the Hathorns' Savannah cargoes— the locomotive and tender brought down from Philadelphia, and the iron rails from Cardiff—confirm the lack of a through-railroad north.[1] Susan may be less well than she admits in her diary, and Jode himself may need a bit of familial encouragement.

On the morning after her twenty-fifth birthday, Susan had written, "Took my leave of Mrs. McNelty just after breakfast and came down on board [the *J. J. Hathorn*]."[2] The trip by coastal steamer to New York will take about forty hours. Writing in pencil that was later, without being rubbed out, inked in, she says, "We glide along so nicely it seems as if there could never be danger."[3] The danger may be the treacherous shoals off Cape Hatteras, or Susan may be alluding to the widely feared hazard to steamship travel during this period: a boiler explosion. The Hathorns themselves have good economic reasons to fear steamships, with their potential to take freight—therefore their livelihood—from sailing ships, as steamships had already taken passengers. But Susan passes over her fears and writes next of the Gulf Stream's traffic and abundant sea life: "Have passed several vessels, and have been surrounded by porpoises

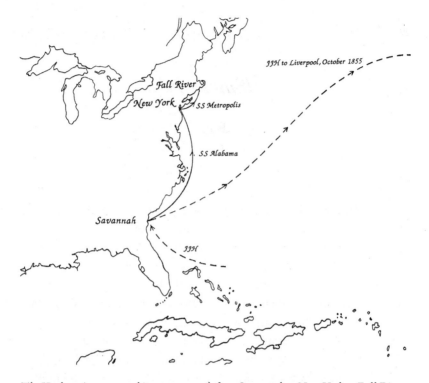

The Hathorns' two steamship voyages north from Savannah to New York to Fall River, September 9–12, 1855, are approximated here. The broken line indicates the J. J. Hathorn's arrival at Savannah in August 1855 and Jode's subsequent voyage to Liverpool in October.

all day. Quantities of flying fish too. Feared this morning the day would be tedious, but it has not."[4] Susan appreciates the steamer's independence from the vagaries of wind and wave; she notes that the headwind "is something that does not much trouble a steamer," and that they will be in New York the next day.[5]

The Hathorns' *Alabama* was one of four nineteenth-century vessels so named, three of them steam powered. Running a regular north-south ferry service between southern ports and New York City during the 1850s, the *Alabama* on which Susan and Jode traveled was a 1,261-ton

The steamship Alabama, *shown here with sails set, took the Hathorns from Savannah to New York.*

side-wheel steamer built by William H. Webb of Greenpoint, New York.[6] The wooden hulls of the *Alabama* and the later famous clipper *Celestial* were launched simultaneously at the Webb yard on January 19, 1850, with the fitting-out taking another year. At 214 feet 4 inches long, 35 feet 2 inches wide, and 22 feet deep, the *Alabama* had 31-foot paddle wheels, making it capable of a speed of ten knots. On its first New York–Savannah run in January 1851, cabin fare cost $25. Susan lists on September 8 a fare to New York of $20 in her account book; despite the economic inflation then in progress, competition on the run may have driven fares down. Susan's $20-fare entry also suggests that again she is recording her individual expenses.[7]

During her Monday at sea on the *Alabama*, Susan stays in her cabin and sews and reads, but by Tuesday morning, she can scarcely contain her excitement. She is following their progress in her diary more than once a day: "9 A.M. Had a beautiful night—the whole passage, there has scarcely been a "ripple" on the water. This morning the Jersey shore is plainly distinguishable. Think to reach N. York by 10 o'clock."[8] Later that day, she notes their brief morning stop in New York: "Do not know exactly the time we arrived—somewhere about half past ten—took a cab to the U.S. Hotel where we dined."

The hotel at which Susan and Jode stopped between steamers "was for one generation New York's most important hotel, standing from 1831 to 1902 just inland from Schermerhorn Row."

> For half a century this structure, first as Holt's Hotel, and later as the United States Hotel, was the most prominent landmark on the East River side of Manhattan south of the [site of the] Brooklyn Bridge. Its location well illustrates the role that its Seaport surroundings played in the growth of the city and continent whose great gateway it formed.[9]

A fascinating example of ingenuity and enterprise, the U.S. Hotel was built with a fortune reportedly amassed by Stephen Holt by selling cheap "shilling" lunches prepared with produce from Fulton Street Market. Susan's incessant needlework had a parallel in the sewing efforts of the indefatigable Mrs. Holt, who spent six years sewing "no fewer than 1500 towels, 400 pairs of sheets with matching ruffled pillow cases, 250 bed ticks, and 300 patchwork quilts (the latter often made of pieces no larger than a two-shilling coin)."[10]

Situated at Fulton and Water Streets, the hotel boasted one of the first flat roofs in New York with "a promenade 80 feet above the ground," and a domed tower topped by a semaphore for relaying ship-arrival information. The 165-room hotel was 134 feet high, with a steam engine operating a lift for baggage (but none for passengers), turning spits, grinding cutlery, and pumping water from a five-hundred-foot deep well. A shipmasters' mecca, the hotel had an expansive hundred-foot-long grand dining room with a twenty-foot ceiling, two smaller dining rooms, and twenty-five "parlours"; particularly popular with sea captains was a bar in the tower topside, with its sweeping view of the port's activity.[11] By the time Susan visited the U.S. Hotel, it had an extensive range of water closets "not equaled by any similar establishment in the United States."[12]

The Hathorns' stay could hardly have allowed Jode time for more than a quick drink in the captains' aerie. As Susan continues her account

The U.S. Hotel, at the corner of Fulton and Water Streets in New York, was that port's landmark for visiting shipmasters, and the Hathorns took a brief respite there on their steamer trip north.

of that September 11, "Left there at four for the 'Metropolis' one of the most beautiful boats I ever saw. Everything is of the best. The supper excellent—servants attentive. Capt. Gerrish of the 'McBiddle' came down with us."[13] Though five steamships named *Metropolis* appear in the mid-nineteenth-century maritime records,[14] it can be established that the Hathorns traveled from New York on the gargantuan 2,108-ton wooden-hulled side-wheeler launched April 20, 1854, in the Green-

The steamship Metropolis, *a much larger and more luxurious vessel than the* Alabama, *took the Hathorns from New York to Fall River.*

point shipyard of Sneden and Whitlock.[15] It served the Fall River Line on the New York–Newport–Fall River run. Susan had more reason to worry on the *Metropolis* than on the *Alabama*, for the *Metropolis* in 1857 held an inferior A2 *Lloyds'* rating; its "Security against Fire" was deemed "Insufficient," and the inspector's remark was "Boilers on guard." [16]

Nevertheless the *Metropolis* was "one of the most celebrated American steamboats of the time, being an advancement in ideas of construction." Just two months before Susan and Jode traveled on the *Metropolis*, it recorded its fastest run between New York and Fall River, eight hours twenty-one minutes, averaging nearly 19 knots, so it is no wonder Susan says she felt she was nearly flying. An immensely successful ship, the *Metropolis* was bigger, faster, and better in every way: it provided sleeping accommodations for six hundred passengers; its engine reportedly had the largest cylinder that up to that time had ever been cast—105.25 inches in diameter, with a twelve-foot stroke; its cruising speed was 20 miles an hour; and its decorations "of the most elegant description." [17]

Yet Susan's final review of the *Metropolis* was less ecstatic. Even deluxe cabins in the mid-nineteenth-century were little more than closets that inspired grumblings from Harriet Beecher Stowe and Charles Dickens, to name two famous literary voyagers of the period.[18] "Last night the cabin was so hot I scarce slept at all," Susan says of her own overnight aboard the *Metropolis*. Susan records details of that eventful September 12, 1855: the sleepless night, the arrival in Fall River, the train trip to Boston and brief layover there, the perennial travelers' frustration with slow baggage, a second train trip to Richmond, and at last, a joyous family reception:

Had a little nap until twelve — then dressed myself ready for the cars. Got in about four. Reached Boston by seven or before — but it took an age to get the Baggage. Went to the NE House, where after a lunch, I tumbled into bed. At half past 11, went to the Depot. The rout{e} was very dusty, and the cars very hot, so the ride was not so pleasant. Arrived at home by 7 P.M. — found the house in a muster, preparing for a collation.[19]

Even with that, the long day was not over. Susan and Jode would spend their first night back in Richmond at his sister's home, where there was visiting and debriefing: "Went up to Sally's and spent the night—sat up until one and did not go to sleep until past two."

🦞

The house on Front Street in which Sally Hathorn Brown and her husband, Lemuel, lived in 1855 was only steps from the large brick Hathorn Block in Richmond, and just around the corner from Richmond House. Sally's house is a logical first-night stop for the young captain and mother-to-be; Susan makes no mention of Brown's being there, which suggests that Lemuel Brown, himself a coastering captain, may be away.[20] Sally, with her toddler, Benicia, is the ideal hostess for Susan after the long journey, and as the next few months unfold, the two will spend many days together and become extremely close. But on the first day after Susan and Jode return, the rest of the relatives "well nigh devour" them, according to Susan. Typical mid-September Maine weather greets them the following day, which after Savannah's heat and "musquitoes" is welcome to Susan: "Rainy this morning, but cleared off cool," she writes.[21]

Susan and Jode have reached Richmond, but their travels are not over.

After a year's absence, everyone is eager to see them, and they begin a complete round of visits to family and friends. On the morning of September 13, Susan says she "Came home about ten, and began to unpack."[22] Where is this "home?" Though Susan never specifies, the diary clearly indicates it to be Richmond House, the boardinghouse that Jefferson and Sally Hathorn built and operated, and that census records show was the senior Hathorns' residence during the census years of 1850 and 1860, and also Susan's residence in 1860. Richmond House occupies the lot on Main Street directly adjacent to the Hathorn Block, and Jode and his bride, heirs apparent to the Hathorn business interests, might be expected to reside there as well, if only temporarily.

During their midday dinner, Susan's brother Llewellyn "made his appearance—came out for Fanny," and that afternoon, Susan and Jode go out to the Post Road to visit Susan's family. Her sister Lucy's mother-in-law is quite ill:

> . . . went out to Father's with them, called at Aunt Rhoda's — found them well with the exception of Paulina. Lucy and Mother were at Mrs. Ring's — she is very sick indeed. . . . Amasa came up at eight and brought Lucy home from Mrs. Ring's. . . . We sat up and talked until twelve — when I began to grow sleepy.[23]

The Hathorns stay the night and Friday dawns quite cool, when Susan says, "was glad to put on woolen stockings and drawers this morning."[24] She expresses further concern about Mrs. Ring, to whose home Lucy and her husband, Amasa, go that morning. Susan and Jode have another set of relatives to visit at her brother Hosea Lennan's. Susan's diary makes clear the tight interrelationship of family and business among the Lennans: Hosea is in the ship supplying business in Gardiner, and Amasa Ring, his brother-in-law, works in the business with him. Because of Amasa's mother's illness, Susan's other brother, Llew, will stand in for him at work:

> Jode and I went down to Gardiner — got to Hosea's about eleven. Found all well and very happy to see us. Had a nice time. Mary dismissed her school

and spent the afternoon with us. Sis is going to father's tonight with Llew,
who came down to help Hosea in place of Amasa. [25]

Here Susan mentions another of her siblings, Mary, who is teaching
school, having taken up (perhaps at the same school) where Susan left
off when she married Jode. "Mary is going to Richmond with us," Susan
writes, "to spend tomorrow." [26] It is another long day. "We did not get
to Mrs. Hathorn's until seven P.M.," Susan writes. The evening brings
visitors to Richmond House, one of them "Mr. E. Small," a relative of
Mrs. Hathorn's and a maritime associate of Jefferson Hathorn's who
would later command the *J. J. Hathorn.* The evening of September 14
also brings a visit from "Brown and Sally to spend the evening." [27]

Susan exercises her penchant for order and returns to her sewing on
the next "fine cool breezy day," when she reports, "I put my things to
rights this morning—took me all the forenoon. Mary sewed on Jode's
shirt. Then I put the buttons on the new shirts and mended his stockings." [28] There is more scurrying about that afternoon, as Molly (Mary)
had to get back to Gardiner on the train:

After she went away I went up to Sally's{,} and Capt. H. & Jode came up to
tea, so we had a family supper. Played a game of "Aggravation" in the eve-
ning. When we came home, [29] *found Miss O. Waite had arrived. Poor San-*
derson Robinson was buried today. He died the day we came home. [30]

Susan calls the next day, Sunday the sixteenth, a "dull, cloudy day—
after dinner, began to rain but only in showers," and Sally (whose name
Susan sometimes writes as *Salle*) and Brown bring their baby down and
take tea; it is also the day of another Richmond funeral, that of "Mrs. D.
Blanchard." [31]

With the start of the new week, the Hathorn family has important business to transact, and since they have apparently waited for Jode's return
to do so, this may in part explain Jode's decision to come to Maine with
Susan. On that cloudy, warm September 17, Susan writes: "The property
of J. J. Hathorn was sold today, and the house has been full of company.

Capt. Hathorn bought 'Willow Dale' for Jode." J. J. Hathorn, Jefferson's younger brother and business partner, had died at the age of thirty-five in March of 1854,[32] leaving an estate that included interests in several pieces of real estate.[33] "Willow Dale" is not a place-name now known in Richmond, but Susan is apparently speaking of a piece of J. J. Hathorn's real estate, and Jack Hathorn did own property along Front Street to the north of the Brown house. In view of the imminent birth of their first child, Jefferson Hathorn might have wanted this nearby, riverfront land for Jode and Susan's future home. The area's topography evokes the name Susan gives in her diary: the major Mill Brook watershed has filled the area with willow trees, and the area between Mill Brook and the Kennebec is the clay hill known as "Hathorn Hill."[34] Because no recorded deeds connect Jode Hathorn to any land, and because J. J. Hathorn's probate records do not so name any piece of real estate, tracing this piece of property to Jode is not possible. The events of 1856 may explain why a transfer to Jode was never completed.

September 17 is a happy day for Susan, with a procession of visitors paying social calls on the returning voyagers. Susan records the comings and goings of friends and family at the Hathorn household that busy Monday: "Miss Waite was here, but went over to Mrs. Foster's to spend the night. Mr. & Mrs. Foster called—Frank Small, and Capt. C. Blair. Then Dr. Libby & wife, Capt. Blair & Lucy spent the evening with us." Frank Small is a relative of Jode's mother, whose maiden name was Small; the Blairs were friends and business associates of Jefferson Hathorn's, and Captain Blair was a maritime colleague. The Blairs were a prosperous family who owned a large piece of land directly across Mill Creek from Hathorn Hill, and Mrs. Harriet Libby, the doctor's wife, was by birth a Blair. Dr. Libby was the Richmond physician who reported to the state on the cholera epidemic. Captain Lemuel C. Blair, his brother-in-law, was involved in the West Indies trade, like the Hathorns.

That day was remarkable for another reason: "Mr. Bickford came in the 3 o'clock train & brought the chest—all things safe."[35] Mr. Bickford, the *J. J. Hathorn*'s first mate, was entrusted with the sea chest that

Susan reported packing with the Hathorns' worldly goods in Savannah. The next morning, Susan appears to have had enough of the Richmond social scene and is ready to get back to business:

> *A rainy day, for which I am thankful. So much company yesterday I scarce sewed a stitch. This morning I got up early, and sorted over my things a little, which came in the chest yesterday. Then sewed on Jode's shirt. It has rained so hard, have had no company today.*[36]

This flurry of visiting recognizes not only Susan and Jode's homecoming but also Jode's imminent leave-taking. Susan displaces this thought, giving it no expression in her diary, and instead pays almost obsessive attention to Jode's clothing:

> *Finished Jode's new shirt — mended old ones and cut down the binding to his new ones. After dinner, made him two collars.*
>
> *I have sewed on Jode's shirt collars, have made three or four.*
>
> *I made the remainder of Jode's collars, and marked them and his other clothing.*
>
> *Pleasant today and the sun very hot, Ironed four shirts for Jode, and a dozen collars — this morning — then packed his things for the boat.*[37]

On Wednesday evening, just as more company is leaving, Susan and Jode learn how short their time at home together in Richmond really is.

> *Mrs. Barnard & Miss Reed . . . had just taken their departure when Mr. Steward came in with a despatch, that the Barque was chartered, and wanted Jode to start for Savannah Friday. Do not know as he will go until next Tuesday.*[38]

The next day, Thursday, Susan and Jode will celebrate their first wedding anniversary.

🕊

On September 20, 1855, which dawned frosty and remained cool, Susan looks back. "Just a year ago, we were married—it has seemed a short year." But that day and the next, Hathorn house is abustle, with Jode taking his leave to visit his Hathorn relatives in Dresden, and Susan going to the Lennans':

We have been full of company as usual — Mr. Harwood here, from Savannah, to dinner — Sally spent the afternoon, and Aunt and Uncle Dole the evening.

After dinner, there were callers, and I did not do much — mended my underclothes and put things a little to right. Jode went up to Dresden to see the folks — is not coming back until tomorrow noon.[39]

Apparently staying at the Post Road farm for Saturday night, Susan is coming down with a cold, and she details in pencil the events of her day without Jode:

Cool and cloudy. Rained a little towards noon. I have mended my night dresses, made a bag for my dress pieces and another for my stockings and put my closet in order. Just before dinner, went up to Sally's and got some patterns — found her ironing. Staid until after dinner then came back and got ready to go out to father's. It was real cold, and I took a little more in addition to what I had, so I sneezed finely all the evening. Lucy was at Mrs. Ring's — Amasa came up after dark and brought Mary — she watched with Mrs. R. who is very slim {ill} indeed.[40]

Susan is in West Richmond, Jode in Dresden: but by that cloudy Sunday, they are back together, for she reports:

Capt & Mrs. Hathorn came out. Hosea, Ann & Mrs. Ricks came up. Lucy, Amasa, Mary and Sis were at home, so that once more us children gathered together at father's house. We staid until after supper, when Jode & I started for the village — got to Father Hathorn's about eight.[41]

From all outward appearances, and from Susan's description, Monday, September 24, is a "pleasant" day, very warm for the time of year. Susan keeps busy with preparations for Jode:

Ironed four shirts for Jode, and a dozen collars — this morning — then packed his things for the boat, at 4 P.M. His father went with him to Bos-

ton, so I am left alone with Mrs. H. and Iffy. Miss Wait was here, but went out calling. [42]

Following upon this entry is perhaps the most revealing of Susan's understated and telling juxtapositions: "After all departed, I made a night dress," she writes. In this seemingly unremarkable report lies a world of information about Susan, her relationship with Jode, and the times and expectations with which Susan lives. As the next day's entry, when she continues this project, makes clear, the "night dress" is the first of the many things she will sew for the baby that will be born in about two months. Susan has waited precisely until Jode is gone, dedicating her sewing time and attention to him while she can.

True to form, once Susan begins sewing for the baby, she is unrelenting. It seems as if a dam has burst: babies appear everywhere, and concern with them becomes paramount. "Am quite tired tonight," she writes the night Jode leaves; "Sally was here this afternoon with the baby." [43] Susan is throwing herself into prodigious preparations for her own baby, it would seem, to cope with her loneliness:

Miss Wait came in about ten and has fitted Mrs. Hathorn's dress. I have mended my box, and sewed on the sacque night dresses. After dinner, went up to Sally's and spent the afternoon.

I have been cutting out a lot of things today and sewing on the sacques. But I do not accomplish much. So many drop in, one cannot sew half the time.

Wrote to Jode this morning — then embroidered the sleeves of two night dresses and run the sides of another. Have sewed the most steadily that I have since I came home. Feels as if I must hurry matters a little. [44]

By Thursday, Susan sees the final evidence of Jode's departure, as she writes, "Capt. Hathorn came home in the last train tonight. Went to N.Y. and saw Jode off." [45] She must do what she must do:

Have accomplished considerable — the six sacques will be completed tonight, after so long a time. Have crocheted the inserting and edge for two today, and almost made them. Have staid in my room as it was not cold. [46]

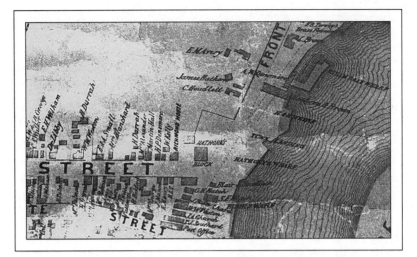

In Richmond, Maine, the Hathorn family lived and worked in the area of Front and Main Streets, shown in this detail from the 1855 Richmond town map. "Hathorn's Block," with its storage building, occupied the large lot on the northwest corner of the intersection, just across from Hathorn's Wharf. Immediately north of that, between the Town Wharf and the Steam Boat Wharf, were the Hathorn & Brown Wharf and Hathorn & Brown Warehouse. Sally Hathorn Brown and her husband, Captain Lemuel Brown, lived in the house just to the north on Front Street. Main Street runs roughly perpendicular to Front, and Richmond House, the Hathorns' boardinghouse, is on the north side of Main, adjacent to the Hathorn Block. It was here that Susan lived with Jode's parents after returning to Richmond in September. The map shows the property of several relatives and neighbors whose names figure in Susan's diary: Bickford, Small, Blair, Southard, Avery, and Witham.

The weather Susan describes is typical of late September in Richmond: frequent cloudy, rainy days, relieved by days of brilliant sunshine and wind, which Susan finds useful "to dry up the mud." [47] As she works on her baby's layette, the bond with Sally and her baby grows stronger. Here is how Susan spends the Saturday after Jode's departure:

Got up quite early — put my room to rights, and sewed the edge on two of the sacques — so they are finished. Then after dinner, went up to Sally's — learned to do the feather stitch [48] and made it around a swathe. Mrs. Nancy

Hathorn came in while I was there and made a long call. Came back home and prepared another band for stitching.[49]

But Susan's life has not turned to "all work and no play," as family and friends make a concerted effort to occupy Susan in this time that must be difficult for her. On Tuesday, for example, "Fanny Foster and Miss Southard called to get something for a levee [reception] for the Library." This call was remarkable for Susan and the Hathorns, since Miss Southard's father, the shipbuilder and owner T. J. Southard, was becoming far and away Richmond's most prosperous man. Interestingly, Miss Southard's call takes place while Jefferson Sr. is out of town; there may well have been feelings of rivalry between the two families.

The Hathorns know well the long separations their work entails, and they have taken Susan into their fold: "In the evening," she writes on her first day after Jode leaves, "Mrs. H. and Iffy, Miss Wait and Mr. D. Stevens came up. Played a game of whist."[50] The Richmond "camp ground," an area set aside for retreats and revival meetings, is having a meeting that week. Susan writes, "The place is full of strangers—the Baptist people have an association."[51] Susan does not number herself among "the Baptist people," but on the following Sunday she indicates that her mother-in-law does: "Miss Wait & Mrs. Hathorn went over to the Baptist house to meeting."[52]

On Wednesday, September 26, Susan writes, "The State Fair is now in session at Gardiner. Would like to attend it," and the steady parade of visitors and guests at Richmond House cannot help Susan from reminiscing about other moonlit nights: "The evening is glorious—so was the last—a full moon—and the air is warm and mild as summer."[53] And on Sunday she has occasion for other retrospection, as she catches up on letter writing: "I have written Misses Brown & Remington and Mary Pollard," recalling her friends in Cardiff and Santiago.[54] "A fine morning," Susan says of that day, "but clouded up towards night and looks like a storm."

Hathorn Block and Richmond House

Susan, cossetted by Richmond relatives and friends yet very much alone at the beginning of October, undertakes an ambitious schedule of sewing for the expected baby and a busy social calendar, as if to distract herself from her grass widowhood. As a Hathorn and a sea captain's wife, Susan can claim a certain social status in Richmond for, up and down the Maine coast, local maritime aristocracies arose in dozens of mid-nineteenth-century towns. One such town was Thomaston, which lies down east of the Kennebec, on the western edge of Penobscot Bay, about seventy miles from Richmond. As one observer described Thomaston, "everybody knew everybody, but not everybody spoke to everybody":

> [I]t was doubtless quarter-deck formality that was responsible for the prevailing custom. A shipmaster who could not speak to a sailor lad on his own ship though he lived next door to him when at home, certainly could not be expected to speak to him when he met him on the streets or at the wharves in Thomaston. And . . . a master's wife could not be expected to condescend to speak to the wives and daughters of those a rank lower than her husband's unless she had excellent reasons for doing so.[1]

In addition, maritime aristocracies had their hierarchies: the "deep-water sea captains, the shipbuilders, the bankers, the ministers and professional men and their families constituted the 'first families,'" while other members of the maritime community lay further from the elite circle.[2] Captains' wives held an enviable, central position in the charmed circle:

[W]hen a man became master of a deep-water craft, not a coaster, he and
his good wife automatically became members of the elect. In many in-
stances the wife was the daughter of a captain and needed no grooming
for her new position. If she were not to the after cabin born[,] she soon
"learned the ropes" and acquired a sophistication all her own. Prosperity
gave her pride. Travel widened her outlook. Varied social contacts gave
her confidence. Every sea cap'n's wife "rigged out" in her silks, satins,
and velvets, adorned with heavy ear rings, and wearing a large cameo on
her firm bosom presented a picture of proud and dignified femininity not
unlike that of the female figurehead. . . . The very bearing of the captain
and his wife discouraged familiarity.[3]

Susan Lennan was not "to the after cabin born," but her intelligence
and education equipped her better than many to appreciate the role of
captain's wife. In view of Susan's pregnancy, it is significant that she does
not return to her parents' home but takes up residence with her in-laws.
As a captain, a shipowner, and a merchant-entrepreneur, Jefferson Hathorn holds a position of prominence in Richmond's social, political, and
business power structure, and Susan, his first son's wife, has left the farm
for good and entered the Hathorns' world.

Despite Susan's privileged position and her efforts to maintain good
cheer, the Maine coast's fall rains and gloom lower her spirits. On the
first day of October, she writes that "it has threatened to rain every hour,
but has only sprinkled a little once." She throws herself headlong into
her sewing: "I have done lots—made two foot blankets—chain stitched
one and feather stitched the other, besides cutting out lots of things."
She notes the comings and goings at Richmond House, and when she
writes that Miss Sarah Foster called for Miss Wait, "who has gone over
there to spend the night," Susan arranges to have company for herself.
"I am going to stay with Sally," she says.[4]

By the next day, Tuesday, Susan is wishing to go to the Gardiner fair
with Sally, yet the weather is uncooperative. Her industrious sewing
continues unabated. She reports that Mrs. Ring has died and the griev-
ing figure of Amasa Ring, Susan's brother-in-law, casts a sad shadow. In
this remarkable entry, Susan summarizes her "little year," and as she

recalls October 2 the previous year, she freely expresses her longing for
Jode and her concern for his safety:

> *A year ago today, we started for Philadelphia to join the Barque. What a
> little year it seems. Today it is raining hard enough — began to pour down
> last night and has only held up a little while this afternoon. Amasa came
> down on business and we spied him as he was going past the window. His
> mother is dead & buried — died a week ago yesterday. Sally and I were going
> to Gardiner if it had not rained. Shall go tomorrow if pleasant. I have done
> lots of work — cross stitched a swathe — made and cross stitched a foot blan-
> ket and made two skirts — they are all ready for embroidering. The rain
> sounds so lonely, it makes me think of the cold storms poor Jode must brave
> this winter.*[5]

The Richmond of 1855 was an exciting, booming place. In 1851 railroad passenger service had come to town,[6] with Richmond on the route
from Portland (the state's largest port), to Bath (the U.S. Customs District seat), to Augusta (the state capital). It was a town where people
dreamed bold dreams, and where some of them came true. During Richmond's most significant economic and population growth—the quarter
of a century between 1850 and 1875—the principal activities had to do
with ships and the sea and the trading of the goods the ships brought,
and in the 1850s the Hathorn family was in the thick of it.

The Hathorns were not the only seafaring-shipbuilding family in
Richmond, however, nor were they the only family whose holdings were
amassed without the boost of inherited wealth. In fact, the fortunes of
the Southard family run as an interesting parallel to the Hathorns'. Susan's diary mentions the Southard women who are her contemporaries:
one was involved in support for the local library, having "called to get
some thing for a levee for the Library," and shortly before her own baby
is born, Susan will note, "Mrs. A. Southard had a young son this morning."[7] A male born to the Southard family would have been cause for
rejoicing, for building a maritime dynasty required sons.

Every maritime family knew the dangers of their way of life. One remarkable monument in a Richmond cemetery has engraved in stone the far-flung character of life at sea, and the paradoxical combination of strength and fragility that defined it. The first name on this stone is that of a captain Susan encountered in Cardiff; the loss of his 867-ton Richmond-built ship *Charter Oak* in 1862 was a tragedy for many families in these reaches of the Kennebec.[8]

CAPT. DANIEL WITHAM

LOST WITH SHIP CHARTER OAK

1813 — 1862

LUCY, HIS WIFE

1813 — 1869

THADDEUS G. THEIR SON

DIED AT CURACAO

1835 — 1853

WM. HENRY THEIR SON

LOST WITH BARK TOMMIE HUSSEY

1846 — 1864

ANDREW PERCY THEIR SON

1848 — 1885

The cemeteries in Richmond and scores of other maritime communities are full of such monuments.

The Southard family had learned that to the sea, a child's gender is immaterial. T. J. Southard's personal tragedy was the loss of a beloved daughter, as well as his grandchild and son-in-law captain, on one of his own ships. Captain Horatio Tallman sailed with his young wife, Delia Southard, and their baby in the *G. W. Morton* in February 1854 from New York for Le Havre. The *Morton* was lost at sea, "never heard from": no ship ever "spoke her" at sea, nor was any wreckage ever found.[9]

The life span of Thomas Jefferson Southard (1802–96), known as T. J. and often described as "the redoubtable," embraced the nineteenth century, and his career stands as a model of nineteenth-century Yankee entrepreneurship; the parallels and differences between his career and Jefferson Hathorn's are worth noting. Tradition says that T. J. initially made his way, barefoot and at the tender age of eleven, from his home in Boothbay Harbor to Richmond. One version says T. J.'s original plan was to see the world as a sailor, though another holds that T. J. had in mind a specific stratagem, a version that better fits the character of the man he would become. T. J.'s plan was to sign on with a Captain Solomon Blanchard to try seafaring on Blanchard's coaster, but the actual experience turned off T. J.'s passion to go to sea.[10]

Not finding life at sea personally agreeable was pivotal to Southard's career. He returned to Richmond and apprenticed himself to the local blacksmith, Andrew Densmore—an experience so significant to him that the "house flag" of Southard vessels would later bear an anvil. In shipbuilding, blacksmiths did the "ironing" of vessels—the fabrication of metal fittings—and tradition has it that T. J. took his pay for one such job in the form of a share in the vessel. T. J. was not one to be content working for others; his vision was ambitious and his spirit entrepreneurial, and he let others do the physical work of shipbuilding while he turned increasingly to supplying capital and managing profits. As his business grew, he built ships by subcontracting out the work of hull, sail, iron, rigging, and fitting-out to others in Richmond. In effect, he provided the leadership that coordinated the Richmond shipbuilding workforce, and he made a lot of money in the process.

Though Jefferson Hathorn was comfortably well-off, T. J. Southard was many times more prosperous, and one explanation for the difference lies in the way the two men used their energies. T. J. Southard immunized himself against the hazards of life at sea—accidents, sinkings, fatal exotic diseases contracted in foreign ports—by staying in Richmond and building ships, while Jefferson Hathorn (and his sons) subjected themselves to these perils on a regular basis. If the land-based J. J. Hathorn had not died in 1854, the Hathorns might have given T. J. Southard more of a run for his money, but a man could not go to sea as much as Jefferson Hathorn did and hope to compete with T. J.'s shipbuilding. Giving Jode the command of the *J. J. Hathorn* suggests that Jefferson Hathorn may have been recasting himself in a land-based role and may have had longer-range plans than he could eventually implement, given the events of 1856.

Like many other energetic entrepreneurs, T. J. Southard did not confine himself to building ships, and it would seem that much of what he touched turned to gold. One story of T. J.'s acumen involves land purchased in Kansas in 1860 for $5,000 and sold in 1882 for $72,000. His boundless industry ran the gamut: he ran a store dealing in dry goods and West Indies goods that regularly grossed $50,000 annually; he was the village postmaster; he served as a director of railroads, telegraph companies, towage companies, and banks; he managed a drugstore, operated a grist mill and a planing mill, built several "business blocks" in Richmond, and became the leading light of the Southard Cotton Mill and of the Southard Manufacturing Company, which was built in 1881 to manufacture seamless grain bags at the rate of 700,000 a year.[11] When all was said and done, however, a list of T. J. Southard's seventy-five ships, totaling nearly 50,000 tons, stands as his most distinct epitaph.[12]

Compared with the Southard family's shipbuilding and -owning, the Hathorns' involvement—including that of both brothers and Jefferson's son-in-law, Lemuel Brown—looks very modest:[13]

Year	Vessel	Rig	Tons	Owner	First Master
1841	Harriet	Brig	160	J. J. Hathorn	T. P. Brown
1842	Importer	Brig	182	J. J. Hathorn	Jefferson Hathorn
1845	Consuelo	Brig	173	T. J. Southard	Jefferson Hathorn
1847	Leo	Brig	136	J. J. Hathorn	P. W. Brown
1847	Masonic	Ship	440	Jefferson Hathorn	Jefferson Hathorn
1848	J. J. Hathorn	Bark	398	J. J. Hathorn	Joseph Small
1855	Melvin	Brig	241	Jefferson Hathorn	Jefferson Hathorn
1857	Columbus	Ship	707	Lemuel Brown	Joseph Small
1859	Richmond	Sch	116	Lemuel Brown	Edward Buker

There are just nine vessels over eighteen years, with a total tonnage of 2,553, or about one-twentieth of the Southard activity. These statistics demonstrate that the Southards kept at it, building and owning bigger vessels over a longer period than the Hathorns. It is curious to note that in 1848, the year that the *J. J. Hathorn* was built, T. J. Southard built a 296-ton bark that he named the *T. J. Southard*, which suggests that at least at that point, a head-to-head rivalry was in progress.

Another important observation one can make in comparing the careers of the Hathorns and the Southards is of the additional vessels with which Jefferson Hathorn's name was associated as first master: the schooner *Texas* (1836), the ship *R. K. Page* (1852), the ship *Pride of America* (1853), the ship *John Sidney* (1855), and the ship *Zouave* (1863).[14] Furthermore, Jefferson Hathorn was at various times master of the following vessels: the ship *Forest King*, the schooner *Gardiner*, the brig *Levant*, the schooner *Mary and Polly*, the schooner *Native*, the schooner *Rebecca*, the brig *Reporter*, the ship *Richmond*, and the ship *St. Paul*.[15] Also, his command of the steamer *Key West* demonstrates his adaptability and flexibility in the face of changing maritime technology.[16] Jefferson Hathorn's choice to remain a man of the sea accounts for much in the difference in the fortunes of Hathorns and Southards. Without J. J. as the land-based manager, and then without Jode and Jeffy, the Hathorn potential was drastically diminished. Perhaps a town like Richmond had room for only one T. J. Southard, however, and less fortunate towns had none.

Nevertheless, the public perception of Jefferson Hathorn was of a successful man, "respected by the public, beloved by a wide circle of friends and blessed with an abundant share of worldly goods." His 1884 obituary in the *Richmond Bee* would give more detail about the Hathorns' place in Richmond than any single document other than the diary. Like Susan's, Jefferson's birthday was in early September, on the second. And like T. J. Southard, he had a personal myth to illustrate his boyhood industry: "the present writer has heard him declare that the first [dollar h]e ever earned was one hundred [cents] which was paid him for cutting a hundred cords of wood," and it is interesting to note that Jefferson's myth involves personal physical labor.

It tells us that Jefferson Hathorn stayed in Dresden on the family place, "Nantucket Farm," until 1832, the year of his marriage to Sally Small, at which point he "purchased what was known as the 'Utley farm' in Pittston." Real life on the Utley farm turned out to be less wonderful than Jefferson had dreamed, like T. J. Southard's experience at sea. In Jefferson's frustration with the farming enterprise, we see a temperament similar to Susan's:

> During the farming season every one was doing his utmost to make and gather the crops; in the winter they had to get up before daylight and feed the products out to the livestock, so that when the spring came, everything was consumed, and the owner of the farm was no richer than he had been at the beginning of the year.[17]

Before he came to Richmond (by this account, in 1835), Jefferson Hathorn had in 1834 purchased the coasting schooner *Native* to make trips between the Kennebec and Boston, "loading his vessel with wood on the outward passage, and bringing back goods for the various towns on the river." When he came to Richmond, he "lost no time in identifying himself with the business interests of the town." At this point he made his "first important venture," building Richmond House. Jefferson Hathorn's obituary, Sagadahoc County records of real property deeds, and census enumerations all corroborate that the family resided at Richmond House thereafter. Jefferson and J. J. formed their partnership and razed the wooden structure in which they had run a store on the northwest corner of Main and Front, and there built the redbrick Hathorn Block.[18]

Jefferson Hathorn's obituary states that from the early 1830s until 1873, he "followed the sea with but little intermission," moving from commands of coasting schooners to larger "West Indiamen," then to the still-larger vessels making transatlantic runs, and finally to the command of the steamer *Key West*, running between New York and Apalachicola, Florida. The *Richmond Bee* would eulogize Jefferson Hathorn's traits:

> Though acting frequently from quick and powerful impulses, the deceased was a man of warm and generous feeling, and was noted for his punctuality in all his engagements. The money which he earned by his enterprise and hard labor, was frequently loaned to deserving individuals whom he saw trying to better their condition.[19]

The Hathorn Block, then about four years old, was depicted as a principal Richmond landmark on the 1855 map. Here the Richmond Bank, of which Jefferson Hathorn was a shareholder, occupies the ground floor facing Front Street, and the Patten & Sturtevant store occupies the first floor shop, with its entrance on Main Street.

Known as a staunch Democrat and a man of civic pride and public spirit, Jefferson Hathorn lent financial support to the Richmond Academy and served a term in the Maine state Senate in 1856. Later in life, he enlarged and improved what came to be known as Evergreen Cemetery, described in his obituary as "now in complete order, and a credit to the village." He was characterized as "scrupulously honest" in business affairs and as a "firm Universalist" in his religion.

Captain Hathorn's obituary and the records of the probate of his estate have several direct ties to Susan's diary. The *Richmond Bee* said, "[Captain Hathorn] found a fine occupation in improving the 'Ferry Farm,' a tract of land which he had purchased at the decease of his brother." Situated on the Kennebec at the site of the Richmond ferry, this property appears to be the "Willow Dale" that Susan says "Capt. Hathorn bought . . . for Jode" from the estate of J. J.[20] In addition, the inventory of Jefferson Hathorn's estate bears witness to his activities in the 1850s.[21] The "brick block" it mentions is the Hathorn Block; the real estate inventory includes the "stores" and lot there, the item with the highest valuation on that schedule. The real estate inventory delineates the two careers of Jefferson Hathorn, the man of the sea and the man of the land: his interests in two wharfs and the riverfront commercial property confirm his continued participation in Richmond's maritime activities; his three farms and other land manifest his return to the land. Also listed is Jefferson Hathorn's spiritual space, his pew in the Congregational Church.

Inventory of Jefferson Hathorn's Real Estate

Description	Appraisal
62/80 of South Dwelling in Brick Block +	
60/80 of West ½ of Stable & Lot	1550.00
All of North Welling on Brick Block +	
½ of East Stable + Lot	2000.00
7¹/₈₀ of Block Stores + Lot	4437.50
¹³/₁₆ " " Wharf	609.32
Ferry Farm	2500.00
½ of Thomas Wharf + Building	370.00
Lot in the Town of Dresden	25.00
Lot of Land in Bowdoinham	50.00
The Joseph Brown Farm in the Town of Pownal	1865.00
The Blair Farm in Richmond	4000.00
His interest in The Blair Cemetery	500.00
Row No 10 in the Congregational Church	30.00
	17941.82

Source: Sagadahoc County, Maine, Probate Records, vol. 203.

The inventory of Jefferson Hathorn's "personal estate" gives evidence of his role in the community: his stock in the Richmond Academy, his stock in the Richmond National Bank and the Building and Loan Association, and the curious $1.00 stake representing ten shares in T. J. Southard's Richmond Manufacturing Association. Jefferson Hathorn's October 1885 inventory of household goods ("including Safe and silverware") lists the trappings of a burgher-farmer, including his 112 tons of hay, his expensive horse, his sleigh and wagons and harnesses, his tools, and his plows and cultivator and mowing machine.[22]

❧

Some thirty years earlier, however, Susan is not concerned with real estate or mowing machines, but with the trip she wants to take to Gardiner. This Gardiner trip may be another attempt at diverting herself; as she finishes her entry for October 3—after an accounting of the baby's "swathes" she is furiously turning out and despite the rained-out library "Levee"—she incidentally discloses the real problem:

> *Still raining hard — has poured all day, so our Gardiner visit is still in prospect. But we have had a nice time sew{ing}. I made two swathes — completed them about eleven — then run the scallops for the bottom of a skirt — it was quite a job. Finished one breadth and was tired enough tonight. We did not go to sleep last night until after two — the rain poured down and the wind blew very hard in gusts — Iffy staid all night with us. The concert or rather Levee for the benefit of the Library was deferred until tomorrow, when it will take place rain or shine. No Letters from Jode.*[23]

The fall rains continue. "This makes the third day the rain has poured down—every thing is afloat," Susan writes on the following day as she adds embroidery to "the skirt," putting "the eyelets and leaves into one breadth." Finally, rain or shine, the library's benefit takes place. Susan doesn't say whether she attends; either the rain prevented her from attending or she did not choose to go, or it was not pleasant. But "Father H. made us a call to see how the widows fared," she writes, which confirms that Lemuel Brown, too, is away at sea again.[24]

As the week ends and the rain abates, Susan's entry for Friday shows her in better spirits; here too, in a varied and lively passage, she reveals that the reason has more to do with Jode than the weather.

Cloudy this morning, but really began to clear off about eight, and has been a very pleasant warm day for the season. I finished my skirt about eleven — came down home, and got the rest of the flannels that were completed, together with the six night gowns and shirts and carried them up to Sally's and ironed them. Took me until past one — Miss Sissy hurt her arm, so we came down home with her, and the house has been full of company. Dr. Boynton, E. Small, Mrs. Wheeler & little boy & Misses Reed and Wait — All but the G{?} to tea. Llew came out with some apples to sell & called — if I had not been so tired, should have gone home with him. Had a good long letter from Jode — suppose he will be off for Liverpool by tomorrow or sooner.[25]

Jode's "good long letter" may also have inspired Susan's cheerful description of the next springlike day: "The brooks were running this morning when I opened the window and the air was so mild and balmy. I could not have believed it October, had not the hues of the trees told the tale."[26] Not even an afternoon rain and being left alone at Richmond House ("Mrs. H. went up to Sally's after dinner") can spoil Susan's sense of well-being. "I have spent the day in my chamber," she writes, "sewing for dear life on the second little skirt—have made eyelet holes around the bottom—have done one breadth—and considerable of the second."[27]

Susan's unflagging work on baby clothes continues the next week. On Monday, she writes, "I have finished working the second skirt—the button hole . . . edge is very neat and pretty. Also feather-stitched with orange silk my fourth foot blanket."[28] But she says that Sally's baby is sick, and "Mrs. Hathorn came up and spent the most of the afternoon." By Tuesday morning, "a fine day," Susan is in her Mount Holyoke mode: "Got up early and built the fire," she says, getting right to work on the sewing—"sewed the waist onto the foot-blanket I made yesterday. Got Mrs. E. Avery's blanket, and took off the pattern."[29]

That afternoon, Susan finally gets her wish to go to Gardiner, but before she leaves, her friends Theresa Patten and Frances Foster, and Eben and Isaac Small, who are relatives and business associates of Jefferson's, visit her at Richmond House. The fair was only one reason Susan wanted to go to Gardiner, for two of her siblings, Lucy and Hosea, live there.

> *After dinner got ready and went to the depot in time for the three o'clock train. . . . When I got to Gardiner, found Hosea at the depot — went up to Lucy's. Kate Swan spent the evening with us. I made one skirt all but embroidering it about the bottom.*[30]

Susan pronounces Wednesday another "fine day" and gives a detailed account of the domestic arrangements in Lucy's home, and of the rearrangements that are to take place. "Old Mrs. Hartigan has been here helping Lucy iron," Susan says, adding that she herself "accomplished considerable—made the other skirt—took off the braid pattern and got it ready to work and run the scallops of the other. Also sewed the edge on my fifth skirt."[31]

Susan's younger sister, Mary, arrives in Gardiner after dinner, and characteristically, Susan at first camouflages her sisters' preparations for the birth of her baby: "Lucy went down street shopping. We partly set the parlor to rights for a sick room—got her bureau down, and cleared it out. Lucy did a lot of shopping for me."[32] Among the "lot of shopping" is the purchase of diaper material, and Susan notes the published report of Jode's departure from Savannah:

> *Have done pretty well today considering my many interruptions. Have scallop{ed} the bottom of one skirt and sewed the edge on a shirt. Also cut off a dozen diapers. Saw by the Boston Journal of last night, Jode cleared the 3d of this month.*[33]

Lucy Ring is six years older than Susan, and by 1855, she has two children herself, a son James (born in 1848) and a daughter Lucy (born in 1849). Business directories show that Amasa Ring had a ships' stores business, a chandlery, in Gardiner, for outfitting and supplying ships prior to voyages. Whether the "Lucy" Susan refers to in her October 11 diary entry is her sister or her six-year-old niece, Amasa Ring appears to have been successful enough in his work to provide luxuries for his family. Susan says that she "helped Lucy clear away to go over to

Mrs. Gordon's to get her riding habit fitted. She staid until past twelve and came home to dinner with Amasa. After dinner she went to ride on horse back." [34]

By Saturday, the lovely fall weather has left Gardiner—"it is welting," Susan says of the rain—so the Ring household makes itself busy indoors. Now Susan is not only making diapers at full tilt but also altering Lucy's maternity clothes for herself, while the rearranging proceeds:

> *I made the other dozen diaper towels this forenoon besides helping Lucy cut her pie apples and do her morning work. At noon, Amasa brought down the bed and carpet for the parlor, and Mary and I put the room to rights — it looks nice and pleasant. Then I overhauled Lucy's old clothes, and got out enough to make me two dozen more diapers.* [35]

Because the point on the Post Road [36] where Susan's family lived is equidistant from Richmond and Gardiner, it is not surprising that some of James Lennan's children live in Gardiner, at the time the larger community. Gardiner's proximity to the state capital, Augusta, makes it a logical site for the state fair, and for a gathering of the Lennans and the Hathorns, as is seen in Susan's record of the week.

> *Amasa went out home — I got ready to go with him, but Hosea & Ann came along, and said father & mother were coming, so I staid behind.*

> *Got home about ten. Just got the fire burning, when Mrs. Hathorn & Sally came — Jep came up to dinner — Fanny & Llew & Benny Flanders were here too. . . . Hosea came up and carried Lucy & me to the Fair. Saw all there was to be seen — which was not much. Mrs. Weston, August Ring, Jenny Purei, Capt. Lancaster and several other old acquaintances I saw there.*

> *The last momentous day of the Fair. . . . Llewellyn & Mother came down, and all hands went this afternoon to see the horseback performance of the*

Ladies. I kept house. A little Lancaster girl won the first prize. Lucy ran her
horse against another and was thrown off, but not at all injured. Father &
Iffy went home.[37]

As the fair draws to a close, Susan's diary tells of the extended family:
Thursday's entry notes, "Mother [Mrs. Hathorn] went to Mrs. Mc-
Causland's and Sally came here"; Friday's reports that after a horseback
ride with Hosea and tea, Sally "went down street and called on Mrs.
McCausland who has a nice 'gal child,'" born that afternoon,[38] which
suggests Mrs. Hathorn may have been among the women attending the
birth.

The harmonious blending of Hathorns and Lennans is evident in Susan's diary. She records that on Friday afternoon she, her two sisters Lucy
and Mary, and her sister-in-law Sally Brown went to Hosea's—"had a
nice time"—and then "came back to Lucy's to stay all night, as all Sally's
baby things were here."[39] It is with Sally that Susan travels back to
Richmond on the next day, a warm, foggy Indian summer Saturday:

We got up early — Sally and I packed our budgets & then I sat down and
finished my blanket. Had just completed it when Jose came to carry us to the
depot. Waited a long while, but found Mare Whitney there, who came down
with us.[40]

"All well at home," Susan reports, and at the close of that eventful week,
she says, "Found a letter here from Jode—he probably sailed the 7th
[of] this month."[41]

The next week's entries are unaccountably kept in blue ink, not Susan's usual black, and Susan compresses events to even fewer words. Yet
she seems content and busy, with a long list of visitors and family coming and going at Richmond House: Mr. Dinslow, her brother Llewellyn,
"Little Joseph Dinslow," Sally and her baby, "Brown," Abby Stinson,
Mrs. Barnard, Mrs. L. Small, Captain C. Blair, and Isaac, Eben, and
Henrietta Small.[42] "The air is as warm as spring," she writes, "and the
brooks are running, so it seems more vernal than autumnal."[43] She remarks on the beautiful evenings and a "glorious" full moon that week,
on the twenty-third. From Richmond House, Susan can glimpse and

hear the river, and she notes that the tides are very high, "and there is quite a freshet again." In addition, Susan's densely populated entries this week further define the Hathorn family: she remarks on the visits of Mrs. Hathorn's Small relatives, on "Jep"'s going to school, on Brown coming in from a voyage, and on "Father" going to "a Railroad meeting in Augusta." [44]

At Richmond House another nest is being prepared, presumably for Susan and the baby's residence after her confinement in Gardiner. To make room for Susan and the baby, one Richmond House resident, Sarah, is displaced from her quarters, a change that will have its repercussions: "Mother began her house cleaning today—cleaned out the hall, and set up a bed for Sarah there—I am to take Sarah's room—have got the stove up there." [45] Susan has been working hard on the baby clothes for two weeks now, and she shows little sign of letting up:

. . . *made up two pieces of the diaper Lucy got for me.*

. . . *finished the diapers, bringing my number up to six dozens. After dinner began to chain stitch the skirt, the pattern for which, I prepared last week.*

I have not accomplished much of my sewing — finished Ann's collar however & have done some on my skirt.

Finished my skirt at last — it has been more trouble than either of the others.

I finished sewing the edge on a shirt, and began to feather stitch a blanket. Got it over half done.

. . . *unpacked my budgets, and partly ran the scallops for my second blanket.*

I have sewed steadily, scalloped two sides of a blanket & more than half of the third side.

I finished my blanket — after its conclusion, pressed it, also the other one — they look pretty — ironed the two shirts I had in the wash, and cut out my three nice ones, and worked a little on them.

I could not sew much on account of . . . my arm was sore — have managed to make one shirt complete, and part of the second.

I have had a nice time to sew. Made the other two little shirts, and cut out four dresses.

I have progressed finely — have made one dress, and the waist of the second, all but the belt. Hoped to have three complete by tomorrow night.

I have had a nice time to sew — have completed the third slip — have only one more cross-barred one to make. [46]

After this spate of baby sewing, Susan proceeds with her announced intentions to fix up her new Richmond House room during the end of the last full week in October. She throws herself into the project bright and early that Monday, making new curtains and going to the furniture store, where she purchases "a sink and bed-stead, but did not find a bureau to suit me." The same day, Mrs. Hathorn "took up the carpet from the kitchen, shook it and put it down in my chamber so it looks 'quite much' already." Susan notes that she has written again to Jode.[47] The following day, Susan reports making

. . . a shoe case for my room this morning, then measured for my bed-tick and mother went in to the store and got it for me. As the slip was begun {the previous afternoon}, I thought I would finish it, before commencing on the tick. [48]

By midweek, Susan is feeling satisfied with the progress on her room, saying she has done "famously in the work line." She enumerates:

Ironed three slips and three shirts this morning — then tore off my bed ticks — made the pillows, bolster, and well nigh completed the feather bed tick, and with mother's help, made the straw tick. So that dreaded job is well over. [49]

Jode's mother is housecleaning and his father has "put up the stoves, which made a heap of dirt for her, as he cleared out the chimney," and he has been "cementing the floor." Besides this domestic duty, Captain Hathorn has been doing maritime duty, coming to the aid of fellow shipbuilder George Farrin (which Susan writes as "Ferrin"), who is having difficulty with one of his vessels, and paying a business-social call at Sally's: "Father has worked on Mr. Ferrin's ship getting her out of the mud, and this evening, he & Mother went up to Sally's to visit the Capt. & his wife boarding there." [50]

One can easily imagine Susan deciding that, in case the baby is early, she will have everything ready by the end of October. With the completion of the feather tick on Thursday, November 1, Susan has accomplished her stated goal: "to get my room in order and have all things in readiness for a case of emergency." [51]

The Nest

By 1855, Jefferson Hathorn's tight-knit family had become a tiny maritime fiefdom. Jode is afar, questing and conquering, while Susan remains in his family's protection. Lemuel Brown might be viewed as a second knight, and the younger son Jeffy, like a page, is training for his own life at sea. That Jefferson Hathorn, lord of the manor, has to "cement the kitchen floor," "put up the stoves," and toil to get Mr. Farrin's ship out of the mud are the mundane realities of his time and circumstance.

By the first week of November and for no specified reason, Susan's first plan to have her baby in Gardiner has changed. She busies herself making her living arrangements at Richmond House increasingly more complete and permanent. During the first weekend of November, Susan writes, "Molly wrote me, that she or Lucy would come up Monday in the boat,"[1] and on Monday says, "Lucy came down in the boat and brought me a nice bureau. I changed my things into it."[2] Furnishing her room occupies Susan during that following week: "I put every thing to rights I could in my room—then swept and dusted the chamber I have occupied."[3] On the following day, we see why she must have her room "to rights": she is expecting her brother Llewellyn, who is to bring her things from the Post Road farm. He does not show up as planned: "Thought Llewellyn would come out today without fail, but he has not made his appearance."[4] Because it is raining on Thursday, Susan puts the time to good use working more on baby clothes ("I have worked nearly all the scallops on the little petticoat—besides sewing the edges onto the lawn dress and putting in the ribbon, &c"[5]).

164

As Susan describes the things she places on her mantel, it is impossible for her thoughts not to turn to Cuba: the Sunday of going shelling on the Trinidad beach, the rum (and perhaps camphor) that figured in the cargoes of the *J. J. Hathorn*, and certainly, Jode: "Have also arranged a jar of shells for my mantle shelf, to sit beside the rum bottle & camphor. All I lack is my bed, and that has not yet appeared."[6] The mention of the missing bed may be a coincidence, but the metaphoric connection to Susan's missing husband seems clear.

On the same Indian summer November Thursday when Susan writes to her husband, she says her mother-in-law "has been cleaning house—the cook room, and has not sat down for the day." With the cleaning of the cellar that Saturday, Mrs. Hathorn finishes her fall housecleaning—"a bad job well over," Susan says.[7] Finally, on Friday Susan's brother Llewellyn arrives, bearing what Susan calls her "housenture"—presumably her household goods/dowry/hope chest:

This has been a beautiful day — warm and sunny, but the travelling is very bad indeed. So said Llewellyn, who made his appearance out here, about eleven o'clock, with my "housenture." The folks were all well at home.[8]

This arrival of Susan's possessions completes her "fixing up." Though Susan has not set up her own separate household, this arrangement is an acceptable one to her, and was common at the time, especially among maritime families. Though extended-family living of the early nineteenth century was starting to give way to nuclear family households, seamen's wives often threw themselves on the mercy of their families, and even a captain's wife, particularly one recently married and about to have her first child, could well expect to reside with parents or in-laws, particularly if they themselves were maritime people.[9]

Susan has put down her roots at Richmond House. In the "furniture account" that appears on the unused July ledger page of her diary, Susan's accounts corroborate the furnishing of what had been "Sarah's room." Susan details expenditures totaling $28.74, listing her purchases of materials for making the bed ticking and confirming the deliveries her diary describes:[10]

Oct. 29   Sink $3.50

           Bed stead... 6.00

      30   Bed ticking for 18-½ yds for Straw

           & 13-¼ yds for featherbed 3.33

           Chamber set—wash bowl & pitcher........................... 1.00

Nov. 5   Bureau 14.00

      6   Looking glass 91

         ....$28.74

In the diary's ledger section is also Susan's "baby account," listing purchases reaching back to London, with the practical alongside the extravagant:[11]

JUNE

23   6 yds print at .14 per yd................................... .84

     8 yds. Flannel at .72 per yd............................... 5.76

30   6 "   "   " .60....................................... 3.60

         "   .54....................................... 3.24

AUGUST

25   8 yds Cotton Cloth 1.40

SEPTEMBER

27   Embroidery silk.. .37

OCTOBER

8   Cotton cloth & 2 skeins orange silk...................... .13

    36 yds Diaper 4.50

    4 yd cross barred 1.68

    12 skeins silk .36   edge & inserting .9.................. .45

    ¾ yd Linen .... .58

16   2½ yds Edging .15   3 yds Edging .10.................... .25

NOVEMBER

1   Ribbon, Paste, Tape, Bobbin, & Inserting .... .76

Winter comes early to Maine, and in various guises. "Woke up this morning, and found a little coat of snow on the ground—the first of the season. But it did not long remain on," Susan writes on November 4, and the following morning reports, "the ground was white with frost, and frozen quite hard." [12] Her time at sea would have given Susan a new perspective on the power of the weather, and in Richmond she could see afresh the role weather plays for land-based maritime people. She reports, "Father went over to Wiscasset," [13] Jefferson Hathorn having availed himself of the break in the weather to make the roughly thirteen-mile trip to the county seat of Lincoln County, another port and shipbuilding town at the head of Sheepscot Bay. [14]

Winter may have come, but the weather temporarily moderates. In Susan's entry for one Sunday, she gives a glimpse of a surprising tomboy streak within this somewhat fussy embroidering woman. One sees how close a presence the river is in her life: "One of the prettiest fall days that can be imagined—warm and sunny—the river looks like spring. The boys have improved the time beech-cutting—almost wished I could go myself." [15]

Who are these boys? Jefferson Jr.—the Iffy/Jeffy/Jep she often refers to affectionately—certainly would be one; possibly she would also include Brown and her own brothers, but hardly Captain Hathorn himself. And the boys may include the other Hathorn son, Volney; no record of him is found other than the gravestone that says he lived from 1844 to 1856. [16] In this brief revelation of Susan's independent, unconventional side, one sees the suggestion of strengths she will need in the years after 1855.

Life at Richmond House is not all tranquillity. In her customary pointed style, Susan reports a difficulty (which has continued from the end of October) and goes right on with her sewing: "Sarah has declared her intention of abiding with us no longer, unless she has a better place to sleep, so I suppose she will decamp tomorrow. I have worked one pattern today on the skirt, and run it twice." [17] This Sarah (whose last name Susan does not mention) appears to be a semipermanent boarder

*These two nineteenth-century winter views look in opposite directions on Richmond's un-
paved Main Street. In the top view, looking west, the large white shuttered building on
the right side of the street is Richmond House; the dark building at the right front is the
Hathorn Block. The bottom view looks down Main Street's slope toward the Kennebec
River, visible beyond the "Coal Office" on the far side of Front Street. Clearly visible on
the north side of Main, near the bare tree, is the three-story shuttered white clapboard
Richmond House, and beyond it and the bare tree, the redbrick side elevation of the
Hathorn Block.*

doing domestic work in return for her keep, a common boardinghouse arrangement. Sarah's feathers are soon smoothed, for on the very next day, Susan writes—her tone speaking the volumes that her direct statement does not—"This Sara will conclude to remain with us a while longer."[18] The normally careful speller Susan misspells Sarah's name and makes her sound foolish.

While this domestic tempest brews, maritime Richmond has seen a major event: the launching of the second of the three new Southard vessels built in Richmond in 1855, the 524-ton ship *Flora Southard*, first captained by Warren Day. "The 'Flora Southard' in which Eben & Isaac Small [sailed], went today," Susan records on November 7. The maritime activities of the Hathorns figure in several of Susan's entries around this time, including that of November 12, when Susan has her mind on her husband and her eye on the calendar: "Just two months ago today Jode and I came home from Savannah. It seems a long time."[19]

By mid November, Richmond shipbuilders realize the window of opportunity is narrowing to get the summer's new vessels to sea before ice closes the Kennebec until spring. This sense of urgency and impatience underlies Susan's report, "Father and Jep are still hard at work on the Brig—get along but slowly."[20] If the vessel's name was known at the time (including to Captain Hathorn), Susan does not give it. The 241-ton brig will be named the *Melvin*, the sole vessel built for Jefferson Hathorn during 1855 and the only vessel he had built between his last joint venture with his brother J. J. (the immense 1,826-ton ship *Pride of America*, built in 1853) and the 707-ton ship *Columbus* he and Lemuel Brown would have built in 1857.[21]

Susan's diary and the maritime records corroborate each other, recording Captain Hathorn as the *Melvin*'s first master. Susan's entry for Thursday, November 22, reads:

Thanksgiving Day. And as cold blustering, uncomfortable a day, as we ever have in winter. Full eight inches of snow fell yesterday and last night, and is blown into heaps. Father got his Brig away about eleven, after a hard forenoon's work, and got to Bath with her in an hour and three quarters. Lots of other shipping went down at the same time.[22]

Bath is as far as Captain Hathorn gets with the *Melvin*. Just two days later, on the Saturday after Thanksgiving, Susan writes in her diary, "Father came home in the three o'clock train to spend the sabbath."

The fact is, Captain Hathorn has a compelling reason to return to Richmond House that weekend—his new grandchild.

TUESDAY, 20.
A cold day — the coldest of the season. Little Baby Hathorn was born this morning about seven o'clock. I am quite comfortable.
   It begins to snow a little tonight.[23]

In this shortest of her diary's entries—a mere twenty-nine words—Susan records her baby's birth. It seems remarkable that she is writing anything, and while it is possible she is writing up events on a later date, the brevity of the entry suggests she is keeping her diary in "real time." The brevity, detail, and immediacy of the following day's entry similarly convey its authenticity:

A snowy day.
   Baby Hathorn and Mother very well indeed. Good Doctor Colby {called} today to see how we were prospering. Sally here tonight and weighed the Baby — eight pounds and a half!
   Mrs. A. Southard had a young son this morning.[24]

What should one make of the fact that Susan neither calls the baby by a name nor makes any mention of whether her baby is a boy or girl, yet in recording the birth of a Southard heir, mentions immediately that Mrs. A. Southard has a "young son?" Following Susan's references to the baby, a curious pattern emerges:

Little Baby Hathorn born this morning. [November 20]
Sally here tonight and weighed the Baby. [November 21]
Baby is good and I am comfortable. [November 22]

Baby eats and sleeps alternately. [November 23]

Mary says this is the only baby she ever knew to be good when you wanted it to be. [November 24]

I am quite smart today and baby as good as a pig. [November 25]

Baby is still good as a pig. [November 27]

. . . have dressed baby for the first time. [November 28]

I dressed the Baby again today. . . . Baby begins to be a little more troublesome. [November 29]

Only on November 30, a full ten days after the baby's birth, do we learn that the baby is a girl. In that day's entry, Susan finally uses a feminine pronoun in a terse allusion to one of those less-than-ideal mornings with her infant: "fussed with baby the whole forenoon—she is not nearly so good as she was." [25]

Knowing Susan's interest in detailed reports of matters of health, the birth of this good-sized baby must have been uncomplicated; had there been serious difficulties, Susan would not likely have shrunk from mentioning them. Susan never says in her diary who attended the birth; on the day immediately following she had written, "Good Doctor Colby [called] today to see how we were prospering," and Dr. Colby will attend Susan over the last six weeks of the diary.

Nothing about Susan's recuperation from the actual birth seems extraordinary. She gradually regains her strength, being "on the mending hand" by Friday, becoming "quite smart" by Sunday. [26] By the next Wednesday, she "Feels real smart tonight"—so smart that she reports having "written a little too for the first time—a letter to Jode," presumably to tell him about the baby's birth. That same day, the domination of the Hathorns' lives by the sea is clear in an entry that says that Captain Hathorn could not get the *Melvin* away from Bath: "As the wind was ahead, Father came home this afternoon again." [27] Susan's account book shows a gift of $10.00 "Re'd of Capt. Hathorn" on November 26.

Susan's letter to Jode has not survived, but we can assume she sent it to Liverpool, the *J. J. Hathorn*'s destination upon leaving Savannah. With port records for Savannah destroyed during the Civil War, no outgoing cargo documents, crew lists, or ship's articles on this voyage survive.

The *Shipping and Commercial List* reports that the *J. J. Hathorn* cleared Savannah for Liverpool on October 3 and arrived in Liverpool on November 10—a fine Atlantic crossing of four and a half weeks.[28] As Susan writes at the end of the month, however, she would not know that Jode has been in Liverpool for nearly three weeks, or that he had reached Liverpool at all, for the *Shipping and Commercial List* does not list the *J. J. Hathorn*'s arrival until the issue of December 5.

All of Richmond, however, seems to know about the new Hathorn baby, and a large segment of the population seems to be paying calls at Richmond House. First, Mrs. George Bickford, the wife of the *J. J. Hathorn*'s first mate, "came in" on the afternoon of the twenty-second, and with that, the parade of visitors commenced. On the Friday after the baby was born, Susan has several callers: "Mrs. Costellow and her sister Mrs. Tibbetts called here this afternoon and Mrs. Revel Bickford this evening. Sally came down too with Martha Robinson—she is the same Martha as in days of yore."[29] In addition to Captain Hathorn coming back from Bath that cold November weekend, Susan writes that on Sunday morning "about eleven o'clock, Mother, Llewellyn and Fanny came out—they thought the baby a wonderful child. They staid until three."[30] On Monday, Mrs. Frances Small comes by, finding Susan sitting up "almost half the time" and feeling "quite smart."[31] Later that week, calls from Mrs. Frank Small, "Mrs. Tibbets (Formerly Harriet Reed)," and Mrs. Boynton seem to cheer Susan.

Prior to the baby's birth, Susan repeatedly mentions her "swollen feet," which may have been symptomatic of preeclampsia, a potentially serious problem.[32] As early as November 10, she writes "my feet swell so very badly, I can scarce step on them." A few days later, she pronounces November 15 "A glorious day—too pretty to stay at home," and goes on to say, "but I have been obliged to tarry there, for my feet are so swollen I can scarce step." That glorious day is followed by a stormy one ("the rain has fallen in heavy showers"), and the weather and Susan's feet are taking their toll on Susan's spirits: "I have felt sort of blue today—my feet are so dreadfully swollen. I can scarce step, and they pain one constantly."[33] Despite a cold turn in the weather that weekend, Susan sets out up the hill for Sally's house on Saturday in a flurry of activity often seen in women about to deliver their babies. She writes in her diary:

> *Pleasant today, but clouded up and seems to look very much like snow. It is quite cold too — colder than we have had it for a long while. Late night the ground froze hard and the puddles have not thawed all day long. I took a walk up to Sally's this morning to see if it would help my* <u>big feet</u>.[34]

After the baby's birth, Susan's complaints about her swollen feet cease; however, her entry for the day one week after the baby's birth foreshadows another difficulty. While she talks about a baby as good as a pig and herself feeling quite smart, her diary shows signs of mild postpartum depression, and she is producing more milk than the baby is drinking.

> *Pleasant but very windy — smoked me out again in my room. Sally came down and fitted me a waist. I have so much milk it keeps me wet from head to foot so I wear Sally's shells and the waist keeps them on. I am on the mending hand — sometimes feel better and then again not so smart. Baby is still as good as a pig.*[35]

Women who have breast-fed know that a baby "as good as a pig" may simply be one too placid and content to empty the mother's breasts, and a backlog of milk leads to problems. Susan is, in addition, troubled by what she calls "cankers," reporting that her mouth is so full of them "I can scarcely eat a mouthful."[36] Susan's spirits could be much better. By the ninth day after the birth, she reports unenthusiastically having "sewed a stitch or two and knit a very little" and concludes by remarking, "Baby begins to be a little more troublesome." She says she is feeling "dumpish."[37]

By the end of November, the honeymoon with the baby is definitely over. On the last day of the month, Susan writes that her little daughter "is not nearly so good as she was," and on December 1 puts into plain language that realization which sooner or later comes to all parents of newborns: "This little lady is some more trouble than formerly."[38]

Swift Ships

At the beginning of December, Susan, secure in her Richmond House bed, has settled with her ten-day-old baby into a kind of maternal hibernation. A week earlier she had written, "The wind blows a hurricane and sends the smoke out in puffs into my room, but I am cuddled down so snug in bed, I do not mind it." [1] Mother and baby are learning the difficult lessons of adjusting to one another's schedules. "Baby slept the whole forenoon, until half past one—then I dressed her and had just completed the operation, when Mrs. Barnard called," Susan records. [2]

Her newborn's "good" behavior—sleeping the whole morning long—is having an unexpected bad effect. She writes, "I am very smart, but have pretty sore breasts just now," and says that the canker in her mouth—a problem Susan has reported twice earlier—is somewhat better. [3] With a mother's milk supply naturally copious following birth, often there is discomfort until milk supply and baby's demand adjust to each other. If a baby sleeps a great deal and nurses irregularly, the mother's breasts become inflamed and, if the situation persists, infected. So it is not surprising that a week later Susan writes, "I have been dosing my breasts today, as they are a little caked and one of them quite painful. Seem to be worse tonight." [4] The dubious blessing of an abundance of milk continues as a problem in Susan's diary entries from the second and third week of December, when the baby is about three and a half weeks old:

> *I am better today than yesterday. A little cake still in one breast, but nothing like last night. Stormy today.*

{T}his afternoon doctored my "lump." Think it is better.

Father came out after me, but as my breast pained me, did not go. Dr. Colby thought there was danger of an abscess in the left one.

. . . am poultising yet — those bunches seem as stubborn as ever — are not at all painful.

Another glorious day — it does seem too bad for a body to be hived up in the house in such weather. The Doctor called this morning — says both sores will prove abscesses — the left one will probably be ready to lance day after tomorrow. It is not very painful.[5]

Susan's medical problem in itself is obviously troubling her, and Jode's being away can only compound the situation. Despite the support of the Hathorns, Sally Brown, and Susan's own family, Susan's diary entries are those of a woman who sounds very much alone. With Christmas approaching, one can be sure Susan is recalling the same time a year earlier, when she and Jode were newlyweds sailing toward Cuba and on to Europe on the *J. J. Hathorn*; such a thought must only intensify Susan's distress. She writes of the twenty-first as "Fair, but looking tonight like snow," and goes on to report graphically,

This has been a sort of blue day with me. The abscess has not been very painful, but it affects me all over — body as well as spirits. It has not come to a head and the Doctor thought best not to lance it until tomorrow when it would be rotted more. Tonight my arm is pretty lame.[6]

On the next day, Saturday, Susan says that her father "came out after me again today, but I could not go," so her health is now isolating her from her parents. Later in that day's entry, her family, sensitive to her situation, comes through for her. She writes, "Amasa came out on business, and Llew came out with him. Am brought my bonnet." The bonnet might have cheered Susan, and it is a good thing, after Dr. Colby's visit earlier that day: "The Doctor lanced the abscess on the left side—there was as much as a cup full of matter. It was not so bad as I thought it would be—more in dreading than in reality."[7] In her entry for Christmas Eve, Susan announces cheerfully, "My abscess is discharging nicely,"

but to her sole confidant, her diary, she describes a Christmas Day that
sounds like a disaster:

> *I am bluer than indigo today — my troubles seem to thicken — nipples sore —*
> *one bleeding and the other cracked half across. The abscess on my right breast*
> *seems about ready to break — all raw, and smarts <u>pleasantly</u>.*[8]

The next day Susan at least is somewhat better physically: "My second
abscess broke this afternoon, and discharged a quantity. Feel better and
stronger than I have for some time."[9]

In the final week of December, Susan's reports on her infection continue with further clinical detail. Despite a final, brave New Year's attempt to put the best possible face on things, her condition does not
really improve:

> *Baby has been cross today — I have hardly had her out of my arms. The*
> *Doctor called again today — thought my left breast should be lanced again so*
> *I did it myself. He thinks now I stand a fair chance to get up once more.*[10]

Unfortunately, the "cankers" that Susan has been describing as infect-
ing her mouth have found a new victim. Two days after Christmas, she
writes in her diary, "I think I am on the mending hand although I fear
my left breast will break—it looks badly about the nipple. Baby is
good, but her mouth is full of canker. My sore mouth is better."[11] The
"canker" in Susan's baby's mouth recalls a similar problem Susan had at
sea, possibly stemming from a nutritional deficiency. Twice following
the baby's birth and before mentioning the baby's infection, Susan complains about the "canker": "My mouth too is so full of canker, I can
scarcely eat a mouthful," she writes nine days after the birth, and about
a week later reports, "The canker is better in my mouth."[12] It appears
Susan may have unwittingly transmitted her infection to the baby.

❧

Looking back over the year in which Susan's plain and fancy sewing is
such a constant theme, it is telling that she writes when her baby is
about two and half weeks old: "Find my time for working will be more
limited than formerly."[13] Susan's diary makes more than 340 notations
of domestic duties, and of those, fewer than sixty do not relate to Susan's

sewing or needlework; of those, many involve the maintenance and completion of sewing projects, such as their washing and ironing (see appendix E for a listing of Susan's projects in chronological order). Though Susan now has a new small creature to endow with the products of her needle, she recognizes that with motherhood, her time for the pleasures of sewing will be greatly diminished.

Whatever her feelings by late December, throughout the fall Susan was diligent, if not obsessive, in sewing for her baby. Once she got Jode outfitted for his voyage in September, with the exception of sewing the mattress ticks and other bedding for her room at Richmond House, a "collar for Ann," and one or two necessities for herself, Susan has been unstinting in her efforts to outfit her baby with beautiful and sometimes elaborately decorated clothes. These parallel the gift of Jode's slippers in a very direct way as an expression of her affection for ones closest to her. She never spends her time and energy making things willy-nilly and she is very selective in her choice of recipients. Only five people, other than herself, are mentioned in the diary as beneficiaries of her sewing or embroidering: Jode, the baby, her sisters-in-law Sally and Ann, and Captain Dickerson, the Hathorns' Savannah host for whose new boat she quickly made a "flag" as a bread-and-butter gift.[14] Significantly, at the close of the year she mentions sewing a gift for Sally ("I have made out to finish the shoe case for Sally"[15]), the woman with whom she has established a very close bond.

Ever practical, Susan finds it a pleasurable duty to see to her own dress, and on the first of December she turns to a project that she had under way for herself when the baby was born: "I have felt pretty smart—have worked a little on that skirt that I was jabbing upon when Baby came to town. This little lady is some more trouble than formerly."[16] A few days later, Susan finishes the skirt, and with that out of the way, turns to an even more ambitious project, a bunting with a "thibet"-lined hood for the baby. She and Mrs. Hathorn go shopping for the materials.

Still fine weather, and such smooth traveling I cannot help wishing myself taking a trip out to Father's. It seems as if such warm pleasant weather could not last long. Mother and I went up to Libby's, Toothaker's, and Miss

Clack's shopping — I bought baby a cloak, Thibet[17] *for a hood, ribbon for my bonnet, and a dress.*[18]

The shopping expedition may have been more than Susan was up to, for the next several days' entries omit any mention of the hood or Susan's work on it. Finally, four days later, she reports having "cut out a part of the little Thibet hood and embroidered it," before "Baby woke up after dinner and worried a while."[19] The hood is not reported as finished at the end of December, which is unusual in that Susan records the finishing of projects, and this one would seem worth her noting. Her account book, however, contains entries supplementing Susan's December diary. On the fifteenth she purchased ribbon for the unfinished hood, and as late as the twenty-fourth, bought three cents' worth of "wadding," presumably an interlining or batting with which to quilt the still-unfinished hood or its lining.

Perhaps most momentous among the account book entries is that made on December 24, when Susan buys her baby a cradle. Susan lists the expenditures in her "baby" account for December, with the year's total, as follows:

7	Thibet for cloak	1.32
	Thibet for Hood	.28
15	Ribbon for Hood	.20
24	Cradle	1.50
	Silk .21 Wadding for hood .03	.24

Her "regular" account of personal expenses for December also includes, among the year's total of just over $150, an unusual expenditure—for presumably medicinal spirits—on December 22:[20]

7	Ribbon for Bonnet trimming 4 yds	1.40
	9 yds Calico for Dress	1.00
22	Fixing bonnet	2.00
	Brandy	.75
	Buttons	.05
	Envelopes	.08
		$151.66

The irresistible combination of the recuperating Susan, her new baby, and Richmond House's central location in town produces a procession of visitors both varied and almost constant. Family members, naturally, are frequently on hand, with Sally figuring most prominently in Susan's diary, but with Mary/Molly, Amasa, Lucy, "Sis" (Lucy Jr.), Brown, Llewellyn, Hosea, and Ann, with the Hathorns being mentioned frequently as well. Others who rate mention in Susan's diary (and the dates of their December visits) are Mrs. Barnard (3); Mrs. George and Mrs. Witham (4); a boarder named Mrs. Bowman (6); Miss Lucy Decker and Mr. (Edward or Revel) Bickford (11); Sally's baby, Benicia (16); Dr. Colby (17, 19, 28); Miss Reed (19); Mrs. Dinslow, Mrs. Avery, and Fidelia Foster (20); Frank Small and Mrs. Timothy Tibbetts (21); Mr. Bickford and Mr. True (23); Mrs. Colby, Mary Whitney, and "Uncle Dole" (29); Mrs. Barnard and her two daughters (29); and Margaret and Dexter (31).

But the most welcome sight on Christmas Eve is Captain Hathorn, returning from the maiden voyage of his newly built brig, the *Melvin*, after delivering it to Providence, Rhode Island. Maiden voyages are sea-trials—ones that not all vessels successfully pass—so there was reason for concern about Captain Hathorn's safety. On December 11, a Tuesday, Susan had reported that Mr. Bickford[21] "came in and spent the greater part of the evening. We heard tonight Father had just arrived at New Bedford."[22] That Thursday, she had written, "Got a letter from Father—he had a hard passage—is now at Providence."[23] On the twentieth she had a letter from her father-in-law that says "he will be home next week."[24] With unmistakable relief Susan writes on Christmas Eve: "Father came back in the three o'clock train!" She clearly feels an admiration for and a strong bond with her father-in-law; several times she reports their success as whist partners, another indication of their compatibility. In fact, on New Year's Eve, Susan writes of a marathon match: "Brown and Sally spent the evening—played five games of whist—Father & I against Mother & Brown and won every time."[25]

🐾

During evenings of card playing in Richmond, it is hard to imagine the Hathorns, Susan in particular, not turning in conversation to similar evenings' entertainment in foreign ports earlier in 1855. Susan's and

Jode's thoughts would certainly be with each other that Christmas, their separation all the more heartfelt because of the new baby. Susan had mentioned writing to Jode, presumably to announce the baby's birth, on November 28. The next time she reports writing to him is with a group of letters she wrote on December 30 ("I have written Miss Wait, Jode, and Mary Pollard today—have felt nicely" [26]).

Surely, however, Susan would have written to Jode at other times during the month between. She takes such clear pleasure and strength from the letters she gets from him, and yet she relates almost nothing of their contents. "Got a letter from Jode this afternoon," she writes on December 3, and then five days later, another: "Got a letter from Jode—not much news, just commenced loading." [27] A week later, Susan observes Jode's birthday in an entry that spans and encapsulates her experience. The occasion so carries her away that she gives us an unexpected glimpse of a Hathorn intimacy:

FRIDAY, 14.

Jode's birth day! he is twenty three years old. Would like to pinch his ears for him. It has been quite mild and the sun has shown out as warm as September. This forenoon, I worked on the baby's hood and this afternoon doctored my "lump." Think it is better. Sally came down and spent the evening. Got a letter from Jode — he is well and prospering. If pleasant tomorrow, shall make a trip to Gardiner. [28]

Susan receives still more mail on the twentieth, when she has letters from each of the Captains Hathorn—one from Liverpool, one from Providence: "Got a letter from father and from Jode. Father is coming home next week." [29]

Even allowing for the slowest mail steamer on the Atlantic and missed rail connections, most letters would have traveled between Liverpool and Richmond within three weeks. With any luck, a letter could arrive in two weeks or less. If Susan wrote to Jode on November 28, he would receive the word of the baby around his own birthday on December 14, so at least in theory, Jode's response could have reached Susan by the end of the year. Because the Liverpool consular posts show the *J. J. Hathorn* as clearing customs for Aspinwall on December 15, it is possible (though not completely certain) that Jode would have received Susan's letter about the baby in time for his response to reach her by December 31.[30] Another family member would probably have written him about the baby, which would add another week and increase the likelihood that he had learned of the birth. Assuming he had, and assuming he wrote Susan immediately, the letter Susan received from him on December 20 may have been about the baby. Unless Susan received a letter from Jode between December 20 and the end of the year and does not mention it in her diary, or received one early in January, the letter on the twentieth would appear to be the last Jode wrote from Liverpool.

In 1855 the U.S. consul in Liverpool was Jode's distant relative Nathaniel Hawthorne, whose Bowdoin College friendship with President Franklin Pierce resulted in Hawthorne's sinecure in the British port. Though Hawthorne's notebooks from this "consular period" are voluminous, he takes no note that Jode appeared before him as a matter routine in maritime law, though the deputy, and not the consul himself, may have received the *J. J. Hathorn*'s officers and the ship's documents. Among the Liverpool consular records, however, is the incoming crew list for the *J. J. Hathorn* (erroneously designated a "ship") showing "J. S. Hathorn, Geo. A. Bickford, and C. H. Fredson" as captain and mates upon its arrival in Liverpool, November 10, 1855.[31]

While Jefferson Hathorn's safe return may have gladdened Susan, it may incidentally have heightened her anxiety about Jode's safety. She has not reported a happy Christmas, and the problem is in part family dynamics. Her otherwise-staunch stalwart, Sally Hathorn Brown, has gone with her husband, Lemuel, and baby, Benicia, to visit the Brown relatives in Pownal. Susan writes on Sunday the twenty-third, "Sally is going to Pounal tomorrow," and again mentions on Monday, the twenty-fourth, "Sally & Brown have gone to Pounal."[32] Pownal is about twenty-five miles away, southwest of Richmond and midway between Brunswick and Portland, but it must seem like the other side of the world to Susan. She writes, "A dull Christmas day enough—snowing as hard as it can. There is neither sleighing, nor wheeling—skating nor sliding"; this is the day on which Susan says she is "bluer than indigo"—out of order physically and out of sorts emotionally.[33]

In the year's final entries, Susan disregards the diary's printed format.

The J. J. Hathorn's *crew list for its 1855 Savannah-Liverpool-Aspinwall voyage shows the bark departing Savannah on October 6, arriving Liverpool November 10, and departing Liverpool for Aspinwall on December 15, carrying "general" cargo. Jode (J. S. Hathorn) is shown as master and George Bickford as first mate, with an inbound crew of thirteen able-bodied men, and an outbound crew of twelve. If James Thompson disembarked the vessel in Liverpool lacking proof of his citizenship, he may have been detained there.*

In addition to the usual subjects, these entries contain an array of concerns common to Susan's life, and to her time and place, among which infant mortality leads the list. Susan's fears for her own baby's health may be just beneath the surface of her account of Ellen's dying baby (the child of the sister of Susan's brother-in-law, Amasa Ring). The Browns' return ("Brown & Sally came back from Pounal in the three o'clock train"[34]) lifts Susan's spirits for New Year's Eve. As she writes her diary's last entry, she is looking forward to a New Year's Day at Sally's house, thinking of her husband, Jode, and recapitulating a year in which she has traveled far, seen much, and experienced profound changes.

Sunday, Dec. 30th
Snowed hard this forenoon, but cleared off and was pleasant after dinner.
Amasa came down to see how Ellen's baby was — it was very sick indeed, and he had hardly left the house before they sent to say it was dying.

I have written Miss Wait, Jode, and Mary Pollard today — have felt nicely. Sally & Brown came down and spent the evening.

Monday. Dec., 31st
The last day of the year — how differently we are situated from the first day of this same year. Then I had no care — was far from home and friends, and knew not when I should see either. How the "little one" claims my attention — Jode is many a league away, but all other friends are near.

I am quite smart today, and baby pretty good — have drawn off the pattern for Mother's flannel skirt, besides straightening that for her cotton one. We have been full of company — Margaret and Dexter called this forenoon. Father was here to dinner. Llew called after dinner and Brown and Sally spent the evening — played five games of whist — father & I against Mother & Brown and won every time.

We are going up to Sally's to spend <u>new year's</u>, if nothing happens.[35]

So Susan's diary ends as informally as it began, and at another arbitrary boundary imposed by the calendar. It has been a year of change and growth, and of joy and sadness and pleasure and pain; yet the diary's ending raises other questions to which we feel compelled to seek answers. What happened to Susan? What was the rest of her life like? What happened to Jode? What happened to the bark *J. J. Hathorn*, and to Captain Jefferson, and to Sally Brown? And most perplexing of all, what happened to the baby girl, to whom Susan never gives a name in her diary?

First, Susan herself gives one final clue in this bound book, listing two dates during the following year on which she made expenditures for furniture.[36] The first date, October 25, 1856, lists:

> 4 chairs $2.16
> 1 Stand 1.00
> Toilet Table 1.75
> Towel Rack .... .60

The purchase of four chairs indicates that Susan's physical household is expanding beyond the single-room stage; at this price, the chairs would seem to be for a kitchen, and it is interesting that Susan purchases them, rather than gets them from a family store of furniture. The stand and toilet table would seem to be filling out a bedroom's furnishings; the towel rack could be for either bedroom or kitchen.

The other date, about two and a half weeks later, November 10, 1856, suggests an even more expansive situation:

> Sofa 34.00
> 6 chairs 24.00
> Rocking chair 10.00

At $4 each, these six chairs seem clearly destined for a dining room, compared with the fifty-cent ones purchased earlier. At $34, this sofa is a major purchase, and at $10, the rocking chair would be for the parlor, not for the porch.

With these entries, Susan has written her last in her diary. But the furniture suggests the further story that unfolds as supporting sources move out of the background and into the foreground. Among these are census and maritime records, supplemented by contemporaneous publications—newspapers and shipping lists. In addition, there is Richmond, Maine, itself, where Jefferson Hathorn left a legacy of two still-visible public works for Richmond: the redbrick Hathorn Block, and the cemetery, sited on what was known as Blair Farm, which he devoted his later years to "improving." Perhaps that is the place to begin.

Evergreen is a New England cemetery that evokes the spare theatrical images of Thornton Wilder's *Our Town*. Set off by an arched wrought-iron gateway, Evergreen lies down a lane off Chestnut Street, which angles off of Main Street to the northwest, toward the Post Road (U.S. 201) and Gardiner. It is essentially one of the old Blair Farm's wide meadows, partly enclosed by a stand of Maine hardwoods and conifers. Two gray gravel two-track lanes in each direction divide the cemetery into nine sections, with another lane around the perimeter.

Approached from the entrance, the Hathorn plot lies on the right side of the right-hand lane, about two thirds of the way back. Here simple, matching Masonic headstones mark Jefferson and Sally Small Hathorn's graves: carved white marble represents altar tables with fringed covers, with the Masonic compass and square surrounding the letter *G* and a closed book on the stone's top surface. Jefferson had definite ideas about headstones, for his will specified that his be in design and material like that of his late first wife. Jefferson's says simply, "BORN SEPT. 2, 1808, DIED FEB. 5, 1885," and his wife Sally's reads, "SALLY. WIFE OF CAPT. J. HATHORN. DIED APR. 20, 1872. AE. 60."

Another pair of markers identical to Jefferson's (except that they lack the Masonic emblem) bear the inscriptions "SALLY, WIFE OF LEMUEL BROWN, BORN MAR. 14, 1834, DIED SEPT. 30, 1889," and "LEMUEL BROWN, BORN JAN. 30, 1821, DIED FEB. 7, 1890." Here too are the marked graves of Jefferson's father, John Hathorn,[37] and his first wife, "Elizabeth G.", whose small, elegant black slate marker, cleanly incised with a weeping willow and urn, is a classic of its style and time. A smaller, less ornate black slate marker memorializes Elizabeth, Joannah, and Gowing, three young children of John and Elizabeth who died at different times between 1800 and 1803. Nearby is Jode's brother Volney, who died on February 2, 1856.

The rest of the Hathorn markers begin to tell the story we are looking for. Here we learn the name of Susan and Jode's baby—it was Josephine F.—and her simple, small marker next to her father's bears a relief carving of a violet plant and the words "daughter of Joseph and Susan L. HATHORN. died Mar. 29, 1858. Aged 2 yrs. 4 mos."

The two remaining headstones, for Joseph S. Hathorn and Jefferson

Hathorn Jr., read as many do in certain New England communities where whole families made their livelihoods on the sea. They also tell, like many other stones, sad stories of men who died young pursuing that life. The grave of Jode's brother Jeffy—Susan's beloved "Iffy"—is marked with a broken shaft monument, a type often used for men lost at sea. It simultaneously commemorates another loss for the Hathorn family, being inscribed as follows:

> In memory of
> JEFFERSON,
> son of Capt. J. &
> Sally Hathorn,
> who sailed from
> Liverpool, in Barque
> J.J. Hathorn.
> Feb. 14, 1861
> for Havana
> AE. 20 yrs.

The *J. J. Hathorn* never reached Havana. From the *J. J. Hathorn*'s last visit to Liverpool, two poignant documents survive. The first is an entry in the consular records showing inward cargo (1,007 bales of cotton from Mobile), outward cargo ("general" for "Havannah"), listing the then-owners and their shares—Lemuel Brown, $^6/_{32}$, John B. Stuart, $^5/_{32}$, Jefferson Hathorn, $^6/_{32}$, and Marshall J. Hagar, $^6/_{32}$, all of Richmond; Joseph Small, $^5/_{32}$, of Pownal; Eben Small Jr., $^4/_{32}$, of Dresden, Maine—and finally, listing the crew arriving from Mobile, noting the usual rash of "desertions," which amounted to roughly all but the officers plus probably either the cook or steward:[38]

> E. Small Jr., Master
> J. Hathorn, Mate
> J. Gardiner, 2nd Mate
> J. Smith
> W. Carter (deserted at Liverpool)
> R. Williams (deserted at Liverpool)

J. Allen (deserted at Liverpool)

J. Sykes (deserted at Liverpool)

M. Kelly (deserted at Liverpool)

W. Call

T. Ashton (deserted at Liverpool)

J. Denny (deserted at Liverpool)

The other document is a Public Instrument of Protest registered with the U.S. vice consul at Liverpool, Henry Wilding, on January 22, 1861. This pro forma document was basically the way a captain covered himself in the event consignees made claims that cargo was damaged en route. The instrument is literally a boilerplate deposition; below the printed formulaic introduction the particulars of the case are penned in (here italicized) and sworn to by Master Eben Small, the mates Jefferson Hathorn Jr. and John Gardiner, and the two non-deserting crew members, William Coll (or Call) and the x-mark of John Smith:

That the said *Ship* [*sic*] being then staunch, tight, and strong, well manned and well provided with sails and rigging, with cables and anchors, and every other thing requisite and necessary for the intended voyage, her cargo well and sufficiently stowed and dunnaged, the hatches properly secured, caulked and battened, having been laden at *Mobile* with a cargo of *Cotton bound for this port on the 11 day of December . . . Nothing worthy of particular remark happened until the 29 of said month which came in with heavy squalls . . . 1 AM we set close reefed both topsails. Latter part continued hard squalls and a very heavy sea and the ship laboured greatly and shipped much water. . . . The 6 of January about 7 PM the wind increasing to a Gale from the North we hove up the mainsail and hauled up the spanker. Middle part we had heavy Gales from WNW with squalls and hail. About 3 AM the foretopsail was split while we were trying to furl it. About 4 AM the maintopsail was split while we were taking it in. We then hauled down the Jib and run under the Foresail. The Gale was very heavy with hard squalls and a high sea, the ship labouring greatly and shipping large quantities of water over all. . . . The 15 about 7 PM we hauled up the foresail having heavy increasing Gales from the South. 7.30 we close reefed the Topsails the Gale increasing with a heavy sea and the ship labouring greatly. . . .*[39]

While the descriptions of storms in protest documents are formulaic, in this case it is also foreboding, considering what awaited the *J. J. Hathorn* on its 1861 departure from Liverpool.

❧

Jode's headstone, the design of which is similar to his grandfather's, is decorated with an anchor and chain and reads:

CAPT. JOSEPH S. HATHORN
DIED AT TRINIDAD
DE CUBA
MAY 8, 1856.
AE. 23 YRS. 5 MOS.

To trace Jode and the *J. J. Hathorn* one must patch together sketchy and incomplete port records with *Shipping and Commercial List* announcements. These show that Jode took the ship in December 1855 from Liverpool to Aspinwall, on the Atlantic coast of the Panamanian Isthmus, and from there, to Trinidad de Cuba. What happened in Trinidad de Cuba is not known. According to the outgoing consular notation, Jode was still listed as the captain of the *J. J. Hathorn* when it cleared for departure from Trinidad on May 15, which is a week to the day after the date when his gravestone says he died. The consular schedule of arrivals and departures is irregular in another way: it records having exacted from the *J. J. Hathorn* the extraordinarily high sum of $20 in fees "and evidence," a remarkable amount on a ledger page where the highest of the other twenty-eight fees is $5.75, and the usual runs about $3.00. There is no mention of Jode's death in any of the consular despatches from Trinidad de Cuba, or from the larger nearby port of Santiago, or from the embassy in Havana. Was the extraordinary fee assessed for a death certification that has since been lost?

The next logical place to look is at the destination listed by the Trinidad consul: "Falmouth," presumably the Maine coastal port midway between Portland and Bath. The Falmouth port records do not exist in the National Archives. The *Richmond Bee* had not begun publication at that point, and the other midcoast newspapers do not mention Jode's death.

One can say with certainty, however, that Jode never saw his daughter Josephine, nor did Susan ever see him again after that dizzying week of family visits in September 1855, when the world literally lay before them and everything seemed possible.

Susan's grave is not in the Hathorn family plot, though it is at Evergreen Cemetery. It is across the lane and a bit farther on from the Hathorns' plot, in the shadow of a black granite block-obelisk. Like other family members', Susan's grave is marked by a small gray granite headstone, hers saying simply, "S.L.H.L.," and to her left lies the grave of her second husband, whose reads, "A. LIBBY." The west front of the large center stone reads:

ABIAL LIBBY

OCT. 1, 1822 – JAN. 3, 1898.

And the east side says:

HARRIET L. BLAIR

SEPT. 13, 1829 – OCT. 28, 1862.

SUSAN L. H. LIBBY

SEPT. 7, 1830 – DEC. 2, 1906.

The Evergreen stones suggest only the outlines: of the life that Susan led in Richmond after Jode's death, returning as a young widow to a second career as a schoolteacher; of the Hathorns' further losses of Josephine and Jeffy; of the Lemuel Browns' moving away to New York City; of Abial Libby's Civil War journal written from near Chancellorsville[40] and his leaving the service to care for his dying first wife, Harriet; of the marriage in 1865 of Susan and Abial Libby and the birth of their three children; of Susan's relationship with her step-daughter Lizzy, who would go to Paris to study French and eventually move with her husband to Cass City, Michigan, taking with her some family photographs and two needlepoint tapestries Susan made.[41] The life Susan Libby's obituaries sketch would seem to have grown perfectly out of the Susan Hathorn of the 1855 diary:

Mrs. Susan L. H. Libby, widow of the late Dr. Abial Libby, died at the home of her son, Rev. F. J. Libby in Magnolia, Mass., after a long illness. Mrs. Libby was a woman that was loved by everybody who came in contact with her. Educated and refined, possessed of one of the most amiable dispositions, she endeared herself to all and the people of Richmond mourn her loss. She was born September 7, 1830, the daughter of James and Lucy Lennan. She studied at Mount Holyoke College and afterwards taught school for a number of years in Richmond. Her first husband was the late Joseph Hathorne [*sic*]. She was afterward married to Dr. Abial Libby, who died in January, 1898. In 1898 and 1899 she took an extensive European trip. For the past eighteen months she has made her home with her son, F. J. Libby.

Mrs. Libby was one of the directors of the Sunshine Club of this town, and . . . was always active in church work and had been very helpful in many manners pertaining to the best interests of the town where she had lived so long. It was she who was instrumental in sending a little cripple[d] girl to the Sunshine free bed of the Eye and Ear Infirmary in Portland, . . . one of the numberless kind deeds performed by this lady.

She is survived by a sister, Mrs. Francis Hildreth of Boston, a brother, Hosea Lennan of Gardiner, and three children, Alice M. Libby, a teacher in Omaha, Nebraska, Frances L. Libby of Ma[g]nolia, Mass., and Rev. F. J. Libby of Magnolia. The funeral was held Friday afternoon from the Congregational church, the Rev. George C. DeMoot officiating. The interment will be in the B[l]air Cemetery.

                              .   .   .

This has been a week of funerals in Richmond. Wednesday news was received of the death of Mrs. Susan Libby of Magnolia, Mass., a former resident of Richmond. Death occurred Wednesday morning. Mrs. Libby had lived for the past four years in Magnolia. Her body will be brought to Richmond. Her son, Rev. S. [*sic*] J. Libby, and her daughters, Alice and Francis [*sic*], will accompany their mother's body home. Mrs. Libby was a woman remar[k]ably well informed on the topics of the day, and always had been active in church work. She was 77 [*sic*] years old and her home always had been in Richmond, until she went to Magnolia four years ago, where her son is Pastor of the Congregational church. Mrs. Libby's girl-hood home was on the Post Road. She was the daughter of James and Lucy Hildreth Lennon [*sic*] of Richmond. At sixteen she taught school.

This photographic portrait of Susan, from 1877, was taken by McCormick Photographer, 23 Temple Place, Boston.

She was married in 1865 [*sic*] to Capt. Joseph H. [*sic*] Hathorne [*sic*], who was lost at sea [*sic*]. [H]e is buried on a lot in the same lane in the cemetery. Her second husband was Dr. Abial Libby, and three children were born to them, Fred, Alice and Francis [*sic*].

Dr. Libby died nine years ago. After that Mrs. Libby with her family went to Europe. Her son, a Bowdoin graduate, studied at Munick [*sic*]. Returning to this country he took his degree at Andover and afterwards went to Oxford for further study. When he accepted the pasturate of the Magnolia church the family moved there. Mrs. Libby's last visit to Rich-

mond was last Summer. She was ill for several years. Mrs. Libby's funeral
occur[r]ed Friday at the Congregational church in Richmond.[42]

. It seems fitting that Susan shared her last travels abroad with her
children, and although two of Susan and Abial's children married, neither had children of their own.

In the legacies of her needlework and her writings, Susan left a tangible account of her life, times, and personal qualities, and nowhere
more so than in her diary of 1855. Despite the sorrows that losing both
Jode and Josephine must have attached to the diary, she kept this book
safe, verifying how precious they were to her, how significant her memories of them and this year were, and how strong and determined a
woman she was. In her diary's pages one can witness and to a certain
extent relive the year though which Susan Hathorn sailed "chalk ginger
blue." In ways far beyond her actual voyage on the *J. J. Hathorn*, the story
she tells is very much that of a bride's passage.

Letter to Emily Whitten

Mt. Holyoke Seminary, Jan. 8th/52

My dear Emily [L. Whitten, of Topsham, Maine],

I had not forgotten my <u>promise</u> of writing by any means, but I have postponed fulfilling it simply for want of time. I was thinking the day I received your letter that as I had neglected so long to write, I would not delay it till vacation, which will be in a week from today, but as I shall have so many things to do then, I will now steal an hour to enlighten your mind with regard to the wonderful doings of Mt. Holyoke. To begin, the Seminary is situated in a small country village—the houses are very much scattered—quite neat in appearance, and have the look of substantial farmers. There are only two stores in the place, and if the girls wish to trade to any amount, some Wednesday they go down to Springfield or to Northampton. As for the villagers, we know no more of them then we do of the natives of India. We are in a sort of nunnery. I could not but smile at your question of how I <u>liked the people</u>, when I knew not a soul out of the Seminary. The teachers do not wish you to make acquaintances, but if you have friends here, they are willing you should call <u>with permission</u>. At first it seemed very strange here indeed, and I thought I should never get used to the <u>rules</u>, and that I could do nothing without breaking them, but I soon got accustomed to them, and I am perfectly contented and like [it] here <u>very much indeed</u>. Many of the girls were very homesick, but I see no tears now at thoughts of home and I dare say, they will cry as heartily next fall to think they must go away, as they did at first to think they must stay. One can

From The Mount Holyoke College Archives and Special Collections.

get along pretty easy here if she chooses, but if you want to <u>excel</u>,—to graduate in less than <u>four</u> years, you must <u>study</u> for it. There are some here, now, who entered last year, and were obliged to study some of the preparatory studies, who are now behind me, although I have been here but a term. They care no more for their books than to be rid of them the easiest way possible. They will be obliged to stay four years. This term I have finished a whole course of History, which includes Worcester's Elements, Goldsmith's England, Rome, and Greece, and Grimshaw's France, and before the week closes, shall have finished and <u>thoroughly</u> reviewed Robinson's Algebra. And, Emily, as an encouragement if you ever come here, I will say, of all things that I ever <u>got hold of</u>, this Algebra beats them all. I never thought Algebra was very hard till I studied this. We girls have declared if we ever meet Professor Robinson, we will very nearly make him take his exit from this <u>mundane sphere</u>. But I don't care about it now, as long as I shall say good-bye to him this week, and it has done me the most good in the way of thoroughly exercising my brains, of any thing I ever studied. And <u>grammar</u>, I have been obliged to study that. No one can enter here without studying Mr. <u>Green's Analysis</u>. I thought I should lay my grammar <u>on the shelf</u> for the future, but I find I shall be obliged to use it oftener than I anticipated. This Analysis is different from anything I ever met with. Weld's is nothing more than the Alphabet compared with it. It is an excellent work. Next term I shall take Euclid. I expect I shall find it pretty hard, but hope to like it. I hope to enter the middle class, and think I may, but am not certain. My Latin is the only thing that I build my hopes upon. If I had not happened to have Latin for two years, I should think my case hopeless, but as it is, I shall be greatly disappointed if I do not. It is more of an undertaking than I anticipated, and it is much harder than formerly. They used to let a scholar be examined in anything she had studied—now they must review it. Formerly many entered and graduated the same year—now it is almost impossible, even if any one has studied every single study, for you see, everything must be <u>reviewed</u> and it takes longer than you would think. If anyone wants to get a <u>thorough education</u>, come to South Hadley, I say. You cannot fail of <u>being thorough</u>. Every fourth lesson is a review. When you have completed a study, you go all over it and <u>review</u> it, and then every <u>fourth lesson</u> is a review. Before you are examined in the summer, all these studies must again be <u>reviewed</u> for examination. The teachers are competent and faithful. You have a good library (which is a great thing if a body could only get time to read!) and all apparatus that is necessary for explanations of the different studies. You can practise on the piano an hour or a half as you like, but you received no instruction. Vocal music is taught and we sing three times each week. Drawing also and French are free, but I have not had time to attend to either. Shall endeavor to the next term. A Miss Butler, who gives lessons in colored crayon drawing, has been here most of the term—she has had a large class, and many of the pupils have executed some beautiful pictures. The terms are ten dollars per quarter. As for the work, we can almost always do what we like. If the work we prefer is light, we must work an hour and a quarter, if harder, only an hour. You can change at almost any time if you wish. The first of the term, I used to weigh the bread for the morning's breakfast, and make thickening for toast. I changed in a little while, and now I build the morning fires, which is pretty hard but I like it as I gain time. I get all my work done for the day an hour and a quarter before breakfast. I get up at a quarter of four! and if we chance to oversleep, everything is hindered through the day. One morning we did not wake till a whole hour and a quarter after we should, and breakfast was delayed a whole hour and everything else. The girls gave us a vote of thanks for this nice nap. All the pupils must rise at fifteen minutes of five— then a girl goes all over the house and rings a large bell—called a rising bell. At six the tardy bell is struck, and if you are not up then you must give in "Tardy in rising," before all the teachers and the whole school. So it is with every thing—you must not be absent from domestic work—from table—from school exercises—tardy at table—at domestic work-exercises—in rising—in retiring—You must not be absent from church nor delinquent in Composition. These are called recorded items. Every Sat. you must spend four hours on Composition. This is as unalterable as the law of Medes and Persians. You must not leave your fire without putting up the fender. (All the stoves are the open Franklin stove). You must not leave wood on the Zinc or hearth; nor matches out of box, nor must you carry fire unless in a fire pan. These are the fire laws and the only laws we have in school, all the others are rules. You see there is nothing that is not necessary in a family of more than two hundred and fifty pupils. If we did our work only when we pleased, you see we should all starve to death,—and there would be no system about the arrangements. As it is, every thing goes on regularly. Everyone has her regular portion to do and is expected to do it. On Wednesday morning, the Seminary is cleaned from cellar to garret. Each one must do half an hour's extra work. It is not very hard to wash down a flight of twenty stairs all painted or to wash with a handled mop, a space of painted floor as large as a small bedroom, and this is the floor mopping at South Hadley that I have heard folks make so much talk about. If any one is [of] a mind to think it is very hard here, they can persuade themselves that it is, but I think any one with quite delicate health might go through a whole course here, and go away with better health than she entered. I know I should laugh if I were at home, to start out before sun rise and walk a mile in the keen cold wintry air, but I do it here quite often and think nothing of it. I am not obliged to walk before sun-rise, but as it is most convenient to do so, I often do it. You can ride as often as you choose and there you need not walk out but half a mile, but you must pay your ninepence for a ride of four miles out and back again. It is very pleasant riding here and we often do it, but generally I prefer to walk.—Shall I give you the order of exercises for a day? Rise at a quarter of five, do chamber work,—get dressed and head combed and study a half hour before breakfast which is at half past six. Then we always walk one mile and back. We do not walk washing day or recreation day. Then study till half past nine when we have devotions in the Seminary Hall, which continue a half hour. At half past twelve we dine. At half past eight we have silent study hours begin and you must not speak[,] only at the half hour bells. Silent study hours continue from half past eight until 25 minutes after twelve. Then begin at three and continue only an hour, during this term, in the afternoon. Then an hour in the evening. If we had liberty to talk when we pleased we should not study at all. We must not enter rooms except at the five minutes bell before breakfast and for 15 minutes after—at the five min. bell before dinner till two, or a quarter past—and from the 5 min. bell before supper till 15 minutes after. If we could talk and go to one another's rooms just when we chose, the lessons would generally be minus with many. We do all the studying in our rooms. The bells at first plagued me very much indeed. Would you like a list of them for a day? 4.45−5−5.15, 5.45 rising bell. 6 tardy bell. 6.15, 6.25 five minutes bell. 6.30 breakfast. 7, 7.15, 7.30, 8. 8.30. 9.30 devotions. 10, 10.30, 11, 11.30, 12, 12.15. 12.25, five min. 12.30 dinner. 1.15, 1.45, 2.15, 2.30, 2.45, 3.15, 3.45, 4.15−4.30−5 exercises close[,] and till 6 is recreation hour and then you can enter rooms till the supper bell. I told you wrong above, 5.30, 5.45−5.55 five min. 6 supper, 7, 7.30, 8−8.15−8.45−9−9.15−9.45 retiring bell[,] 10 tardy bell. Don't you think it would somewhat puzzle a novice to keep the run of so many bells? We used to run at every bell, but we have got used to them and we know just when we ought to go to any of [?] exercise. The bells are changed in different parts of the term as the studies are arranged differently. The list I have given you is as they were last series which includes the time till Thanksgiving. Then a new series begins which extends to the end of this term.

I have not told you anything of the building—nor of the ground nor the scenery. The landscape is beautiful. Mts. Tom and Holyoke rise frowning against the sky four or five miles distant. During the summer term the scholars always have an excursion to Mt. Holyoke, which they enjoy very much. On the mountain is a large tavern, where you can be provided with a spy glass, and I do not dare to say how many cities and villages you can see. The prospect is almost boundless. Back of the Seminary is Miss Lyon's tomb. It is surrounded by an iron fence and shaded by a large oak. The Seminary is a large building, 4 stories high—of brick. The main building is one hundred and seventy five feet long. The basement is occupied by the domestic hall, dining hall, music room, etc. The second story by the seminary hall, library, parlors, one music room, recitation rooms; the third and fourth as rooms for scholars. There is a long wing, which has been added within a few years, and the out-buildings are connected with the wing and main building and enclose a square, used as a clothes-yard. It is rather hard to room in the fourth story. I roomed there the first four weeks. After those 4 weeks, we move. Each one writes a note to the teacher, telling with whom and in what <u>story</u>, not what room, she would like to be put. If they can possibly accommodate you, they commonly do, unless they think two <u>wild</u> ones want to get together, when they try to put a wild one and a steady one together. I now room in a double room, in the third story of the wing. I have three room-mates, very pleasant girls—one from New York— one from Vermont and one from Gardiner, Me.

As for the examinations—I do not think they are at all to be feared. You do not pass near as severe an examination, as when you go to a committee, Mr. Wheeler and Mr. Clement for instance. In Arithmetic you are examined in the rules as far as through the Progressions; then they write about a dozen or twenty sums on the board for you to do; then you must be examined in Colburn's Mental Arithmetic and you have finished your examination in Mathematics. A slight review of history—a careless glance at geography and Watts on the mind, and grammar is all, unless you have studied Latin—Then you must look over the reader—read here and there a few lines and parse a few words; they can tell if you know any thing about it and you are <u>examined</u>. If you have never studied Latin, you are expected to take it up at once, and you will not be so high in rank, as it is a <u>preparatory</u> study. Every year they raise the standard of the school and it grows harder and harder each year. I have heard, but I could not give it as truth, that it is the intention to introduce Greek, and have the whole course occupy four years—the same as a collegiate course. Within a year or two, they have changed from Day's Algebra to Robinson's, which is much harder.—from Weld's Analysis to Green's.—and next year—every one must to begin the studies of the Junior year, have studied Nepos, else they will be studying the first part of the term only preparatory studies, which will give them no chance to enter the middle class. Within five or six years, Latin has been introduced. If you come here (and I will apply for you if you wish it) I would advise you to take Latin at once, and Algebra. Those things will carry you a long way in this Seminary. I think you would be delighted here,—at first you would be a little homesick perhaps—but you would soon get over it,—and be as happy as I am, which is saying a great deal. If you do not come, if ever you come within twenty miles of the place, come and visit the school—you would be astonished to see how conveniently every thing is arranged—the domestic hall—the recitation hall—everything about the whole building—and you would wonder as I do, that one woman could have planned it all. The portrait of Miss Lyon hangs in the Seminary hall in a large heavy gilt frame. She was quite plain in appearance and not very preposs[ess]ing in manners, I am told.

If you do not like to do your own washing—you can have it done by a poor woman who lives close by and takes the washing of the Seminary girls. I believe the expense for the year is about ten dollars—it would vary as you had much or little to wash.

The rooms are not carpeted. You can carpet them if you choose—each has a bed with a straw tick and I thought when I first came, a wonderful hard mattress—shovel—tongs—table lamp—pail etc., etc. You can fix your room as nicely as you please and there are many little things which you can bring from home which will be of great use to you. My room-mates are old scholars and they have every thing convenient. Our room is as nice as a parlor,—it has a brussels carpet—a nice tidy on our stand—a nice table covering—and we all had some pretty books on top, so that it looks quite nice,—pretty muslin curtains—tied with pink ribbons—an old rocking chair—and we took our trunks and turned them into lounges;—we bought patch and made some cotton ticks and filled them with hay, and they look as nice as can be. I think you would feel quite at home in 88, which is the number of our room.

I have written as fast as I could for my life, with many interruptions, with bad pen-ink and holding my paper in my lap, so you must excuse this, and admit I have at least written a Long letter. I have not told of half I wanted to— but you must come and find out the rest yourself. Mary would be at home here perfectly—she would want to live here always.—Give my love to all the friends. Pray do not let any one see this for I have written in the greatest haste. I have told you all that will be useful to you, that I can think of, and I think you had better come here.

We have had some fine lectures—one by President Hitchcock of Amherst College on his travels in Europe. He is the author of a very distinguished work on Geology. Last night, Professor Hopkins of Williams College delivered a lecture on the ruins of Ninevah.—It was intensely interesting. That college has lately had an addition to their cabinet. Two idols of Ninevah. He thinks one of them is the God Nisroch, before which Sennecharib was slain as he was worshipping it. One image is seven feet high and is a human figure—dressed in a sort of robe or toga—its right hand is extended and holds a cone. On the head is a sort of turban, with a double fold. On the shoulders is carved three daggers. The other image is a human figure except the head, which is an eagle. He had a stone, which was written on with the same characters as are inscribed on these figures, and it is supposed and pretty clearly proved, that this writing was done before Alexander the [G]reat, about 6 centuries. Oh the lecture was so interesting. How you would have enjoyed it. Give my love to Mary Frank, your mother and father. Don't let your father see this or he will criticise it I fear. I can imagine him now putting on his glasses and after inspecting it, he lays it down and says, Why I should think Miss L—— might do better than that. Mary, you could beat her, I think. So don't you let any body see this.

In haste,

Susan.

"A Three Years Cruise in the Ship Graduate"

On a pleasant September morning in the fall of 1849, I set out from my quiet mountain home, for the distant port, where the ship that was to take me [on] a long eventful voyage lay anchored. The tears of my brothers and sisters were mingled with my own; for until now, I had never left my childhood home, and it cost me an effort to say "Good-Bye" to all its loved ones, and to take a last farewell of its familiar haunts. Three years must elapse, before I would again behold them. What a long time they were in there in the future. How many sad things might happen, ere they passed away, and what changes might come o'er that little spot, where memory would love to linger. But hope gilded the future, and shed her cheering light on its shadowy darkness, and whispered of the joy of meeting after that long absence, and amid the blessings of my good old father, and the prayers of my affectionate mother; the last hurried tearful words were spoken, and I was on my way.

I will pass over the home sickness—the heartsickness, the long and weary journey—the many good resolutions formed for the future—the pleasant memories of the past—the repentant feelings for some unkind words or deeds, that now would gladly be recalled. I will pass these over.

In a few days, I gazed upon the noble barque; that was to be my home. She was the largest, I had ever seen, and for thirteen years, had gallantly braved the

From The Mount Holyoke College Archives and Special Collections. The manuscript appears to be in two copyists' handwriting, neither of which strongly resembles that of Susan's very legible letter and diary or her punctuation style. This text has been greatly abridged to eliminate the many illegibilities. The title was underlined as shown above.

storms. As I first saw her, by the silvery moonlight, no stars or stripes were streaming from her topmast, nor crescent flaunted in the breeze; but on a field of blue gleamed a snowy cross, encircled by a halo of light. And methought we might look up to this, when warm and weary with the toilsome cares of life, and it would cheer us onward in the rugged way.

But where was the mind that planned this noble structure—so that its semblance is seen in many a distant land? Where the untiring spirit, that patiently, zealously wrought on amid disappointments and trials, that watched its progress with intensest interest, and finally triumphed in its completions? Wher[e] the genius, that first guided it among the dangerous shoals and quicksands, and with unerring judgment, brought it safe to port. Alas that death is in the world!

On the day appointed for the ship to sail, with a fair breeze, and a pleasant sun, we steered from port. Our large crew, consisting of about two hundred and twenty were mostly novices, and surely none ever deserved the name of "land lubbers," more truly than did we. Of necessity, the discipline on board was strict—rules and regulations seemed interminable, and transgressions were frequent. But as we grew accustomed to the service, the rules seemed less onerous, and we found it ever possible to mind them all.

We were a motley crew, of almost every shade but black—the dark, fiery child of the sunny south—the pale cheek of the north—the [olive] of the distant isles and the stranger from the far west—all had met together. It required no little skill we could see to mould this mass of mind—to manage the varied dispositions—to curb the haughty temper of some—to rule the wayward spirit of another, and still administer justice to all. But our pleasant and beloved commander was competent to the task, and each officer lent efficient aid, by vigilance and faithfulness to duty.

But I had quite forgotten to say, whither we were bound. It was not to the golden land, where many turn their prow to find an early, and mayhap, dishonored grave. But we were first to bend our course to the classic shores of Greece—the fairest home of the arts and sciences, and the chosen retreat of the muses, repa[i]ring amid the blue waters of a sunny clime. . . . Fain would we have tarried long in this land of the scholar's lore, but we might not linger. Favoring breezes filled our sails, and a short passage brought our bark to the Tibur's shore. The sceptre has long since fallen from the hand of the world's mistress, and Rome lives but in the days gone by. . . . No wonder that we gazed with feelings of mingled awe and admiration, as the gilded spires of that fallen city, faded from the eye.

Far behind we left the E[truscan?] land; and the cultured hills and smiling dales of France tempted us to pause. The warlike Gaul, that bravely battled with the Roman legion, would scarce recognise in the polished Parisian, a descendant of his race. The diadem encircles no longer the brow of a Charlemagne, and the galliant chevalier rallies not around a Bourbon's banner. . . . As the rival sister beckoned across the channel, we wound the parting haunt to "La Belle France," and joyously greeted England.

The eye of the ocean's mistress is not turned backward to the past, glorious though that past may be—nor does it rest upon the present; but far into the future. . . . The glory of the coming years shall dim the memory of the olden time. Proudly England rests in her security, and her safeguard is her people's love. May her name stand ever as now, high on the list of fame. When the swelling sail bore us from her happy shores; we parted with her, as from a friend we loved. What port would next receive us?

Our passage had been thus far prosperous. Storms had sometimes crossed our pathways, but the sailor knows full well old ocean's surface is easily ruffled. Things on shipboard had progressed as they ever do; and dispite our large number we had none been idle. There was ever something to keep brain and fingers busy.

We were scarc[e]ly off the coast of England; when a dense fog completely enveloped us, and here our troubles began. Starless night succe[e]ded sunless days, and as our ship drove onward; we lost our reckoning, and our where-a-bouts was a problem we could not solve. Sailors are generally superstitious, and we began carefully to notice every sign; but this only involved us the more deeply in trouble. Our situation was truly critical—the sharp and jagged rocks; that surround the barren desert isle of . . . equations kept us in terrible suspense, and I tremble even now at the thoughts of those fathomless depths. . . . But another drop was added to our cup of sorrow, as the phantom, shadowy forms of a Binomial Theorem presented itself to view. Steadily on it came, through the misty darkness, but it met strong hearts and ready hands, and like the ghosts of old, it vanished like a passing dream. Only those who have experienced the terrible dangers of the ocean, can appreciate our feelings, as at length the . . . misty shroud rolled slowly away, and the cheering beams of the sun gladdened our hearts.

We found we had drifted in our course, to a land where we were strangers. Far as the eye could reach; its craggy highlands skirted the horizon, and the blue peaks lost in the distance mingled with the sky. Its shores were bold and rugged, and a practised foot must scale its toilsome summit. But when once these dizzy heights were mounted, the unsurpassed grandeur of the landscape might well make one forget the strife and weary way. . . . A pilgrim of the

Roman time, known in the legends of the past as Marcus Tullius Cicero, climbed up and up that giddy steep, and left a name forever written in the annals of the Earth. . . .

At the mountain[']s base lay a lovely and romantic glade, like a precious stone in costly setting. We might wander the wide world over; but we could not find its like. The far famed beauty of the cashmere nob would suffer, when compared with Virgil's dell, ornamented as it was, but nature[']s handiwork, and all that art could desire.

We coasted many months, along the Latin shore, and gathered many a gem to store in our caskets. We dearly loved those rocky headlands, and through the remainder of the voyage, their tall peaks girdled the horizon; sometimes melting away in the dim distance, till their shadowy outline was completely lost, and then standing boldly out like sentinels to guard the shore.

What a cheerless place was that old, but still flourishing settlement of Grammarville, where we were next obliged to put in through stress of weather. It looked worn and weather beaten, and the damp moss of centuries covered the rocks that lined its coast. Among the many buildings that bore a general resemblance to one another, I noticed a substantial structure, the residen[ce] of Lindley Murray, which rose in proud prominence, above its neighbors, and whose outline had seemingly been made a model for the rest, but their minor points of finish, fancy had dictated. Mossy and grey with years, it reminded one of the baronial castles of the feudal age. Thickly scattered about the sub[u]rbs were houses of recent origin, and there seemed no end to their multiplication.

After having made a thorough acquaintance with the people, we put out from Grammarville, with the intention of visiting the dominions of the fair Queen Flora, and ere long the turrets of her beautiful palace, half hidden though they were by clustering foliage, announced our close proximity. Language will fail me to do justice to this place. The country was one continuous garden, where flowers of every hue gave their perfume to the passing zephyr. Arranged with studied negligence and nicest taste, were the graceful many elms, the drooping willows—the hardy, stormdaring oak—the quivering ash—the sighing pine—the maples in their sombre garb, and the many magnificent trees of a tropical climate. Arbors overrun by the rare climbers of the south were thrown across the cultured walks, and strange parasites entwined themselves about the loftiest Magnolia. . . . We had now well nigh arrived at the end of the first year and as we looked back upon its joys and sorrows that had gone forever the weeks seemed shorter than we had deemed them as we stood on the threshold of our father[']s cot. . . . And we were told that when we had dropped our anchor in

Euclid's harbor we should have a short respite from labors. Accordingly we looked forward to the arrival there with considerable interest. A pleasant summer day was drawing to a close as the triangular spires on [the] antique roof[s] of the little town in that harbor met our eyes. . . .

. . . While here many of our crew left. We parted with them sadly we had enjoyed the same pleasures and suffered the same hardships partaking of the same vessel and had truly become attached to each other; most of them we shall meet no more below. Those who remained were promoted in office. And when the ship was again in readiness for sea and the list of seamen complete . . . we cheerily plowed the way to the distant land of Evidences. The good king Alexander who presides . . . in these realms is . . . a person of great depth of thought [and] fond of disputation and it requires some study to fathom all his sayings.

. .,. I think it was about this time we discovered Newman's peninsula and its placid loveliness slowed our sails awhile [to] rest amidst its beauties. Here were many treasures carefully preserved of inhabitants of nations which had long been absent from earth. . . .

As we put out to sea [again] a heavy spray [rose] up which drove our ship from her course and work. . . . Fortunately for us Physiology lighthouse was ahead, built on a Rock promontory that runs out for miles into the sea, its retreating shores form a safe harbor for the tempest tost. . . . Columbus['] sailors never sent up a more joyous shout when that fair island of the tropics rewarded their labors than did the graduates . . . when we reached this place of safety. . . .

Could we realize the circling months of the second year had flown. . . . and again our ranks were thinned, but luckily there has never been as great a difficulty in finding a sufficiency of hands to man the Graduate; and soon two hundred and fifty sailors trod her deck and [as] a fair wind sprang, we put out to sea.

But dangers awaited us—a hurricane and we came near making our next trip to the bottom. However a kind Providence watched over us and preserved us from the threatened destruction and we gladly entered the first place of safety that presented itself. As we caught a peep of the town in the distance we imagined we had been driven again into Euclid's harbor. There certainly was a familiar look about the place and yet it did not seem the same. There was more complexity of form about the buildings and their appearance was far more imposing. The people informed us they were a Colony from the Harbor. But we perceived at once that they had far surpassed the mother country. They treated us with kindness and consideration—gave us every opportunity of studying their structures; and I trust we left with the firm conviction that we had gained something of discipline by the proceeding.

Not far from this place is a celebrated island name[d] on modern maps as Hitchcock's vineyard. It is the largest island known having a diameter of about eight thousand miles and a circumference of about twenty-five thousand—and comprehending many millions of square miles in extent. . . . Every species of soil necessary for the production of the countless variety of plants that administer to the pleasure or support of man was here furnished without stint. And here too were the record books of time that told how the surges of the ocean had once rolled in desolation over a buried world. Here were the footprints of a mammoth race that freely roamed the forests—and mayhap had these days exist[e]nce and passed away ere man was formed from dust. Here were the planets of other days that decked the face of nature when the earth was new. Strange tales of the past these told, but none could fail to give them credence. . . .

Unfortunately for us we at this time entered the strait of Logic. The passage was difficult and dangerous and it required the most skillful management to navigate it in safety. If we shunned Scylla on one side, it was only to be drawn into Charybdis on the other. The pointed rocks hidden beneath the turb[i]d water threatened death to the unwary sailor. Where ever we attempted to land the premises were liable to give way beneath our feet and precipitate us headlong. . . . a vision dawned upon us and led us to suppose we were approaching fairy ground. Spread out before us in its loveliness and stretching away into the distance was one of the fairest landscapes eyes ever beheld. I[t] could have received no more fitting name than Paradise. We left this summit port in our whole three years voyage with sorrow: and the cruel future we soon experienced rendered this pleasant time peculiarly dear to our memories. When so near the end of our voyage we deemed its trials and hardships over—when the thoughts of soon meeting the loved ones from whom we had been so long severed filled our minds you may judge how near being forever disappointed our bright hopes for the future came when I tell you our ship struck the fatal reef of Butter! But gallantly she bore up and though the shock made every timber in her quiver the next moment she moved calmly on and a joyous shout went up from her deck that made the air resound. Thanks! We were safe! A few days after we reached our harbor and the inmates of the Graduate rowed safely to the shore to the chorus of Holyoke [F]orever.

Susan [H]. Lennan.

Hol. Sem. July 27, 1852   Transcribed Aug. 8th [illeg.] "36"

Susan Hathorn's Diary

Covers: 21 cm × 17.4 cm; blue and black marbled boards, corners worn. Black embossed and gilt-stripped backstrip.

Pages: 20.5 cm × 16.5 cm. Pale blue lined paper. 6 gatherings of 8 leaves, plus 3 gatherings of 6 leaves, plus separate title-page leaf printed recto and verso (corresponding separate leaf cut from back). Total pages, 134. 1.35 cm thick.

Printed format: Title page reads, "Daily Journal for 1855. Published annually by Kiggins & Kellogg, Publishers, Blank Book Manufacturers, and Wholesale Booksellers and Stationers, 88 John Street, New-York."

Diary format, Monday–Wednesday on left pages, Thursday–Saturday on right. Months and dates printed.

Account book format, Accounts Receivable and Accounts Payable, 2 months per page.

Manuscript: Kept almost entirely in black ink, occasional sections in blue, some entries with visible pencil beneath. Fine, legible hand.

Lines of Descent

❧❀❧

Hathorn

John Hathorn (12/28/1720 – 1777) [Jode's great-great-grandfather]
married (1742) Esther Wyman (? – ?)

John Hathorn (1/19/1744 – 4/11/1815)
married (11/27/1766) Tabitha Going (? – ?)

John Hathorn (9/29/1767 – 10/31/1848)
married (6/3/1790) Elizabeth Gray (? – 6/15/1802)
married (8/1803) Elizabeth Bickford (? – ?)

Jefferson Hathorn (9/2/1805 – 2/5/1885)
married (2/23/1832) Sally Small (? – 4/10/1872)
married (1878) Emma Moore (? – ?)

Joseph S. Hathorn (12/13/1832 – 5/8/1856)
married (9/20/1854) Susan Hildreth Lennan (9/7/1830 – 12/12/1906)

Josephine Hathorn (11/20/1855 – 3/29/1858)

Lennan

David Lennan (11/26/1765 – 12/7/1861) [Susan's grandfather]
married Agness [maiden name not known] (? – ?)

James Lennan (10/26/1796–?)
married Lucy Hildreth (1804 or 1805–4/24/1869)

Susan Hildreth Lennan (9/7/1830–12/12/1906)
married (9/20/1854) Joseph S. Hathorn

Josephine Hathorn (11/20/1855–3/29/1858)

The Hathorn line of descent is according to Sinnet (1946); the Lennan line is according to the research of John A. Robbins Jr., Richmond Historical and Cultural Society.

Susan's Work

Date	Task or Project	For	Notation
1/1	Embroidered shoes	Jode	"begun to work a pair"
1/2	Embroidered shoes	Jode	Worked steadily
1/3	Embroidered shoes	Jode	Finished front
1/4	Embroidered shoes	Jode	Out of needed color
1/5	Embroidered shoes	Jode	Needs shade
1/6	Embroidered shoes	Jode	Working around needed color
1/8	Embroidered shoes	Jode	Finished one
1/9	Embroidered shoes	Jode	Too dark to work
1/9	Knitted	SH	"knit a long way"on blue stocking
1/10	Knitted		
1/10	Washed		Skinned hands, deferred to Hannah
1/11	Embroidered shoes	Jode	Too warm
1/13	Embroidered shoes	Jode	
1/13	Ironed	Jode	Shirts (8)
1/15	Embroidered shoes	Jode	
1/16	Baked		Cupcakes (2), ginger crackers (a host of)
1/16	Washed		
1/17	Embroidered shoes	Jode	
1/19	Crocheted		
1/19	Embroidered shoes	Jode	
1/22	Mended stockings		Friend Jane crocheted
1/23	Sewing	Jode	Hemstitched handkerchiefs
1/24	Embroidered shoes	Jode	
1/24	Ironed		
1/26	Washed		

(continued)

Date	Task or Project	For	Notation
1/27	Crocheted		
2/5	Housecleaned		
2/5	Ironed		
2/6	Bookkeeping	Jode	
2/6	Fumigated bedbugs		
2/7	Embroidered shoes	Jode	
2/9	Housecleaned		
2/9	Tied up fruit		
2/9	Bookkeeping	Jode	
2/10	Embroidered shoes	Jode	
2/12	Embroidered shoes	Jode	
2/13	Embroidered shoes	Jode	One back done, began the other
2/15	"Worked a little"		
2/16	Embroidered shoes	Jode	Second back done, size questioned
2/16	Embroidered shoes	Jode	Black ground done, out of worsted
2/19	Mended	SH	Calico dress
2/19	Sewed	SH	Pink gingham apron
2/19	Washed		
2/20	Sewed	SH	Green cashmere dress
2/20	Washed		Finished what was begun on 2/19
2/21	Embroidered shoes		"I think I shall keep for myself"
2/21	Ironed		
2/21	Mended	Jode	Shirts and stockings
2/21	Sewed	SH	Green cashmere dress
2/22	Embroidered shoes		"I could not let them be"
2/22	Ironed		
2/22	Starched		Shirts (10)
2/23	Ironed		Shirts (10), etc.
2/27	Sewed	SH	Green cashmere dress
2/28	Embroidered shoes		Jode's done, Susan "lacks one shade"
2/28	Washed		
3/1	Ironed		
3/1	Sewed	SH	Green cashmere dress
3/2			
3/2	Sewed	SH	Finished green cashmere dress
3/3	"Set about"	SH	Barege de Laine dress
3/3	Housecleaned		
3/3	Washed	Jode	Black pants and silk neckerchief
3/5	Washed		
3/6	Ironed		
3/6	Mended	Jode	Shirts

Date	Task or Project	For	Notation
3/6	Repaired	SH	Barege de Laine dress
3/6	Worked buttonholes		Nightdresses
3/7	Repaired	SH	Barege de Laine dress
3/7	Sewed	SH	Barege skirt
3/8	Quilted	SH	Gingham dress onto skirt
3/10	Cut out	SH	Chemise
3/10	Ironed	SH	Barege de Laine, wrapper, Barege
3/10	Washed	SH	Barege de Laine, wrapper, Barege
3/10	Worked buttonholes	SH	Chemise
3/12	Washed		
3/13	Ironed		Poor luck with starched clothes
3/14	"Scaled up Jode's writing"		
3/14	Sewed		Chemise
3/16	Sewed	SH	Chemise
3/17	Braided rags		For rug
3/17	Sewed	SH	Finished chemise
3/19	Braided rags		For rug
3/19	Sewed		Mat
3/20	Sewed		Mat
3/23	Sewed		Orange peel quilt piecing
3/24	Sewed		Orange peel quilt piecing
3/24	Sewed		Back to sleeve
3/26	Embroidered shoes	SH	
3/28	Embroidered shoes	SH	
3/29	Embroidered shoes	SH	Finished last pair
3/29	Mended		Purse fringe
3/20	Sewed		Patchwork
4/3	Knitted	SH	Blue stocking
4/4	Bound	Jode	"General Chart"
4/4	Knitted	SH	Blue stocking, finished one, began another
4/5	Housecleaned		
4/5	Knitted	SH	Blue stocking
4/5	Knitted	SH	Cappiola
4/5	Sewed, embroidered		nightcap
4/6	Knitted		Cappiola
4/10	Embroidered		Pin cushion
4/10	"Finished"		"all work"
4/10	Knitted	SH	Cappiola
4/11	Embroidered		Dahlia mat

(continued)

Date	Task or Project	For	Notation
4/12	Embroidered		Another dahlia mat
4/13	Embroidered	Sis Ring	Lamp mat
4/13	Knitted	SH	Blue stocking
4/14	Knitted		
4/19	Housecleaned		
4/20	Pasted		Scrapbook
4/24	Knitted	SH	Blue stocking
4/25	Pasted		Scrapbook
4/26	Pasted		Scrapbook
4/27	Drew		Winter piece
4/27	Pasted		Scrapbook
4/28	Baked		Ginger snaps and sugar cakes
4/28	Drew		Winter piece
5/2	Mended	Both	Clothes
5/3	Mended	Jode	Shirts
5/5	Wrote "receipts" for cooking		From Mrs. Hale's book
5/7	Wrote receipts for cooking		From Mrs. Hale's book
5/8	Wrote receipts for cooking		From Mrs. Hale's book
5/9	Drew		
5/9	Packed	SH	
5/17	Sewed		Calico aprons (2)
5/18	Mended		Stockings, flannels
5/18	Sewed	SH	Linen chemise, cut out at sea
5/19	Hemmed	Jode	Silk handkerchiefs (2)
5/20	Leatherworked		Cut out patterns for flowers and leaves
5/20	Leatherworked		Cut out "card rack"
5/20	Leatherworked		Leaves
5/21	Sewed	SH	Brown muslin skirt
5/21	Sewed, "run the breadths"	SH	Blue plaid dress
5/21	Sewed, "run the breadths"	SH	Reddish pink lawn
5/21	Sewed, made flounces	SH	Blue "all wool de Laine"
5/23	Sewed	SH	Trimming on green dress
5/23	Sewed	SH	Linen chemise finished
5/26	Ironed and starched		Bad luck
5/28	Bookkeeping		"our and ship's accounts"
5/28	Sewed		Shirts

Date	Task or Project	For	Notation
5/29	Embroidered	SH	Shoes, oak leaves and coral
5/29	Sewed		Shirts, one finished
5/30	Sewed		Shirts, one finished
6/2	Embroidered	SH	Shoes, oak leaves and coral
6/4	Embroidered	SH	Shoes, oak leaves and coral
6/4	Knitted		Cotton stocking
6/5	Knitted	SH	
6/5	Quilted	SH	Alpaca skirt
6/6	Knitted	SH	
6/6	Quilted	SH	Skirt, nearly finished
6/7	Bound	SH	Skirt with velvet
6/7	Knitted	SH	All evening
6/7	Quilted	SH	Skirt, finished
6/8	Cleaned		Carpet, stateroom, cabin
6/9	Embroidered	SH	Shoes, oak leaves and coral
6/13	Mended	Jode	Gloves, clothes, handk
6/14	Mended		
6/15	Washed		Stockings, handkerchief, collars; washed gloves with milk
6/15	Hemmed	Ship	Tablecloths (3)
6/15	Ironed and starched		
6/15	Sewed	SH	Linen chemise, cut out at sea
6/16	Leatherworked		From the Misses Brown
7/2	Leatherworked		[Jode varnished it]
7/2	Sewed		Shirt, one all but sleeves
7/3	Bookkeeping		Settle up accounts
7/3	Sewed		Shirt, one all but one sleeve
7/4	Sewed		Shirts, finished 3rd began 4th
7/5	Sewed		Shirts, finished 4th, cut out 5th
7/6	Sewed		Shirt, finished body, sleeves of 5th
7/7	Leatherworked		Sea too rough
7/7	Sewed		Shirts, finished 5th, cut out 9 more
7/9	Sewed		Shirt, made body
7/10	Sewed		Shirts, finished 6th, worked on 7th
7/11	Sewed		Shirt, nearly finished 7th
7/12	Cleaned		Stateroom
7/12	Leatherworked		All P.M.
7/12	Mended	Jode	Pants
7/12	Sewed		Shirt, finished 7th
7/13	Leatherworked		
7/13	Sewed		Shirt, made body of 8th

(*continued*)

Date	Task or Project	For	Notation
7/14	Sewed		Shirt, finished 8th
7/15	Leatherworked		Admonishes self to do better next week
7/16	Sewed		Shirt, 9th all but assembled
7/17	Sewed		Shirts, finished 9th, began 10th
7/18	Sewed		Shirt, finished 10th
7/19	Sewed		Shirt, worked on 11th
7/19			[Jode made card case frame & vase bottom]
7/20	Sewed		Shirt, finished 11th
7/21	Sewed		Shirt, finished 12th
7/23	Leatherworked	Lucy, SH	Wreath for Lucy's vase; leaves/flowers for SH's inkstand
7/24	Leatherworked	SH	Sweated over flowers for inkstand bottom
7/25	Leatherworked	SH	Wreath for inkstand
7/26	Leatherworked		[Jode helped with card case]
7/27	Housecleaned		Cabin
7/27	Mended	Jode	Underwear
7/31			[Jode made SH a spool stand]
7/31	Sewed	Jode	Made slippers larger, were too small
8/1	Mended	Jode	Coats
8/1	Sewed	Jode	Made slippers larger, were too small
8/2	Quilted		Skirt, outside from Mrs. Hathorn
8/3	Quilted		
8/3			[Jode made fancy capstan cover]
8/4	Quilted	SH	Skirt, outside from Mrs. Hathorn, finishes
8/6	Housecleaned		Stateroom
8/7	Embroidered		Slippers, oak leaf & coral
8/8	Embroidered		Slippers, oak leaf & coral
8/9	Embroidered		Slippers, oak leaf & coral
8/10	Embroidered		Slippers, oak leaf & coral, lost pattern overboard
8/11	Embroidered		Slippers, oak leaf & coral
8/13	Embroidered		Slippers, oak leaf & coral
8/14	Embroidered		Slippers, oak leaf & coral
8/15	Embroidered		Slippers finished & fit
8/16	Housecleaned		
8/16	Knitted		
8/20	Crocheted		Edging
8/21	Crocheted		Edging

Date	Task or Project	For	Notation
8/22	Crocheted		Edging
8/22	Sewed		
8/27	Crocheted		
8/27	Sewed	Capt. Dickerson	Flag for Capt. D's boat
8/28	Cut out		Patterns
8/28	Sewed	Capt. D	Stars on flag
8/31	Crocheted		Edging
8/31	Sewed		
9/1	Crocheted		
9/6	Sewed		Shirts, made one & hemstitched
9/7	Sewed		Shirt, made another & hemstitched
9/10	Sewed		
9/15	Mended	Jode	Stockings
9/15	Sewed		Buttons on Jode's new shirts
9/18	Sewed	Jode	Shirt
9/19	Sewed	Jode	Shirt
9/19	Sewed	Jode	Collars
9/20	Sewed	Jode	Collars
9/21	Marked	Jode	Collars and other clothing
9/21	Mended	SH	Underclothes
9/21	Sewed	Jode	Collars
9/22	Housecleaned		Closet in order
9/22	Mended	SH	Nightdresses
9/22	Sewed	SH	Bag for dress pieces and stockings
9/24	Ironed	Jode	Shirts and collars
9/24	Packed	Jode	For boat
9/24	Sewed		Nightdress
9/25	Mended	SH	Box
9/25	Sewed	Baby	Sacque nightdresses
9/26	Cut out	Baby	"a lot of things"
9/26	Sewed	Baby	Sacques
9/27	Embroidered	Baby	Sleeves of two nightdresses
9/27	Sewed	Baby	Nightdress
9/28	Crocheted	Baby	Edging for sacques
9/28	Sewed	Baby	Six sacques completed
9/29	Cut out	Baby	Another band for stitching
9/29	Embroidered	Baby	Learned featherstitch, made it on swathe
9/29	Sewed	Baby	Edging on two more sacques
10/1	Cut out	Baby	"a lot of things"
10/1	Embroidered	Baby	Two foot blankets

(continued)

Date	Task or Project	For	Notation
10/1	Sewed	Baby	Two foot blankets
10/3	Run	Baby	Scallops for bottom of a skirt
10/3	Sewed	Baby	Two swathes
10/4	Sewed	Baby	Skirt, buttonhole & eyelets & leaves
10/5	Sewed	Baby	Finished skirt
10/6	Sewed	Baby	"second little skirt"
10/8	Embroidered		Featherstitched with orange silk, 4th foot blanket
10/8	Sewed	Baby	Finished second skirt
10/9	Copied		Pattern
10/9	Sewed	Baby	Waist onto foot blanket made on 10/8
10/9	Sewed	Baby	One skirt, except embroidering bottom
10/10	Sewed	Baby	Other skirt
10/10	Sewed	Baby	Edge of 5th skirt
10/12	Sewed	Baby	"steadily all day . . . made up 2 pieces of diaper"
10/13	Sewed	Baby	Other diaper towels
10/15	Embroidered	Baby	Chain stitch skirt
10/15	Sewed	Baby	Finished diapers (now 6 doz)
10/16	Embroidered	Baby	Chain stitch skirt
10/16	Sewed	Ann	Collar
10/18	Embroidered	Baby	Chain stitch skirt, finished
10/19	Sewed	Baby	Edging, featherstitched a blanket
10/20	Sewed	Baby	Blanket, finished
10/22	Sewed	Baby	Blanket, scalloped sides
10/23	Cut out		Three nice shirts
10/23	Ironed		Two shirts
10/23	Sewed	Baby	Blanket, finished
10/24	Sewed		One shirt complete, and part of second
10/25	Cut out	Baby	Four dresses
10/25	Sewed	Baby	"the other two little shirts"
10/26	Sewed	Baby	Made one dress, waist of 2nd, except belt
10/27	Sewed		Third slip, only one more cross-barred slip to make
10/29	Sewed	House	Curtains
10/29	Sewed		Waist to 4th slip
10/29	Shopped	House	For furniture
10/30	Made		Shoe case

Date	Task or Project	For	Notation
10/30	Measured	House	For bed tick
10/30	Sewed		Finished slip
10/31	Ironed		Slips (3) and shirts (3)
10/31	Made	House	Pillows, bolster, featherbed tick, straw tick
11/1	Sewed	House	Feather tick
11/1	Sewed	SH	Skirt for "boughten waist"
11/1	Sewed	Baby	Began lawn dress
11/2	Sewed	Baby	Tucks in skirt to lawn dress, made skirt, began waist
11/2	Sewed		Put braid on 2 slips, looped 3rd with ribbon
11/3	Sewed	Baby	Finished the "little lawn dress"
11/3	Sewed		Fixed the sleeves of other slips
11/3	Sewed		Sewed on buttons, etc.
11/5	Sewed	Baby	Waists for best petticoat & foot blanket from linen
11/6	Housecleaned		Room
11/6	Ironed		Slips (3)
11/6	Sewed		Skirt onto waist Lucy bought
11/6	Sewed		Last pettiskirt
11/7	Copied pattern	House	Cushion
11/7	Run	SH	Scallops for my skirt
11/8	Housekept		Arranged jar of shells
11/8	Sewed	Baby	Scallops on "the little petticoat"
11/8	Sewed		Edges onto lawn dress, putting in ribbon
11/9	Sewed	Baby	"my best and last foot-blanket"
11/9	Sewed		Scalloping skirt finished, "run down seams"
11/10	Copied pattern		Petticoat, and run design, bunch of grapes
11/10	Made	SH	Pincushion
11/10	Mended	SH	Stockings
11/12	Embroidered		Pattern on skirt
11/13	Embroidered		Pattern on skirt
11/13	Knitted		
11/14	Embroidered		Pattern on skirt
11/14	"Run"		Pattern twice
11/15	Embroidered		Pattern on skirt
11/16	Embroidered		Pattern on skirt

(continued)

Date	Task or Project	For	Notation
11/16	"Run"		Pattern (2 or 3)
11/17	Embroidered		Pattern, fixed cushion
11/17	"Run"		Pattern, rest of
11/19	Sewed		Skirt
11/29	Housekept		Set room to rights
11/29	Knitted		"a very little"
11/29	Sewed		"a stitch or two"
11/30	Knitted		
12/1	Sewed		Skirt "I was jabbing upon when Baby came"
12/4	Sewed		Skirt
12/5	Sewed		Skirt completed
12/7	Knitted		
12/7	Shopped		At Libby's Toothakers & Miss Clack's
12/10	Sewed		Sleeves and lining to calico dress
12/11	Cut out	Baby	"part of the little Thibet hood"
12/11	Embroidered	Baby	Thibet hood
12/13	Embroidered	Baby	Thibet hood
12/14	Embroidered	Baby	Thibet hood
12/28	Sewed	Sally	Shoe case
12/31	Drew off	Mother	Pattern for mother's flannel skirt
12/31	Straightened	Mother	Pattern for cotton skirt

Susan's Accounts

ACCOUNT BOOK SECTION
OF SUSAN HATHORN'S 1855 DIARY

To personal Expenses $151.66
" Furniture 28.74
" Baby Fixings... 30.14

Cash Account

January

17	Paid negro for carrying budgets............................	.20
19	To hair comb	.30
	Doll for Sis Ring	.15
	Eight pairs of Cotton Stockings............................	2.00
	Loose Wrapper or Blouse...................................	1.50
25	Fan	2.12½
	[Total]..	6.27

February

	Amount brought over......................................	6.27
2	6 Towels at $7 per Dozen	$3.50
8	Linen Lawn Dress	4.45
"	Negro Wench	.40

24   2 yds Cambric...   .50
      6 skeins worsted..   .10
      [Total]...$15.22

March

      Amount brought over...................................$15.22
[a column of "To"'s but nothing filled in]

April

[same as March]

May

 1   Amount brought over...................................$15.22
 2   1 Pr Gaiter Boots & 2 prs Slippers.......................   3.75
      Cashmere Shawl..   14.00
      Mantilla...   6.50
      Undersleeves...   .75
      Four Collars..   3.55
      2 Pairs of Gloves..   1.00
      2 Calico Aprons..   .28
      24 yds. Lawn...   2.88
      20 yds. Blue Plaid.......................................   5.50
      15 yds. Blue All wool de Laine...........................   5.55
17   1 Crochet Collar...   .33
      2 Pocket handkerh'f's for girls & 1 vase for Lucy.........   .75
      Toys for Sis Ring & Fanny...............................   .36
      1 Box of Thread...   .40
      "Sunny Memories" and "Fashion & Famine"...............   .75
18   Making Embroidered Slippers............................   1.12
      Crochet Hooks, Books, Patterns, &c., Pins...............   1.08
      Velvet trimming for Green dress.........................   .37
      2 Pairs Black Cashmere stockings........................   .81
      4 Rolls wadding...   .41
      1 Bunch knitting cotton.................................   .31
19   oz. Sewing Silk...   .37
      2 Prs. Scissors...   .87
      5 yds. Lining for Blue de Laine.........................   .45
23   Sewing silk for   "   "   "...........................   .03

24	Visit to Tower with Book	.43
	Gloves, Piping, Fruit &c.	.63
26	Hair Band .75 Frizettes .50 Velvet Ribbon	1.87
	Board 2 weeks and 2 days	17.00
	Fare to Gravesend	.37
	[Subtotal]	$87.69
	Visit to St. Paul's Cathedral .50 Crochet Patterns .12	.62

June

16	Carriage hire	$4.32
19	Leather for Leather work	1.92
	Shoe maker's Punch	.60
	Naptha and Gum Shellac	.24
	Carriage Hire	1.68
23	Round Pounce for Leather work	.24
	Inserting and Edge for Chemisette	.42
	Edging and inserting for Linen Chemises	1.12
	Postage	.26
	Oranges	.24
25	Postage to Vermont	.24
	Spirits of [?] Wine	.72
	Gum Shellac	.12
	[Subtotal]	$99.81
	[Carried over from end of May]	.62
	[Year-to-date total]	$100.43

July
[no entries; at sea]

August

To cash on hand	10.25
To cash from Sallie	1.12

September

4	Negro wench .25 Cloth & needles [.20]	.45
6	Paper Fan .08 Apples .08 Palmetto Fan .03	.19
8	Fare from Savannah to N. York	20.00
	Board at Mrs. McNelty's 2 days	4.00

Apples .14, 1 Trunk 3.00 .... 3.14
Fare from N.Y. to Richmond............................ 13.25
13   Horse hire 1.62
18   Borax .03—Postage .06—Cambric .07 .... .16
24   8 yds Calico for Sarah 1.00
27   Letter stamps .51, Envelopes & Paper .40 .... .91
[Year-to-date total]..................................... $145.15

October

9   Fare to Gardiner—Hack & Porter .... .63
18   Fruit... .05
20   Fare to Richmond .30   Porter .25 .... .55
[Year-to-date total]..................................... $146.38

November

[Amount brought over] $146.38

December

7   Ribbon for Bonnet trimming 4 yds....................... 1.40
     9 yds Calico for Dress 1.00
22   Fixing bonnet 2.00
     Brandy .... .75
     Buttons... .05
     Envelopes.. .08
     [Year-to-date total]..................................... $151.66

[At this point the "Bills Payable/Receivable" section begins. On the January page, Susan has written:]

Nov. 26   Re'd of Capt. Hathorn $10.00

[On the June Bills Payable/Receivable page she keeps a "baby fixings" account:]

June

23   6 yds print at .14 per yd................................ .84
     8 yds. Flannel at .72 per yd. 5.76

6 "   "   " .60 .... 3.60
6 "   "   " .54 .... 3.24

Aug. 25 8 yds Cotton Cloth.. 1.44

Sept. 27 Embroidery silk .... .37

Oct. 8 Cotton cloth & 2 skeins orange silk...................... .13
            36 yds Diaper 4.50
            4 yd cross barred 1.68
            12 skeins silk .36   edge & inserting .9 .... .45
            ¾ yd Linen.. .58
       16 2½ yds Edging .15   3 yds Edging .10 .... .25

Nov. 1 Ribbon, Paste, Tape, Bobbin, & Inserting .... .76
        5 Bought waist... 3.00

Dec. 7 Thibet for cloak 1.32
            Thibet for Hood.. .28
       15 Ribbon for Hood.. .20
       24 Cradle 1.50
            Silk .21 Wadding for hood .03............................ .24
            [Total expenditures]....................................$30.14

[The July page bears the following "furniture account":]

Oct. 29 Sink $3.50
            Bed stead 6.00
       30 Bed ticking 18½ yds for Straw & 13¼ yds for
            featherbed 3.33
            Chamber set—wash bowl & pitcher........................ 1.00
Nov. 5 Bureau... 14.00
        6 Looking Glass .... .91
            [Total]..$28.74

10/25 1856 4 chairs $2.16
            1 Stand 1.00

	Toilet Table	1.75
	Towel Rack	.60
11/10	Sofa	34.00
	6 chairs	24.00
	Rocking chair	10.00
	[Total for furniture	$102.25]

On the November page, the right half of which has been torn away, the following items are listed in pencil that has been almost completely erased. This "inventory" list is not dated, but was probably written sometime during 1855. It includes: "Stockings, 4 pairs; Stays, 2 pairs; White dress; Green dress; Saque & skirt; Dressing gown; Traveling dress; Black silk sacque; 4 Chemises; 3 prs. Drawers; 5 night gowns; 4 night caps; 1 white skirt; 3 [towels?]; 4 collars; 2 slipper [topsides?]."

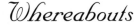

Whereabouts

Susan Hathorn's Travels, 1855, According to Her Diary

1/1	Grand Turk Passage
1/3	Santiago, Cuba
2/16	Cay Blanco, Trinidad de Cuba
3/2	Port Casilda
3/5	Near Antigua
3/23	Salt Cay
3/25	Gun Cay
5/8	The Downs, Beachy Head, Dover
5/9	Gravesend, Thames, London
5/10	Misses Bragge's, America Square, London
5/26	Gravesend, Dover
5/30	Scilly Islands
6/4	Anchoring ground (Bristol Channel)
6/12	Cardiff
6/27	"the Roads" (Cardiff)
6/28	At sea
8/18	Duboy Island and Light, Tybee Light [Savannah]
8/19	Savannah River
8/25	"Montgomery" (Captain Dickerson's home) through 9/5
9/5	Savannah, Mrs. McNelty's
9/9	*Alabama*, Savannah to New York
9/11	New York City, U.S. Hotel
9/11	*Metropolis*, New York to Boston
9/12	Boston, "N.E. House"
9/12	Richmond

The J. J. Hathorn's Coordinates, 1855

꧁

	Date	Time	Lat.	Long.	Comment
1	1/2	16:00	20.27	72.07	Grand Turk
2	2/12	Night	19.24	77.01	Santiago, Cuba
3	2/13	Night	19.47	78.10	
4	2/14	08:00		79.53	
5		12:00	20.43	79.53	
6		16:00		79.75	
7		Sunset		80.01	
8	2/15	Morning		80.22	
9		12:00	21.31	80.15	
10		16:00		80.07	
11	2/16				Cay Blanco, Trinidad
12	3/15	16:00		80.16	Trinidad de Cuba
13		Sunset	21.15	80.18	
14	3/16	Morning	20.40	81.05	Dead reckoning
15		12:00	20.57		
16		16:00		81.32	
17	3/17	08:00		79.00	
18		12:00	20.31		
19		16:00		83.21	
20	3/18	08:00		85.03	
21		12:00	21.30		
22		16:00		85.10	
23	3/19	08:00		85.59	
24		12:00	23.07	85.49	Double altitudes
25		16:00		85.39	
26	3/20	Morning	22.56	85.28	Sumner's
27		12:00	22.58		

	Date	Time	Lat.	Long.	Comment
28		16:00		85.55	
29	3/21	Morning	22.48	84.18	
30	3/22	08:00	23.15	83.42	
31	3/23	08:00	23.30	80.56	Sumner's, Salt Cay
32		12:00	23.41		
33		16:00		80.39	
34	3/24	Morning		80.43	
35		12:00	21.18		
36		17:00	24.35	79.56	
37	3/25	12:00	25.38		Gun Cay
38		16:00		79.46	
39	3/26	Morning		79.50	
40		12:00	30.16		
41		16:00		79.32	
42	3/27	Morning		79.50	
43		12:00	30.16		
44	3/28	08:00		78.47	
45		12:00	31.08		
46		16:00		78.22	
47	3/29	12:00	31.55		
48		16:00	32.00	77.00	
49	3/30			76.40	
50	4/1	12:00	34.48		
51		16:00		75.13	
52	4/2	08:00		73.13	
53		12:00	35.48		
54		16:00		71.48	
55	4/3	08:00		69.04	
56		12:00	36.02		
57		16:00		68.11	
58	4/4	12:00	35.08		
59		16:00		65.47	
60	4/5	08:00	36.14	65.35	
61	4/6	Morning		63.00	
62		12:00	38.02		
63	4/7	16:00	40.17	58.28	Dead reckoning
64	4/8	12:00	40.20	54.40	
65	4/9	16:00	41.50	52.52	Dead reckoning
66	4/10	16:00	42.42	49.43	
67	4/11	16:00	42.20	47.14	
68	4/12	Morning		46.13	
69		12:00	42.54		

	Date	Time	Lat.	Long.	Comment
70		16:00	43.12	45.03	Dead reckoning
71	4/13	Morning		42.38	
72		12:00	44.56		
73		16:00	45.10		
74	4/14	08:00		38.09	
75		12:00	47.00		
76		16:00	47.21	36.40	
77	4/15	08:00		35.55	
78		12:00	47.56		
79		16:00	47.36	34.49	
80	4/16	16:00	47.51	33.10	
81	4/17	16:00	48.07	28.41	Dead reckoning
82	4/18	08:00		26.51	
83		12:00	48.06		
84		16:00	48.06	26.30	Dead reckoning
85	4/19	12:00	48.00		Dead reckoning
86		16:00		25.22	
87	4/20	12:00	48.09		
88		16:00		24.46	
89	4/21	Morning		24.09	
90		Night		20.31	
91	4/23	16:00	49.40	19.05	
92	4/24			17.50	Dead reckoning
93			50.00		Imperfect meridian
94	4/25	16:00	50.00	16.50	"Summs"
95	4/26	12:00	49.48		
96		16:00	49.46	15.30	
97	4/27	16:00	49.42	13.16	
98	4/28	16:00	49.53	13.20	
99	4/30	16:00	48.03	12.09	
100	4/30	16:00	48.27	10.25	
101	5/1	08:00	48.06	9.15	
102		16:00	48.12	8.18	
103	5/2	16:00	48.25	8.34	
104	5/3	16:00	48.26	7.57	
105	5/4	16:00	48.18	7.14	Dead reckoning
106	5/5		48.15	8.00	
107	5/6	16:00	49.24	5.05	
108	5/7	16:00	50.24	1.25	The Downs, Beachy Head, Dover
109	5/9				Gravesend
110	5/26				Gravesend, Dover
111	5/30	16:30	49.50	4.35	Scilly Isles

	Date	Time	Lat.	Long.	Comment
112	6/4				"anchoring ground," Bristol Channel
113	6/29	16:00	50.36	6.34	Dead reckoning
114	6/30	16:00	50.08	9.14	
115	7/2	16:00	50.08	11.05	No observation
116	7/3	16:00	49.45	11.30	
117	7/4	18:00	49.00	14.04	
118	7/5	16:00	47.45	14.52	
119	7/6	16:00	47.22	15.01	
120	7/7	16:00	47.40	17.38	
121	7/8	16:00	44.18	18.47	"chalk ginger blue"
122	7/9	16:00	40.50	20.00	
123	7/10	16:00	38.00	20.08	
124	7/11	16:00	36.10		
125	7/12	16:00	34.30	20.34	
126	7/13	16:00	32.30	22.34	
127	7/14	16:00	30.33	24.04	
128	7/15	16:00	28.31	25.30	
129	7/16	16:00	27.50	28.43	
130	7/17	16:00	27.23	31.40	
131	7/18	16:00	27.21	34.25	
132	7/19	16:00	27.19	37.00	
133	7/20	16:00	27.24	39.14	
134	7/21		27.11	42.38	
135	7/22	16:00	27.05	44.01	
136	7/23	16:00	26.45	46.34	
137	7/24	16:00	26.10	49.06	
138	7/25		26.10	51.14	
139	7/26	16:00	26.00	52.45	
140	7/27	17:00	26.26	54.28	imperfect sight
141	7/28		27.00	56.06	no meridian altitude
142	7/29	16:00	27.45	56.43	
143	7/30	16:00	28.20	56.46	
144	7/31	16:00	28.20	58.11	
145	8/1	16:00	28.00	59.31	
146	8/2	16:00	27.20	61.36	
147	8/3	16:00	26.30	62.49	
148	8/4	16:00	26.05	63.15	
149	8/5	16:00	26.40	64.17	
150	8/6	16:00	26.40	66.22	
151	8/7	16:00	26.30	67.45	
152	8/8	16:00	26.09	69.20	
153	8/9	16:00	26.45	70.03	

	Date	Time	Lat.	Long.	Comment
154	8/10	16:00	26.38	70.25	
155	8/11	16:00	26.14	70.52	
156	8/12	16:00	26.28	71.55	
157	8/13	16:00	26.50	73.44	
158	8/14	16:00	27.30	75.26	
159	8/15	16:00	28.00	76.52	
160	8/16	16:00	28.35	78.52	
161	8/17	16:00	29.50	79.35	
162	8/18				Duboy Island and Light, Tybee Light
163	8/19				Savannah River
164	9/9				aboard SS *Alabama*, Savannah–NY
165	9/11				aboard SS *Metropolis*, NY–Boston

Notes

Introduction

1. David Lennan, b. November 26, 1765, d. December 7, 1861; Agness Lennan, birth and death dates unknown, maiden name not known. Data on the Lennan family are from the *International Genealogical Index* (hereafter IGI), Version 2.18 (1988), and the Webster/Johnson and Webster/Williamson *Vital Records of Gardiner, Maine, to the Year 1892*. Local geographical orientation and genealogical research on the Hathorns and Lennans were provided by John A. Robbins Jr. of the Richmond Historical and Cultural Society and Robbins Historical Research, Inc., and by Danny V. Smith, Gardiner, Maine.

2. The research library at the Maine Maritime Museum at Bath maintains a comprehensive collection of published works on Maine and Kennebec River maritime activity, archives of manuscript materials, and extensive cross-referenced card files of ships and captains with Kennebec area associations.

3. Hildreth genealogical studies center mainly on the forebears of Horace Hildreth, governor of Maine (1945–49) and later ambassador to Pakistan. Horace Hildreth's line of Hildreths and Lucy Hildreth Lennan are not closely related. The main source is Walter Goodwin Davis's *The Ancestry of Sarah Hildreth, 1773–1857, wife of Annis Spear, of Litchfield, Maine*; other Hildreth information appears in the IGI and *Vital Records of Gardiner*.

4. Williamson, *Vital Records of Gardiner*. Susan's siblings were Lucy Fletcher Lennan, b. September 12, 1824, married Amasa S. Ring (date unknown); Hosea Hildreth Lennan, b. October 29, 1827, married Ann Esty (Foy), May 9, 1851; Mary Snow Lennan, b. November 23, 1833, d. May 16, 1870, never married; Llewellyn Lennan, b. March 1, 1835, married Emerline J. Hildreth, August 24, 1862; Joseph Emerson Lennan, b. March 7, 1839, d. January 20, 1850; and Frances Lennan, b. February 12, 1843, who is not documented in the usual sources.

5. James Edward Ring, b. January 21, 1848; Lucy Ellen Ring, b. September 17, 1849. Their other children were born after 1855.

6. Hosea and Ann's two daughters were Anna Sarah Lennan, b. April 16, 1853, d. September 12, 1853, age 5 months; and Alice Few Lennan, b. February 22, 1855,

d. May 10, 1855, age 3 months. Five of Hosea and Ann's seven children would die in infancy; only Frank Foy Lennan, b. April 18, 1865, and William Blake Lennan, b. May 26, 1869, survived childhood.

7.   Twenty-seven was not extraordinarily late for a man to marry in the 1850s and family obligations may have absorbed Llewellyn's attentions before 1862.

8.   The Salem Hathornes, including some maritime people, and their connection to the Maine Hathorns are discussed in Vernon Loggins, *The Hawthornes: The Story of Seven Generations of an American Family*.

The Hathorn name's spelling survived various permutations—Hawthorne, Hauthorne, Harthorne, Hathorne, and Hathorn all are linked. Nineteenth-century customs and records add further variations. The spelling of the family name in the time of the earliest traced English ancestor, Thomas of Bray, Berkshire, England, was *Hathorn*. The *e* was added by his financially and socially successful grandson, the first William. Nathaniel Hawthorne, the American author, added the *w* to his name while a student at Bowdoin College.

9.   *Block*, meaning a large commercial building divided into separate stores, offices, or apartments, is still common in midcoast Maine.   ·

10.   Volney B., who lived only to the age of 12, is something of a mystery. His gravestone is in the Hathorn family plot in Evergreen Cemetery in Richmond, but he is nowhere to be found in other records. Susan never mentions him in the 1855 diary, nor is he enumerated among Jefferson Hathorn's household in the 1850 census, the only one for which he would have been living.

11.   The Mount Holyoke College Archives and Special Collections. See appendix B.

12.   Letter to Emily Whitten, January 8, 1852, The Mount Holyoke College Archives and Special Collections. See appendix A.

13.   Helen Lefkowitz Horowitz, *Alma Mater: Design and Experience in the Women's Colleges from Their Nineteenth-Century Beginnings to the 1930s*, 24–25.

14.   Susan may not have matriculated there realizing that; mid-nineteenth-century higher education for women was undergoing revolutionary times and experimentation. The classical academic curriculum offered to male students and at Mount Holyoke was generally not available to women. See Eleanor Wolf Thompson's *Education for Ladies, 1830–1860: Ideas on Education in Magazines for Women*, especially the chapters, "The Importance of Female Education" and "Normal Schools and Training." Most pertinent to the origins of and practices at the early Mount Holyoke is Horowitz's *Alma Mater*.

15.   Letter to Emily Whitten.

16.   Ibid.

17.   Susan Hathorn's 1855 diary is the property of Special Collections Library, Duke University. Quotations are cited as *SH* followed by month and day. Susan usually wrote her daily entries as single paragraphs; when extended quotes incorporate several days' entries, vertical spacing is used to indicate a change of day. SH, February 17.

18.   Letter to Emily Whitten.

19.   Ibid.

20.   Ibid.

21.   Ibid.

22.   "Coastwise manifest, Bark *J. J. Hathorn*, Port of Philadelphia, October 20, 1854," Box 158, RG 36, National Archives.

January

1.   SH, January 1.
2.   Ibid.
3.   *Shipping and Commercial List and New York Prices Current*, December 20, 1854. Susan follows a common spelling for Santiago, used also by the *Shipping and Commercial List*. Susan's spelling is usually excellent, though occasionally she spells unfamiliar proper names phonetically, later regularizing and correcting the spelling.
4.   SH, January 1.
5.   The *S.* probably stands for Small, the maiden name of Jode's mother, Sally. No documentation of Jode's given middle name has been located. Some port scribes incorrectly report Jode's middle initial as *J.*, as in the vessel's name.
6.   Jode's personal financial share in the *J. J. Hathorn* cannot be documented from surviving records. Most ships' shares of the time are stated in 32nds, and a captain's share generally was about $\frac{4}{32}$. Whether or not Jode technically owned that much, it seems safe to assume that his father, Jefferson Hathorn Sr., owned a substantial share in the vessel at the time, especially in view of the death of his business partner and brother Joseph Jackson Hathorn in 1854.
7.   Susan Burrows Swan discusses the complementarity of "business" and "pleasure" needlework in *Plain & Fancy: American Women and Their Needlework, 1700–1850*. Also see Betty Ring's *Girlhood Embroidery: American Samplers and Pictorial Needlework, 1650–1850* (New York: Alfred A. Knopf, 1993).
8.   SH, January 2.
9.   Ibid.
10.   Susan's usual style is to indicate the degrees with a double quote and the minutes either with a single quote or with no mark at all.
11.   SH, January 2. The "Tortuga" Susan mentions is Ile de la Tortue, a ten-mile-long island lying parallel to the coast about three and one-half miles off Cap-Hatien, Haiti.
12.   SH, January 3.
13.   Ibid.
14.   Ibid. To *heave-to*, a vessel is laid on the wind with sails shortened and trimmed, so as it comes up to the wind it will fall off again and thus make no headway.
15.   SH, January 4.
16.   SH, January 5.
17.   Susan is referring to her older sister, Lucy Fletcher Lennan Ring.
18.   SH, January 6.
19.   Author's italics.
20.   Carroll Smith-Rosenberg's "The Female World of Love and Ritual" (New York: Alfred A. Knopf, 1985) explores one extreme manifestation of this social pattern.
21.   SH, January 7.
22.   SH, January 8.

23. Ibid.

24. SH, January 9.

25. SH, January 10.

26. SH, January 8 and 13. Susan may have misunderstood "pelican" for "penguin."

27. SH, January 10.

28. SH, January 13.

29. SH, January 12.

30. SH, January 11.

31. SH, January 12.

32. SH, January 13.

33. Appendix C describes the manuscript.

34. A railroad train or horse-drawn trolley.

35. SH, January 15.

36. Ibid.

37. SH, January 16.

38. "Brown," to whom Susan always refers by his surname, is Captain Lemuel Brown, the husband of Sally Hathorn Brown, Jode's sister; "Jeffy" is Jefferson Hathorn Jr. (b. April 10, 1840); and "Molly" is Mary Snow Lennan.

39. SH, January 16.

40. SH, January 17.

41. SH, January 18.

42. Bauge is a coarse woolen fabric, often felted on one side.

43. SH, January 18.

44. SH, January 19.

45. SH, January 20. Susan's comment is interesting in view of her February 8 reaction to the same cathedral, and to St. Paul's Cathedral in London.

46. SH, January 23.

47. Ibid.

48. SH, January 25. Susan means a small "boat," not the *J. J. Hathorn*.

49. SH, January 27.

50. SH, January 26.

51. Jode is two years, three months younger than Susan.

52. Richard Henry Dana's *The Seaman's Friend* actually comprises "A plain treatise on practical seamanship," with exhaustive chapters on rigging, sails, knots, etc., and the use thereof, offering a comprehensive handbook on life at sea; a glossary of sea terminology, "Customs and Usages of the Merchant Service"; and "Laws Relating to the Practical Duties of Master and Mariners." The last two detail the relationship of a captain and his men. Content aside, the stylistic personality of *The Seaman's Friend* can hardly be more split; the first section is written in nautical argot, and the others are couched in legal language, footnoted with citations to statutes.

53. Ibid., 189.

54. Ibid., 208. When the ship's medicine chest (the use of which ships often charged against seamen's wages) and ministrations on board are of no avail, the master is obliged to get the man medical attention ashore. All seamen paid a percentage of their wages into "Hospital Money," instituted by maritime legislation in 1798 to establish and sup-

port hospitals for sick and disabled mariners; mariners' hospitals were a common feature of ports around the world. Besides trauma cases resulting from accidents and fights, seamen contracted an array of exotic diseases.

55. SH, January 29.

56. SH, January 31. The captain's leadership was considered more vital to the ship's welfare than was his physical labor.

57. SH, January 30.

58. Ibid.

59. Ibid.

60. Susan's preferred spelling, *barque*, is preserved in quoted material.

There are two fundamental ways of rigging (or putting the sails onto) a sailing vessel: square or fore-and-aft. On a square-rigged ship, the largest and most important sails are basically square in shape and attached ("bent") to yardarms ("yards"), pieces of wood that intersect the stout wooden masts "square" ("athwart"), i.e., at right angles. These yards are, within reason, capable of swiveling to catch the winds that drive the ship.

By the mid–nineteenth century, however, the fully square-rigged ship, specifically designated as a *ship* in registrations and so forth, could be seen to have certain disadvantages. Chief among these was the manpower (and danger) involved in raising, lowering, and reefing sails, which involved sending men aloft to shorten (decrease the area of) sails by gathering and tying them to yards. Fore-and-aft sails, running longitudinally on the vessel, could be raised by a system of blocks and pulleys, and shortened from the bottom. The safety factors are obvious, and the economics here are hardly subtle: more manpower equals more expense equals less profit for the ship. Many maritime cultures had realized that versions of fore-and-aft-rigged vessels, such as schooners, required fewer men to work. From the 1840s onward, the building of barks in New England and Britain increased, marking a kind of temporary evolutionary standoff between square and fore-and-aft rigs, and a move toward the colossal, multimasted, oceangoing schooners (completely fore-and-aft rigged) that would dominate merchant sail at the end of the nineteenth century. On a vessel carrying a crew of ten or eleven, the modified mizzen-mast arrangement could cut manpower costs by 20 percent—two fewer men to pay—and give a sail that would "hold her up to the wind."

61. Basil Lubbock, in *The Western Ocean Packets*, ascribes a February 27–March 12, 1859, passage to the *Dreadnought*, under the command of Captain Samuel Samuels. However, this record crossing is more a technical than an actual one, and even the *Dreadnought*'s times between the real ports of Liverpool and New York (as opposed to between lights or waiting mail boats) were often more on the order of thirty days.

62. Enrollments for the Port of Bath, November 29, 1848, no. 56, vol. 16, RG 36, National Archives, Washington, D.C. The *J. J. Hathorn* was built in John Toothaker's shipyard.

63. Billet heads were said to resemble rolled-up letters, from the French *billet*.

64. *American Lloyds' Registry of American and Foreign Shipping*, 1862 edition, lists the information on the *J. J. Hathorn* as bark number 1418; the *Lloyds'* information is confirmed in several other sources, including the definitive work on Kennebec River shipbuilding, William Avery Baker's *Maritime History of Bath, Maine, and the Kennebec River Region*. References to *Lloyds'* are to the *American Lloyds'*.

65. First Class designations were Classes A1, A1-, and A1½; Second Class designations were Classes A1½- and A2. *Lloyds'* ratings were not carved in stone, as *Lloyds'* explains, "Ship owners desirous of having the character of their vessels restored on the American Lloyds['], must submit to a special examination of Frame, Planking and Fastenings, and put in a state of thorough repair" (xii–xiii).

66. *American Lloyds'*, xii–xiii.

67. The *Lloyds'* 1861 edition tells us the *J. J. Hathorn* was last "metalled" in November of 1858, meaning that its hull was clad with copper below the waterline. An 1861 notation informs us that the ship underwent repairs to the deck cabin in 1860, was fitted with a new deck, and had defective timbers removed and replaced prior to the inspection ("the survey," in marine-insurance parlance) carried out in November of 1860. The nature of these repairs suggests that the *J. J. Hathorn* may either have deteriorated or sustained major damages in a grounding, collision, or fire, though no civil records, such as insurance claims, support this. These extensive repairs become more interesting in light of the *J. J. Hathorn*'s last voyage from Liverpool in February 1861.

February

1. SH, February 1. G. P. R. James (1801–60), a prolific English author of historical romances, enjoyed at midcentury a popularity rivaling that of Dickens and Thackeray.

2. SH, February 2.

3. SH, February 1.

4. SH, February 2.

5. SH, February 3. Rufus's identity is not known; no surviving *J. J. Hathorn* documents include anyone so named.

6. SH, February 3.

7. SH, February 6.

8. SH, February 7.

9. SH, February 6. Chronometers needed frequent calibration.

10. Ibid. The sole Incoming Customs Declaration for the *J. J. Hathorn* surviving in the National Archives—the incoming documentation at Philadelphia (from England) in September 1854—amply demonstrates the complexity of maritime bookkeeping tasks.

11. SH, February 8.

12. Ibid.

13. SH, February 5. See Dana, *The Seaman's Friend*, for descriptions of the mates' responsibilities.

14. SH, February 9.

15. Ibid.

16. SH, February 10.

17. Consular Posts, Santiago, Cuba, January 7, 1851–December 15, 1856 (National Archives, Microfilm T55, roll 4, 166–02), RG 59; National Archives, Washington, D.C.

18. The value is exactly $97,200, from which one should deduct the average of the *J. J. Hathorn*'s duplicated cargo declaration ($3,250), for a total of $93,950. On the outgoing (adjusted for the duplication), the total is $124,400.79.

19. SH, February 12.

20. Joan Druett's compendious *"She Was a Sister Sailor": The Whaling Journals of Mary Brewster, 1845–1851*, discusses many first-person accounts of whaling captains' wives, including their mention of the phenomenon of "land legs."

21. SH, February 14.

22. SH, February 12.

23. SH, February 14.

24. SH, February 15.

25. Frank Shay's *An American Sailor's Treasury: Sea Songs, Chanteys, Legends, and Lore* includes a section on nautical superstitions.

26. SH, February 16. This entry confirms the *J. J. Hathorn*'s cargo as ballast.

27. SH, February 16.

28. SH, February 17.

29. SH, February 20.

30. SH, February 21.

31. SH, February 26 and 28.

32. SH, February 19.

33. SH, February 20.

34. SH, February 25.

35. SH, February 21.

36. SH, February 23.

37. SH, February 16.

38. SH, February 26 and 27.

39. SH, February 27.

40. SH, February 28.

March

1. Susan uses *cask* to mean a specific size of small wooden barrel, but a *cask* is not a standard measure. The standard modern U.S. *hogshead* holds 63 gallons, though in some cases containers called *hogsheads* hold as much as 140 gallons; in U.S. usage, the *barrel* for (nonpetroleum) liquid such as the *J. J. Hathorn* is carrying accommodates 31.5 gallons; the *tierce*, a size of cask usually used for spirits, measures 42 wine gallons.

2. SH, March 1.

3. Aboard mid-nineteenth-century ships, as on land, the main meal of the day was midday "dinner."

4. SH, March 2.

5. In *Two Years Before the Mast*, Dana designates a nearly identical situation as mutiny.

6. Consular Despatches, Trinidad, Cuba (National Archives, Microfilm T699, roll 4), RG 59; National Archives, Washington, D.C.

7. SH, March 2.

8. SH, March 3.

9. SH, March 5.

10. SH, March 6.

11. Large merchant ships sometimes carried a person known as the supercargo to over-

see the safety of the cargo on behalf of the shipowners, to whom the agents had entrusted the cargo. The supercargo position was a sinecure and the person who held it considered an "idler" by the crew. Often called the "ship's cousin," a supercargo was often an actual relative of the shipowners. The father of Jode's distant cousin Nathaniel Hawthorne was a supercargo when he perished at sea.

12. SH, March 7.

13. SH, March 8.

14. An exception to this regulation was made for certain outsized lumber used in shipbuilding, too long to fit into holds; such deck cargo was permitted only during calm seasons.

15. Susan's description of the ship heeling over (March 19: "The ship lays over a great deal and makes it worse than it is") indicates that the Trinidad stevedores did not do a perfect job.

16. SH, March 5.

17. SH, March 6.

18. SH, March 13.

19. SH, March 12. This is a combined Sunday/Monday entry.

20. SH, March 8. The Maine Maritime Museum's Captain's File lists Captain William Mann of Yarmouth, but offers as biographical data only his marriage, which took place in 1852. The Consular Return for Trinidad de Cuba reports his bark *Archimedes'* tonnage as 298.

21. There is no evidence that Susan spoke any Spanish, which may have contributed to her isolation. Susan's letter to Emily Whitten indicates that, besides English, Susan knew only Latin, though she was planning to learn French.

22. SH, March 10. Susan follows the nineteenth-century spelling *musquito* throughout.

23. SH, March 12.

24. SH, March 9. Susan seems to use "cook" and "steward" interchangeably; it is unlikely that both a cook and a steward would have wives accompanying them, or that a vessel of the *J. J. Hathorn*'s size would include both a cook and a steward.

25. SH, March 10.

26. SH, March 12.

27. SH, March 13.

28. George Bickford, a cousin of Jode's on his mother's side, is listed as mate also on the crew list for the *J. J. Hathorn*'s last sailing from Liverpool on February 14, 1861.

29. SH, March 13.

30. SH, March 14.

31. Ibid.

32. SH, March 15.

33. While articles of shipping often addressed the subject of spirits, no articles for the *J. J. Hathorn* have been recovered. In the 1850s some naval vessels still provided the twice daily gill (four fluid ounces) of grog (a dilution of one part rum to one and a half parts water), but the distribution of grog was not a common practice in the merchant fleet. Susan does not mention grog being distributed on the *J. J. Hathorn*.

34. SH, March 1.

35.   Dana, *The Seaman's Friend*, 86–87.

36.   On some vessels, data were first recorded on a slate in the aftercabin by the mate who had just finished his watch, then read and "corrected" by the master, and finally, at the end of each day, transcribed into the permanent logbook by the first mate, who was officially responsible for the log. However, on many smaller merchant vessels, the ship's master kept the log himself. Dana, *The Seaman's Friend*, 134, 145, 198.

37.   Susan Hathorn's accounts are reproduced in full in appendix F.

38.   Susan occasionally refers to *luggage*, but her customary word for suitcases is *budgets*. If she uses *budgets* in its strict sense, her luggage is leather.

39.   SH, January 19.

40.   Carroll Smith-Rosenberg and others have discussed at length the concept of the "woman's sphere."

41.   SH, February 2.

42.   SH, January 25.

43.   SH, March 16. Susan is never able to identify this vessel by name.

44.   SH, March 17.

45.   SH, March 16. See also the reference to Jode's reading of *Old Mortality*, another of the Waverley novels, at the end of this month.

46.   SH, March 17.

47.   SH, March 19 and 20.

48.   SH, March 20.

49.   SH, March 21, 22, and 23.

50.   W. H. MacLeish's *The Gulf Stream* provides more detail on the history and hydrography. Between Florida and Cuba, the stream is known as the Florida Current.

51.   SH, March 27, 28, 29, and 30.

52.   SH, March 31.

53.   SH, March 23, 24, 26, 28, 29, and 30.

April

1.   British archivists at the Guildhall Library of the City of London, the National Maritime Museum in Greenwich, and the Public Records Office in Kew report that official records for the Port of London for the nineteenth century no longer exist, having been discarded earlier in this century, without being microfilmed, as too voluminous to preserve. The assumption that the Hathorns docked at St. Katherine's Dock is based on its proximity to the America Square boardinghouse, as well as to the sugar and spirits warehouses in that quarter. It is possible that the *J. J. Hathorn* docked at the West India Docks, somewhat farther downstream. Susan, however, says nothing about taking the cars or train between the bark and their lodgings, or Jode's commuting daily for the landing of the cargo.

2.   SH, April 2 [1 and 2]. This is a combined Sunday/Monday entry.

3.   SH, April 2.

4.   SH, April 3.

5.   SH, April 4.

6.   SH, April 11.

7.   SH, April 14.

8.   SH, April 5.

9.   SH, April 19 and 20.

10. SH, May 2.

11. SH, May 3, 4, and 5. 'Scouse (or lobscouse), a staple of the maritime diet, was a stew of bits of salt meat, broken biscuits, potatoes, onions, and whatever spices were available.

12. Ships' cooks—whose talents and access to ingredients produced rather poor food—were viewed askance by the working crew as being "idlers"—members of the crew who did not stand normal watch with the sailors. Idlers also included, when present, the ship's carpenter, sailmaker, painter, supercargo, and boatswain; the *J. J. Hathorn*, being a smaller vessel, probably did not have any idler other than the cook. Peter Kemp, *The Oxford Companion to Ships and the Sea*, 414.

   The generally celibate nature of life at sea makes for curious realignments of gender-associated tasks. Sea cooks were almost invariably male, and even if a captain's wife had sailed with the ship, her place was in the aftercabin, not the galley. See Margaret S. Creighton, *Rites and Passages*.

13. SH, April 28.

14. Recent studies comment on motivations for diary writing among nineteenth-century American women, whose diaries fused such impulses as a rigorous work ethic with a confessional purpose and spiritual self-examination. See Mary Anne Wallace, "Days of Joy and Fear: Nineteenth-Century New England Family Life at Sea," and Jane H. Hunter, "Inscribing the Self in the Heart of the Family: Diaries and Girlhood in Late-Victorian America."

15. Though Susan's *cappiola* is either an unrecorded colloquialism or a word of her own invention, she is probably making a close-fitting cap for casual daily wear, meant to control the long hair women wore at this time; patterns for daytime caps—knitted, crocheted, netted—abound in needlework instruction books and periodicals published in the mid-1800s.

16. SH, April 10.

17. SH, April 5.

18. SH, April 4.

19. The term *bluestocking* for a woman of literary or scholarly inclinations dates from the eighteenth century.

20. SH, April 4.

21. The first-time browser in the *Atlas of Pilot Charts* will be struck by the differences in navigation conditions from month to month throughout the year. A large, thin volume that preserves a wealth of data with absolute economy, the *Atlas* is roughly twenty by thirty inches and just nineteen pages thick. It does not present the geographic features of regular navigation charts, but focuses on sailing conditions and calculates statistical averages for decades of collected data about weather and currents on a separate chart for each month. Of land-mass features it shows principally locations of large ports and the general coastline, without location of lights or soundings, although the "100 fathom curve" is indicated around most coastlines.

22. The *Atlas* shows that the distance from Great Abaco Island in the Bahamas to a

midocean point at 43°N 50°W, which the Hathorns passed close to, is 1,674 nautical miles; then the distance from 43°N 50°W to Bishop Rock off the southwest coast of Cornwall (49°40′N 6°34′W) is 1,816 nautical miles. Dr. John Harland and Stanton Crapo provided insight into this navigational problem.

23.   To put this in present-day context, the Blue Ribband (eastbound and westbound) for transatlantic passenger travel is held by the *United States*, for its consecutive July 1952 maiden voyages. The record time is 3 days, 10 hours, 40 minutes; the top speeds of the *United States* on those voyages was in excess of 36 knots. John Malcolm Brinnin's *The Sway of the Grand Saloon* discusses this in detail. The *QE2*'s transatlantic average speed is 28 knots; modern cruise ships normally cannot exceed 18 knots.

24.   *Atlas of Pilot Charts*, April.

25.   SH, April 8, 9, 10, 11, 12, 13, and 14.

26.   SH, April 16. This is a combined Sunday/Monday entry.

27.   SH, April 17, 18, 19, and 20.

28.   SH, April 2.

29.   SH, April 28 and 29, and May 2, 3, and 4.

30.   SH, May 5.

31.   SH, May 7.

32.   SH, May 8.

May

1.   SH, May 10.

2.   *London: The Blue Guide*, 275–76. Named for the ancient St. Katherine's Royal Hospital, founded on the site in 1148 by Queen Matilda, the dock is still in operation as a private yacht basin. See also *Baedecker's London and Its Environs* (1908 edition), 140–44.

3.   Not *American*, as Susan writes it in an atypical slip.

4.   This railroad ran from the East India Dock at Blackwall Reach, past the West India Dock on the Isle of Dogs, on to the Church Street Station. Today Tower Hill Underground Station lies beneath America Square.

5.   "This crescent is remarkably intact with identical terraced houses, each with its semi-mass-produced doorways and well-designed classical detail. South of the crescent is another fragment of Dance's original scheme, a tiny circus, and north of this project a square named America Square, built to commemorate the American Colonies, but now almost derelict." *The Shell Guide to The History of London*, 1981, 295–96. The derelict buildings have since been razed and replaced with high-rise office buildings housing insurance firms.

6.   For discussions of the public perception and social acceptance of maritime people, see, e.g., Valerie Burton's "The Myth of Bachelor Jack: Masculinity, Patriarchy and Seafaring Labour"; Charles P. Kindleberger's *Mariners and Markets*; Richard J. Cleveland's *In the Forecastle; or, Twenty-five Years a Sailor*; Margaret Creighton's "American Mariners and the Rites of Manhood, 1830–1870"; and Basil Greenhill and Denis Stonham's *Seafaring under Sail: The Life of the Merchant Seaman*.

7.   SH, May 10. Susan later corrects her spelling of *Howes* and *Cleaveland*; also, she refers to "the Misses Bragge" in her May 26 entry.

8.   At the sixteen addresses of America Square, *Watkins's Commercial and General London Directory and Court Guide for 1855* lists James Little & Son, builders; Wm. Morse Batho, solicitor; Mrs. Elizbth. Brunton's lodging house; Mrs. Lavinia Brewis's lodging house; James Stanes and Son, china dealers; Brass and Stanes, shipowners; Ford & Curtis, wine and provisions merchants; Miss Elizabeth Bragge's boardinghouse; William J. Creed's boardinghouse; Andrew White, spirit merchant; Mrs. Mary Ellis's boardinghouse; Leach & Clark, ship and insurance agents; Thomas James Lough, merchant and general agent; William Palmer, wine importer; Mrs. Sarah Willis's boardinghouse; and Heisch Cox and Co., merchants.

Earlier in the nineteenth century, Baron Meyer de Rothschild, who would have had compatible interests, reportedly resided at Number 14 America Square. *Watkins's* clearly shows Number 14 jointly occupied in 1855 by Thomas J. Lough, merchant and general agent, and William Palmer, wine importer. Number 14 America Square, badly damaged by World War II bombing in 1941, was subsequently demolished. (*Dictionary of City of London Street Names* [New York: Arco Publishing Co., Inc., 1970], 15.)

9.   Presumably this Jersey is the British Channel Island, not New Jersey, yet the coincidence of the surname of Alexander suggests that the census taker may have confused the two.

10.   By 1855, Number 9 had been absorbed into the Bragge establishment.

11.   Between Numbers 5 and 6 on Crosswall was situated the local "Engine House," and at Number 10, we find the surgeon Andrew Holman. Also on John were three coffeehouses and a boardinghouse in operation. The name of George Street, the short street that crosses Vine north of John, was later changed to India Street.

12.   The Angel was still an operating pub in the mid-1990s. *Watkins's Commercial and General London Directory and Court Guide for 1855* includes the following occupants on John Street: an Australian merchant, five merchants, a ship and insurance agent, two wine merchants, a police inspector, a ship's provision merchant, a pilot agent, an "Engine House," a Mrs. Quinland, two boot and shoe makers, a Mrs. Wight's lodging house, a surgeon, a tailor, a ship agent, a painter, a sugar refiner, a ship broker, Henry J. Sly's "Angel Tavern," the "Hamburg Coffee House," an importer of foreign goods, a cork manufacturer, a cork merchant, an importer of "italian stores," a ship's grocer, Mrs. Sarah Aubery's coffeehouse, a tailor, a stationer and tobacconist, and Mrs. Sarah Coles, listed as a "carrier."

13.   *Watkins's Commercial and General London Directory and Court Guide for 1855.*

14.   SH, May 11.

15.   Ibid.

16.   Kemp, *Oxford Companion to Ships and the Sea*, 810; see also, e.g., Herman Melville's *Redburn*.

17.   SH, May 12. Soule is a prominent mid-nineteenth-century Maine maritime name.

18.   SH, May 12.

19.   SH, May 14 and 15.

20.   SH, May 15.

21.   Mary Anne Wallace's paper "Ocean Sisterhood" and thesis "Days of Joy and Fear" discuss the journal-letter form and its function in the maritime family.

In addition, the archives at Mount Holyoke indicate that journal-letter writing was well established at the college by Susan's time there. Mount Holyoke journal-letters were circulating reports of graduates and former students who had gone abroad on missionary work.

22. SH, May 15.

23. SH, May 16.

24. SH, May 17.

25. Briggs, *Iron Bridge to Crystal Palace*, 165.

26. Quoted in Ibid. 172.

27. SH, May 18. The book Susan has found so absorbing, *The Lofty and the Lowly*, is an episodic escapist romance, an example of the pulp novels published for nineteenth-century female readers.

28. SH, May 18.

29. Ibid.

30. Priscilla Metcalf, *Victorian London*, 19.

31. The *ILN* review denounces "a fearful increase of portraits, one or two of outrageous dimensions." May 12, 1855, 457.

32. Some of the Bragge house sojourners did attend the theater, though Susan did not.

33. *ILN*, May 19, 1855, 476.

34. *ILN*, May 12, 1855, 451.

35. *ILN*, May 26, 1855, 506.

36. SH, May 19.

37. The Thames Tunnel has since 1865 been part of the London underground network, carrying Metropolitan Line subway trains.

38. SH, May 19.

39. SH, May 21.

40. SH, May 10, 12, 16, 18, and 19.

41. SH, May 21.

42. SH, May 22.

43. SH, May 22 and 23.

44. SH, May 24.

45. SH, May 25.

46. Ibid.

47. SH, May 26.

48. Ibid.

June

1. SH, May 27. May 27 and 28 are a combined Sunday/Monday entry.

2. SH, May 27.

3. SH, May 28.

4. Ibid.

5. SH, May 29.

6. Ibid.

7. SH, May 30.
8. Ibid.
9. Harriet Beecher Stowe's steamship voyage was considerably shorter.
10. Harriet Beecher Stowe, *Sunny Memories of Foreign Lands*, 1.
11. Ibid., 1–2.
12. Ibid., 2.
13. Ibid., 2–3.
14. Ibid., 4.
15. Ibid., 5.
16. Ibid., 7.
17. Ibid., 18.
18. SH, May 30. Susan's comment may be relevant in light of Jode's death, eleven months later.
19. SH, May 31.
20. Kemp, *Oxford Companion to Ships and the Sea*, 696. As Kemp explains, sails up to and including topsails have sewn into them two rows of "reef-points" or rope ties, by means of which the sail is pinched or pleated to shorten it.
21. Ibid., 70.
22. SH, May 31.
23. SH, June 1.
24. Ibid.
25. Other than a conviction on slave trafficking charges, little could confirm such an allegation. This "rumor" was reported by John A. Robbins Jr. of Richmond. The only rationale Robbins could offer for the story was that the Hathorn Block had, built some distance into the hill behind it (extending what would be the first story on Front Street), a large cellar area, and he supposed that it could be a place to detain slaves.

However, others indicate this is improbable. African slaves transported to Maine would have been free there; the U.S. Censuses of 1850 and 1860 for Richmond enumerate several free people of color. African slave routes never included the circuitous trip to Maine, and the cellar was more probably for roots, spirits, and semi-perishable goods acquired through maritime trade. Moreover, any vessel used to transport slaves would have to be fitted with shallow decks that would make it unuseable as a cargo vessel.

26. Situated at $51°10'$N $4°40'$W, Lundy Island stands in the Bristol Channel about ten land miles north off Hartland Point in Exmoor. Susan has misunderstood the island's name, confusing it with the Bay of Fundy, which separates Nova Scotia from Maine.
27. SH, June 2.
28. Ibid.
29. SH, June 3. Fannie is probably Frances Fosler, and Hosea Hildreth Lennan is Susan's brother.
30. SH, June 4.
31. SH, June 5.
32. Ibid. The Major alluded to appears in later entries.
33. SH, June 6.
34. *Hunt and Co. Directory*, 12.
35. SH, June 7.

36. SH, June 8.
37. Ibid.
38. SH, June 9.
39. Ibid.
40. Ibid.
41. SH, June 10.
42. Ibid.
43. SH, June 11.
44. Ibid.
45. *Hunt and Co. Directory*, 27.
46. *Imperial Gazetteer*, 706.
47. SH, June 12.
48. SH, June 13. While maritime law required U.S. nationals to return to U.S. ports on the ship on which they left the country, consular files are full of reports on sailors discharged "with cause." Consular reports from Liverpool, for example, where Jode's distant relative Nathaniel Hawthorne was consul at this time, include affidavits of any number of captains and mates who appeared attesting to the circumstances of a crew member's dismissal, death, or desertion.
49. SH, June 15. Susan suggests that at least one of the crew who left the ship in London rejoined it in Cardiff.
50. This is the opinion of Dr. David Perkins, National Museum of Wales Maritime and Industrial Museum, Bute Dock, Cardiff.
51. SH, June 13.
52. SH, June 14 and 15.
53. SH, June 16.
54. SH, June 17.
55. Ibid.
56. SH, June 18.
57. *Shipping and Commercial List* (June 20, 1855), 1.
58. *Shipping and Commercial List* (June 16, 1855), 1. Some of the larger ports categorize their lists by type of vessel, listing full-rigged ships first, then "barques," then schooners, etc. This in part accounts for the lack of exact chronological order in the listing.

The captain of the *Jos. Jones*, arriving May 28, is listed as "Hosmer," probably a reporting error, for Susan and Jode become well enough acquainted with the man to be aware of the correct spelling of his name.

When Susan reports on June 18, "Capt. Wheeler went to Newport," there is either a subsequent change in the captain's plans or Susan has named the wrong captain. Captain Wheeler, a favorite of the Hathorns and Susan in particular, figures in several additional diary entries in Cardiff, and the *Shipping and Commercial List* does not show him departing on June 18.

59. SH, June 19.
60. Ibid.
61. Technically, these are the applications for Seamen's Protection Papers, filed under "An Act for the Relief and Protection of American Seamen." A partial, indexed collection is held in the National Archives. Seamen's Protection Papers Application Abstract

for Plymouth, N.C., January 1–March 31, 1831, box 11, no. 5856, RG 36, National Archives, Washington, D.C.

62.   John A. Robbins Jr., Richmond, Maine, researched the Hathorn genealogical material.

63.   SH, June 22.

64.   Ibid. Susan usually writes *Capt.s* for *Captains*.

65.   SH, June 20.

66.   SH, June 21 and 22.

67.   SH, June 22.

68.   SH, June 23.

69.   SH, June 20 and 21.

70.   SH, June 21 and 23.

71.   SH, June 26.

72.   Ibid.

73.   SH, June 23. Mary Pollard, whom Susan met in January in Santiago, was the Spanish wife of an English physician.

74.   SH, June 24.

75.   Ibid.

76.   SH, June 26.

77.   SH, June 27.

78.   Ibid. Susan will give these letters to the towboat when Jode returns.

79.   SH, June 28.

80.   Ibid. Susan persists in calling the Bristol Channel island "Fundy."

81.   SH, June 20.

82.   SH, June 29 and 30.

83.   Ibid.

July

1.   "The Ship Graduate." See appendix B.

2.   Ibid. The excessive punctuation of the "Ship Graduate" essay is not present in Susan's diary, and so may be the copyists' addition.

3.   SH, July 1.

4.   SH, July 2. This is a combined Sunday/Monday entry.

5.   SH, July 3, 4, 5, 6, and 7.

6.   SH, July 14.

7.   SH, July 19.

8.   SH, July 22.

9.   SH, Accounts, July. See appendix F.

10.   SH, July 2, 4, and 7.

11.   SH, July 8. This is a combined Sunday/Monday entry.

12.   SH, July 9, 10, 12, 13, 14, 15, 16, 18, and 19.

13.   SH, July 20.

14.   SH, July 24 and 25.

15. SH, July 27 and 31, and August 3.
16. SH, August 4.
17. SH, July 3.
18. SH, July 2, 13, 16, 17, 19, 26, and 30, and August 3.
19. SH, July 7 and 22.
20. SH, July 11 and 14.
21. Benicia is named for the California bay where Lemuel Brown's ship was at anchor.
22. SH, July 27.
23. SH, July 31.
24. SH, August 1.
25. SH, August 3 and 2.
26. SH, August 3.
27. SH, August 4.

August

1.   Cholera is an acute infection of the small intestine, and the disease's swift course produces rapid, severe dehydration caused by massive diarrhea. A whole century would pass before tetracycline would enable physicians to eradicate the causative organism in infected patients.

2.   Dr. Abial Libby, Report to the Maine Medical Society, n.d., Richmond Historical and Cultural Society files.

3.   Sturtevant Notes, Richmond Historical and Cultural Society; Walter H. Sturtevant and Ruie L. Curtis, *Richmond on the Kennebec*, 101.

4.   Though both associated with tropical ports and transmitted by mosquito bites, the causes of malaria and yellow fever were not at the time clearly understood.

5.   SH, February 19, 20, and 24. Yellow fever and malaria both involve high fevers; the yellow fever protozoan parasite causes anemia and inflammation of the spleen, and the yellow fever arbovirus attacks the liver, causing jaundice. As early as 1700, quinine was known to be an effective cure for malaria. On the other hand, yellow fever—now considered a "preventable disease" through control of mosquito populations and use of live-virus vaccines—is even today a disease treated for its symptoms, though modern treatment methods have dropped the fatality rate for yellow fever to about 10 percent. (*Encyclopaedia Britannica*, 1976 ed., "malaria" and "yellow fever," *Merck Manual* [Rahway, N.J.: Merck & Co., Inc., 1977], 57–58, 159–62.)

6.   SH, October 2.

7.   SH, March 20. This is the first time Susan alludes to the *J. J. Hathorn's* being in Savannah previously, though her subsequent entries confirm this.

8.   *Shipping and Commercial List and New York Prices Current*, September 23, 1854; October 25, 1854; November 4, 1854; December 20, 1854; May 30, 1855; June 9, 1855; June 20, 1855; July 14, 1855; and August 29, 1855.

9.   SH, August 4.

10. SH, August 16 and 17.

11. SH, August 7, 10, and 11. Nautical logs and diaries use *sail* as both singular and plural in referring to vessels sighted.

12. SH, August 12, 13, and 18.

13. SH, August 5. *Lalla Rookh*, the Irish romantic Thomas Moore's wildly popular orientalist poem that was first published in 1817, clearly was a favorite of mariners, judging from the number of vessels so named.

14. Mary Anne Wallace and Joan Druett have both observed that Susan's secular reading on a Sunday does not adhere to the usual practice among captain's wives.

15. SH, August 6.

16. SH, August 7, 8, 9, and 10.

17. SH, August 11.

18. SH, August 14.

19. SH, August 15.

20. SH, August 20.

21. SH, August 16.

22. SH, August 18.

23. SH, August 19 and 20. This a combined Sunday/Monday entry.

24. SH, August 21.

25. SH, August 22.

26. Ibid.

27. SH, August 23. Susan's initial misspelling of Captain Dickerson's name indicates that the Hathorns were not houseguests of the Dickersons during their November 1854 stop in Savannah.

28. SH, August 24.

29. *Directory of the City of Savannah, for the Year 1850*, 14.

30. *Directory of the City of Savannah*, 1858, 24.

31. *Directory of the City of Savannah*, 1859, 69.

32. The designation *stevedore*, in the *Directory of the City of Savannah*, is misleading.

33. SH, August 27. Montgomery has become a northeast suburb of Savannah.

34. SH, August 27.

35. SH, August 28 and 29.

36. SH, August 29, 30, and 31, and September 1.

37. SH, September 2.

38. SH, August 29 and 30, and September 2, 3, and 4.

39. SH, September 4.

40. SH, September 5.

41. Ibid.

42. SH, September 6.

43. Ibid.

44. SH, September 6 and 7.

45. SH, September 7.

46. *Directory of the City of Savannah*, 1850, 64.

47. *Directory of the City of Savannah*, 1859, 125. Susan spells the boardinghouse keeper's name with an *e*; the city directories' spellings vary.

48. SH, September 8.

September

1. Some 60 percent of the nation's rail mileage in 1850 was in New England and mid-Atlantic states, giving those regions tremendous economic and strategic military advantages that the South sought to negate. The growth of U.S. railroads during the 1850s was phenomenal, more than tripling in that decade (from 9,021 miles in 1850 to 30,626 miles in 1860 [Statistical Abstract of the United States, U.S. Department of Commerce, Washington, D.C.: GPO]). Railroads were to play an important role in the Civil War in carrying troops and supplies, and the South's less extensive railroad system would eventually contribute to the Confederacy's military defeat.

2. SH, September 8.

3. SH, September 9. The combination of writing tools suggests Susan may well have written these entries aboard the *Alabama*.

4. Ibid.

5. SH, September 10.

6. This *Alabama* served in a civilian capacity until it was fitted out for duty at the New York Navy Yard and commissioned on September 30, 1861. According to the *Dictionary of American Naval Fighting Ships* (vol. I., Washington, D.C.: Navy Department, Office of Chief of Naval Operations, 1959), 18, this *Alabama* enjoyed a distinguished subsequent naval career, taking part in the blockade of Charleston, and capturing four (or three, according to Erik Heyl, *Early American Steamers*) vessels between October 1861 and July 1863, during which period it participated in the expedition along the coasts of Florida and Georgia and assisted in the capture of Fernandina, Florida, on March 4, 1862. Following a yellow fever epidemic among the crew in Key West in July 1863, the *Alabama* was ordered to Portsmouth, New Hampshire, for quarantine and decommissioning, but the following May the *Alabama* was recommissioned and returned to action off the North Carolina coast, first in the blockading squadron off Wilmington, assisting in the capture of a blockade runner, and later participating in the two naval bombardments of Fort Fisher. After this action, it operated as an ordnance and dispatch vessel at Hampton Roads, Virginia, and then saw service towing vessels from Hampton Roads to Philadelphia; following decommissioning on July 14, 1885, the *Alabama* was sold and returned to civilian service.

7. A month after the Hathorns' trip, on October 13, 1855, New York port records show that the *Alabama* began extending its southern run beyond Savannah to the ports on Florida's eastern coast, and over the next six years, until the beginning of the Civil War, the *Alabama* would continue on this run (Heyl, *Early American Steamers*, 7).

Heyl's account follows the *Alabama*'s return to civilian service in Florida waters, which was largely unsuccessful. With the Florida routes not economically rewarding, the vessel was sold and moved north, where for about five years she was operated by a company of three Connecticut owners. On March 21, 1878, the *Alabama*'s papers were surrendered with the cryptic notation "Vessel and papers destroyed by fire," though without exact date, location, and cause of the accident.

8. SH, September 10.

9. Norman Brouwer, "The United States Hotel," 6, 9.

10. Ibid., 6.

11. Ibid., 6, 9.

12. Ibid., 9. By 1855, the hotel had left the hands of the impecunious Stephen Holt for those of a Mr. Johnson, who installed the water closets.

13. SH, September 10.

14. Heyl discusses one *Metropolis*, an 878-ton wooden-hulled screw-driven vessel built in 1861, which does not appear in the authoritative "Lytle-Holdcamper List"; this vessel had an eventful career in the Civil War and met an eventually disastrous civilian end. See Heyl, *Early American Steamers*, 255–56.

15. American Steamship Notes, Mariners' Museum Library, put the *Metropolis*'s tonnage at 2,210.

16. *New York Marine Register*, 1857, 328–29. This publication is devoted to steam-powered vessels, similar in format to the *American Lloyds'*.

17. American Steamship Notes, Mariners' Museum Library. Moreover, these notes describe the *Metropolis* as structurally unusual, having been "built on the plans of the ocean steamships of her time, the hull timbers being carried to the second deck, and diagonally braced there by doing away with the hog frame."

18. Charles Dickens bemoaned his accommodations on the "*Britannia* steam packet" in *American Notes*.

19. SH, September 12.

20. Lemuel Brown had by this time restricted his activities to vessels involved in coastal trading, instead of "blue water" (around-the-Cape) ships. This would possibly explain why Lemuel Brown doesn't appear in Susan's account of the homecoming on Tuesday, but then does appear on Friday.

21. SH, September 13 and 14.

22. Ibid.

23. Ibid.

24. SH, September 14.

25. Ibid.

26. Ibid.

27. Ibid.

28. SH, September 15.

29. Presumably back to the Richmond House from Sally and Lemuel Brown's.

30. SH, September 15. Susan later corrects her spelling of Miss Wait's name.

31. SH, September 16.

32. According to Charles Sinnett, "The Sturdy Hathorn Family," J. J. Hathorn was survived by his widow, Mary E. Springer Hathorn, whom he had married in July of 1840, and the two of their five children who survived infancy, Philena W. (b. 1844, married Henry Sawyer, 1861) and Frances B. (b. 1846, married Zaccheus Allen, 1870).

33. In 1868 his widow, Mary, petitioned for a commission to set off and assign her dower rights (that is, divide her interest, presumably so she could dispose of it) in what is still known in Richmond as the "Brickyard Lot."

34. This hill is probably the source of the clay used to make the bricks of the Hathorn Block, as listed among J. J. Hathorn's business activities was the manufacture of bricks.

35. SH, September 17.

36. SH, September 18.

37. SH, September 19, 20, 21, and 24.

38. SH, September 19.

39. SH, September 20 and 21.

40. SH, September 23.

41. Ibid.

42. SH, September 24. "Iffy" is Jefferson Hathorn Jr., Jode's younger brother, who is fifteen. Miss Wait boards at Richmond House.

43. SH, September 24.

44. SH, September 25, 26, and 27.

45. SH, September 27.

46. SH, September 28.

47. Ibid.

48. That Susan did not know the featherstitch is surprising, since it is an easy and rather basic embroidery stitch.

49. SH, September 29.

50. SH, September 25.

51. SH, September 26.

52. SH, September 30.

53. SH, September 26.

54. SH, September 30.

October

1. Aubigne Packard, *A Town That Went to Sea*, 402.

2. Ibid., 404.

3. Ibid.

4. SH, October 1.

5. SH, October 2.

6. Sturtevant and Curtis, *Richmond on the Kennebec*, 91.

7. SH, September 25 and November 21.

8. From a photograph reproduced in *Richmond: A Long View, 1823–1973* (n.p.).

9. Sturtevant and Curtis, *Richmond on the Kennebec*, 39. This section is based on an oral account by Charles Farrin, member of a family of Richmond shipbuilders closely associated with the Hathorns.

10. See Braun, "T. J. Southard," 8, and Mark Hennessy, "Richmond Dreams for Another Jeff Southard," 4. A more dramatic account, Braun's version has T. J. making his trek at age eleven, but Hennessy plainly states that T. J. made his trip in 1819, which would make him a more likely seventeen years old.

11. Braun, "T. J. Southard," 8, and William Hutchinson Rowe, *The Maritime History of Maine: Three Centuries of Shipbuilding and Seafaring*, 157.

12.   William Avery Baker, *Maritime History of Bath, Maine, and the Kennebec River Region*, 956–63. Baker, who is considered the authority, lists seventy-five Southard vessels, but some anecdotal accounts place Southard's output as high as 115 vessels.

13.   It is important to note that "the owner" was the largest but seldom the sole shareholder in a vessel.

14.   This list comes from Baker, *Maritime History*, and the Captain's File at the Maine Maritime Museum Library.

15.   Polly Roberts, longtime secretary of the Richmond Historical Association, had this list (since transferred to the Richmond Historical Association's archives) in her papers at the time of her death, and its entries corroborate many of those in the Captain's File at the Maine Maritime Museum. This list does not give years.

16.   Ibid.

17.   *Richmond Bee* (undated clipping, 1884), from the Richmond Historical Society files.

18.   In the 1990s the Richmond House building still stands on the north side of Main Street a few doors up the hill from Front Street, much as originally configured—a two-story frame building, standing with its gable facing the street—its third floor no longer present.

19.   *Richmond Bee* (undated clipping, 1884).

20.   Ibid. SH, September 17. Jode's death in May 1856 accounts for the fact that Jefferson, not Jode, "improved" the farm.

21.   The complete inventory of Jefferson Hathorn's estate includes evidence of the many accounts owing to him and the estate's small liability to Dr. Abial Libby, who attended his final illness.

22.   An incorrectly computed total of $17,941.82 was filed; it should be $17,936.82. The estate inventory included, among other things, the following:

10 Shares in the Richmond National Bank	1150.00
8 " " " Building Loan Association	1224.00
10 " " " Richmond Manufacturing Association	1.00
2 " " " Richmond Academy	16.00
House Hold Furniture including Safe & silverware	600.00
45 Tons of Pressed Hay on Ferry farm 12.75	573.75
20 " " Loose " " Ferry " 10.50	210.10
35 " " Pressed " " Blair " 12.75	446.25
12 " " Loose " " Blair " 10.50	126.00
1 Horse	125.00
1 Sleigh & Robe	20.00
2 Harness	10.00
1 Platform Scale	6.00
1 Horse Waggon	25.00
1 Buggy Waggon	60.00
1 Jack Screw	5.00
Set of chains 2.00 Blocks & Jawl 3.00	5.00
1 Hay Knife 1.50 Chest of tools 10.	11.50

1 Grind Stone 1.50 1 Grind Stone 3.00 ....   4.50
1 Plow 5.00 1 Plow 2.50 1 Wheel barrow 1.50 ....   9.00
1 Old Mowing Machine 5.00
1 Cultivator 3.00
1 Single Horse Cars or Waggon 22.00

23. SH, October 3.
24. SH, October 4.
25. SH, October 5.
26. SH, October 6.
27. Ibid.
28. SH, October 8.
29. SH, October 9.
30. Ibid.
31. SH, October 10.
32. Ibid.
33. SH, October 11.
34. Ibid.
35. SH, October 13.
36. Presently U.S. Highway 201.
37. SH, October 14, 17, and 18. The last passage's "little Lancaster girl" suggests that the equestrienne Lucy is the younger.
38. SH, October 19.
39. Ibid.
40. SH, October 20.
41. SH, October 21. The *sailing* date of October 7 does not conflict with the October 3 date for clearing customs.
42. SH, October 22, 23, 25, 26, and 27.
43. SH, October 22.
44. SH, October 25. Jefferson Hathorn was a member of the state railway commission, according to his obituary.
45. SH, October 25.
46. SH, October 12, 15, 16, 18, 19, 20, 22, 23, 24, 25, 26, and 27.
47. SH, October 29.
48. SH, October 30.
49. SH, October 31.
50. Ibid.
51. SH, October 27.

November

1. SH, November 3. Richmond is downriver from Gardiner; Susan's preposition is a lapse that her Monday's entry corrects.
2. SH, November 5.

3. SH, November 6.

4. SH, November 7.

5. SH, November 8.

6. Ibid.

7. SH, November 8 and 10.

8. SH, November 9.

9. See the work of Mary Anne Wallace, particularly her master's thesis, "Days of Joy and Fear," and Lisa A. Norling's dissertation relating more specifically to the New England whalefishery, "Captain Ahab Had a Wife."

10. SH, ledger.

11. SH, ledger.

12. SH, November 4 and 5.

13. SH, November 6.

14. Sagadahoc County, in which Richmond is located, split off from Lincoln County in 1853.

15. SH, November 11.

16. The gravestone in the Hathorn family plot in Evergreen Cemetery names Volney as a son of Jefferson Sr. and Sally.

17. SH, November 14.

18. SH, November 15.

19. SH, November 7 and 12.

20. SH, November 15.

21. Baker, *Maritime History*, 956–63. The builder of record is S. C. Colby, though Susan's diary makes clear Capt. Hathorn was personally involved in the *Melvin*'s construction.

22. SH, November 22.

23. SH, November 20.

24. SH, November 21.

25. SH, November 20 to 30.

26. SH, November 23 and 25.

27. SH, November 28.

28. *Shipping and Commercial List*, November 10 and December 5, 1855.

29. SH, November 23.

30. SH, November 25.

31. SH, November 26.

32. The preeclampsia syndrome includes hypertension, albuminuria, and/or edema and may lead to full-blown eclampsia, a potentially fatal condition involving coma and seizures.

33. SH, November 10, 15, and 16.

34. SH, November 17.

35. SH, November 27.

36. SH, November 29.

37. Ibid.

38. SH, November 30 and December 1.

December

1. SH, November 24.
2. SH, December 3.
3. SH, December 4.
4. SH, December 8.
5. SH, December 9, 14, 17, 18, and 19.
6. SH, December 21.
7. SH, December 22.
8. SH, December 25.
9. SH, December 26.
10. SH, December 28.
11. SH, December 27.
12. SH, November 29 and December 5.
13. SH, December 6.
14. This flag project seems to have been neither intricate nor time-consuming.
15. SH, December 28.
16. SH, December 1.
17. "Thibet"—named for the country of Tibet—was a woolen coating fabric finished with a smooth, heavily-felted face.
18. SH, December 7.
19. SH, December 11.
20. SH, ledger.
21. Since "Geo. A. Bickford" is listed as the *J. J. Hathorn*'s first mate on the crew list filed in Liverpool in November 1855, the Mr. Bickford visiting Richmond House in December 1855 may have been Revel or Edward, the man with whom Jefferson Hathorn got his Seaman's Protection Papers in 1822.
22. SH, December 11.
23. SH, December 13.
24. SH, December 20.
25. SH, December 31.
26. SH, December 30.
27. SH, December 3 and 8.
28. SH, December 14.
29. SH, December 20.
30. Consular Posts, Liverpool, England, 1855 (Roll T13), RG 59; National Archives, Washington, D.C.
31. All list their nationality as "USA" with the exception of James Thompson, beside whose name is noted "no proof." Consular Posts, Liverpool, England, 1855, "Public Instruments of Protest," no. 450; RG 59; National Archives, Washington, D.C.
32. SH, December 23 and 24. Susan spells the town as "Pounal."
33. SH, December 25.
34. SH, December 29.
35. SH, December 30 and 31.

36. SH, ledger.

37. The stone reads, "DIED Oct. 2[?]1, 1848 Aged 81 yrs. 1 mo."

38. Port Records of U.S. Consul at Liverpool, 1861, "Outgoing Vessel Certification," no. 186, p. 32, RG 59; National Archives, Washington, D.C.

39. "Public Instruments of Protest," 1861, no. 38; RG 59, National Archives, Washington, D.C.

40. A portion of this anguished diary is in the Maine State Archives, with a submittal letter from Frederick J. Libby, the son of Susan and Abial Libby.

41. The tapestries are in the homes of Fred B. Auten, Cass City, Michigan, Lizzy's grandson, and Charlotte A. Schmidt-Fellner, Riverside, Connecticut, Lizzy's granddaughter.

42. Unattributed texts from Richmond and Gardiner newspapers preserved in typed transcript by the Richmond Historical Society.

Bibliography

⟨✦⟩

Sources

Albion, Robert G., William A. Baker, and Benjamin W. Labaree. *New England and the Sea*. Middletown, Conn.: Wesleyan University Press, for Mystic Seaport Museum, 1972.

American Lloyds' Registry of American and Foreign Shipping. New York: E. & G. W. Blunt, Ferris & Pratt, Steam Book & Job Printers, 1862.

Atlas of Pilot Charts: North Atlantic Ocean. Washington, D.C.: Defense Mapping Agency, Department of Defense (NVPUB 106), Ed. No. 2, n.d.

Baedecker, Karl. *Baedecker's Index of Streets and Plan of London*. N.d. (Maps only.)

———. *Baedecker's London and Its Environs*. Leipzig: Karl Baedecker, Publisher, 1908.

Baker, William Avery. *Maritime History of Bath, Maine, and the Kennebec River Region*. Bath: Maine Maritime Museum, 1973.

Beaver, Patrick. *The Crystal Palace, 1851–1936: A Portrait of Victorian Enterprise*. London: Hugh Evelyn, Ltd., 1970.

Biddlecombe, George. *The Art of Rigging: Containing an Explanation of Terms and Phrases and the Progressive Method of Rigging Expressly Adapted for Sailing Ships*. Salem, Mass.: Marine Research Society, 1925. (Based on *The Elements and Practice of Rigging and Seamanship*, by David Steel, first published in London, 1794.)

Bonham, Julia C. "Feminist and Victorian: The Paradox of the American Seafaring Woman of the Nineteenth Century." *The American Neptune* 37, no. 3 (1977): 203–18.

Boyle, P. *Boyle's City Companion to the Court Guide for the Year 1800*. London: P. Boyle, 1800.

———. *Boyle's City Companion to the Court Guide for the Year 1802*. London: P. Boyle, 1802.

Braun, Priscilla E. "T. J. Southard: 19th Century Entrepreneur," *Maine History News*, April 1972, 8.

Briggs, Asa. *Iron Bridge to Crystal Palace: Impact and Images of the Industrial Revolution*. London: Thames and Hudson / The Ironbridge Gorge Museum, 1979.

Brinnin, John Malcolm. *The Sway of the Grand Saloon*. New York: Delacorte Press / Seymour Lawrence, 1971.

Brouwer, Norman. "The United States Hotel," *South Street Reporter* 6, 4 (1972–73): 6, 9.

257

Burton, Valerie, "The Myth of Bachelor Jack: Masculinity, Patriarchy and Seafaring Labour." In *Jack Tar in History: Essays in the History of Maritime Life and Labour*, 179–
98. Fredericton, New Brunswick: Acadiensis Press, 1991.

Clark, William J. *Commercial Cuba: A Book for Business Men*. New York: Charles Scribner's
Sons, 1898.

Cleveland, Richard J. *In the Forecastle; or, Twenty-five Years a Sailor*. New York: Manhattan
Publishing Company, n.d.

Colcord, Joanna C. "Domestic Life on American Sailing Ships." In *Thirty Years of The
American Neptune*, 8–18. Cambridge: Harvard University Press, 1972.

Creighton, Margaret S. "American Mariners and the Rites of Manhood, 1830–1870."
In *Jack Tar in History: Essays in the History of Maritime Life and Labour*, 143–63. Fredericton, New Brunswick: Acadiensis Press, 1991.

———. *Dogwatch and Liberty Days: Seafaring Life in the Nineteenth Century*. Salem, Mass.:
Peabody Museum of Salem, 1982.

———. "The Private Life of Jack Tar: Sailors at Sea in the Nineteenth Century." Ph.D.
diss., Boston University, 1985.

———. *Rites and Passages*. Cambridge: Cambridge University Press, 1995.

Dana, Richard Henry, Jr. *The Seaman's Friend*. Boston: Thomas Groom & Company,
1845. Reprint, Boston: Library Editions, 1970.

———. *Two Years Before the Mast: A Personal Narrative "Housed on the Wild Sea, with Wild
Usages."* New York: New American Library, 1964.

Davis, Walter Goodwin. *The Ancestry of Sarah Hildreth, 1773–1857, Wife of Annis Spear,
of Litchfield, Maine*. Portland, Maine: Anthoensen Press, 1958.

Dickens, Charles. *American Notes*. New York: The Mershon Company, n.d.

Dodson, Vita. "Those Lady Ships." *Log of Mystic Seaport* 32, 2 (1984): 59–64.

Druett, Joan. "Those Female Journals." *Log of Mystic Seaport* 40 (winter 1989): 115–25.

———, ed. *"She Was a Sister Sailor": The Whaling Journals of Mary Brewster, 1845–1851*.
Mystic, Conn.: Mystic Seaport Museum, 1992.

Duncan, Roger F. *Coastal Maine: A Maritime History*. New York: W. W. Norton & Co.,
1992.

Dye, Ira. "Physical and Social Profiles of Early American Seafarers, 1812–1815." In *Jack
Tar in History: Essays in the History of Maritime Life and Labour*. Fredericton, New
Brunswick: Acadiensis Press, 1991.

FreeHand, Julianna. *A Seafaring Legacy: The Photographs, Diaries, Letters and Memorabilia
of a Maine Sea Captain and His Wife, 1859–1908*. New York: Random House, 1981.

Galloway, David H. *Directory of the City of Savannah, for the Year 1850*. Savannah, Ga.:
Edward C. Councell, 1849.

———. *Directory of the City of Savannah, for the Year 1858*. Savannah, Ga.: George N.
Nichols, Printer, 1858.

A Gazetteer of the World, or Dictionary of Geographical Knowledge. London: A. Fullarton,
1859.

Greenhill, Basil, and Ann Giffard. *The Merchant Sailing Ship: A Photographic History*. New
York: Praeger Publishers, 1970.

———. *Women under Sail: Letters and Journals Concerning Eight Women Travelling or*

Working in Sailing Vessels between 1829 and 1849. New York: Great Albion Books, 1971.

Greenhill, Basil, and Dennis Stonham. *Seafaring under Sail: The Life of the Merchant Seaman.* Annapolis: Naval Institute Press, 1981.

Haller, Stephen A. *Families at Sea: An Examination of the Rich Lore of "Lady Ships" and "Hen Frigates" Circa 1850–1900.* San Francisco: National Maritime Museum Association, 1985.

Harthorn, Wayne, Warren Clark, and Laura Cliff. "William Hathorn of Cushing, Maine." *Essex Genealogist* 7, 2 (1987): 65–66.

Hawthorne, Nathaniel. *The Consular Letters, 1853–1855.* Edited by Bill Ellis. Columbus: Ohio State University Press, 1988.

————. *The English Notebooks.* Edited by Randall Stewart. New York: Russell & Russell, 1962.

Hennessy, Mark. "Richmond Dreams for Another Jeff Southard." *Portland Sunday Telegram and Sunday Press Herald,* February 16, 1947, 1, 4.

Heyl, Erik. *Early American Steamers.* Buffalo, N.Y.: n.p., 1953.

Historic American Buildings Survey, National Park Service, Department of the Interior. *Maine Catalog: A List of Measured Drawings, Photographs and Written Documentation in the Survey.* Augusta, Maine: Maine State Museum, 1974.

Home, Gordon. *The London of Our Grandfathers: A Pictorial Presentation of London As It Was One Hundred Years Ago.* London: Homeland Association, 1927.

Horowitz, Helen Lefkowitz. *Alma Mater: Design and Experience in the Women's Colleges from Their Nineteenth-Century Beginnings to the 1930s.* New York: Alfred A. Knopf, 1984.

Hunt & Co. *Hunt & Co.'s City of Bristol, Newport & Welch [sic] Towns Directory, including Bristol, Bridgend, Cardiff {etc.}* London: B. W. Gardiner, 1848.

Hunter, Jane H. "Inscribing the Self in the Heart of the Family: Diaries and Girlhood in Late-Victorian America." *American Quarterly* 40, 1 (1992): 51–81.

The Imperial Gazetteer of England and Wales. London: A. Fullarton & Co., [1871].

International Genealogical Index, 1988 ed., version 2.18. Salt Lake City, Utah: Corporation of the President of the Church of Jesus Christ of the Latter-day Saints, 1989.

Kemp, Peter, ed. *The Oxford Companion to Ships and the Sea.* New York: Oxford University Press, 1976.

Kindleberger, Charles P. *Mariners and Markets.* New York: New York University Press, 1992.

Larcom, Lucy. *A New England Girlhood, Outlined from Memory.* N.p.: Riverside Press, 1889. Reprint, Williamstown, Mass.: Corner House Publishers, 1977.

Lawrence, Mary Chipman. *The Captain's Best Mate: The Journal of Mary Chipman Lawrence on the Whaler Addison, 1856–1860.* Edited by Stanton Garner. Providence, R.I.: Brown University Press, 1966.

Leading Business Men of Lewiston, Augusta and Vicinity, Embracing, Also, Auburn, Gardiner, Waterville, Oakland, Dexter, Fairfield, Skowhegan, Hallowell, Richmond {etc.}, with an Historical Sketch of Each Place. Boston: Mercantile Publishing Company, 1889.

Libby, Charles T. *The Libby Family in America: 1602–1881.* Portland, Maine: B. Thurston & Co., 1882.

Loggins, Vernon. *The Hawthornes: The Story of Seven Generations of an American Family.* New York: Columbia University Press, 1951. Reprint, New York: Greenwood Press, 1968.

London: The Blue Guide. Edited by Stuart Rossiter. London: Ernest Benn, Ltd.; Chicago: Rand McNally & Co., 1978.

Lubbock, Basil. *The Western Ocean Packets.* Glasgow, Scotland: James Brown & Son Ltd., 1925. Reprint, New York: Dover Publications, 1988.

Lytle, William M., and Forrest R. Holdcamper. *Merchant Steam Vessels of the United States: 1790–1868* ("The Lytle-Holdcamper List"). Revised and edited by C. Bradford Mitchell and Kenneth R. Hall. Staten Island, N.Y.: Steamship Historical Society of America, 1975.

Macgregor, David R. *Merchant Sailing Ships, 1815–1850: Supremacy of Sail.* Annapolis: Naval Institute Press, 1984.

———. *Merchant Sailing Ships, 1850–1875: Heyday of Sail.* Annapolis: Naval Institute Press, 1984.

MacLeish, W. H. *The Gulf Stream.* Boston: Houghton Mifflin Co., 1989.

Melville, Herman. *Redburn* [1849]. New York: Anchor Books, 1957.

Metcalf, Priscilla. *Victorian London.* New York: Praeger Publishers, 1972.

Morison, Samuel Eliot. *The Maritime History of Massachusetts, 1783–1860.* 1921. Reprint, Boston: Northeastern University Press, 1979.

New York Marine Register: A Standard of Classification of American Vessels, and of Such Other Vessels As Visit American Ports. New York: R. C. Root, Anthony & Co., 1857.

Norling, Lisa A. "Captain Ahab Had a Wife: Ideology and Experience in the Lives of New England Maritime Women, 1760–1870." Ph.D. diss., Rutgers University, 1992.

Packard, Aubigne Lermond. *A Town That Went to Sea.* Portland, Maine: Falmouth Publishing House, 1950.

Podmaniczky, Christine, and Earle G. Shettleworth Jr. *Through a Bird's Eye: Nineteenth Century Views of Maine.* Rockland, Maine: William A. Farnsworth Library & Art Museum and the Maine State Museum, 1981.

Preble, George A., and Pa[rtr?]idge. *Complete Schedule of Vessels Built and Registered in the District of Bath, Maine, Commencing at 1783, Giving Rig, Name, Tonnage, Where Built, First Master, Registering Owner, and Hailing Port.* Bath, Maine: Fen. G. Barker & Company, 1878.

Reason, James. *Man in Motion: The Psychology of Travel.* London: Weidenfeld & Nicolson, 1974.

Roberts, Polly, et al. *Richmond: A Long View, 1823–1973.* Richmond, Maine: Richmond Historical & Cultural Society, 1973.

Robinson, John, and George Francis Dowe. *The Sailing Ships of New England: 1607–1907.* Salem, Mass.: Marine Research Society, 1922.

Rowe, William Hutchinson. *The Maritime History of Maine: Three Centuries of Shipbuilding and Seafaring.* New York: W. W. Norton & Co., 1948. Reprint, Gardiner, Maine: Harpswell Press, 1989.

Ryan, Mary P. *The Empire of the Mother: American Writing about Domesticity, 1830–1860.* New York: Institute for Research in History and the Haworth Press, 1982.

Scholten, Catherine M. "'On the Importance of the Obstetrick Art': Changing Customs of Childbirth in America, 1760–1825." In *Women's America*, edited by Linda Kerber and Jane DeHart Mathews, 65–79. New York: Oxford University Press, 1987.

Schwabel, Peg Connally. "Yankee Women at Sea." *New Bedford* 4, 3 (1984): 52–54.

The Shell Guide to the History of London. London: Michael Joseph, 1981.

Sherman, Susan McCooey. "Lace Curtains in the Captain's Quarters." *Log of Mystic Seaport* 20, 1 (1968): 11–14.

Smith-Rosenberg, Carroll. *Disorderly Conduct: Visions of Gender in Victorian America*. New York: Alfred A. Knopf, 1985.

Sturtevant, Walter H., and Ruie L. Curtis. *Richmond on the Kennebec*. Edited by John Daly Fleming. Richmond, Maine: Richmond Historical Committee, 1966.

Swan, Susan Burrows. *Plain and Fancy: American Women and Their Needlework, 1700–1850*. New York: Holt, Rinehart & Winston, 1977.

Thompson, Eleanor Wolf. *Education for Ladies, 1830–1860: Ideas on Education in Magazines for Women*. New York: King's Crown Press [Columbia University Press], 1947.

Ulrich, Laurel Thatcher. *Good Wives: Image and Reality in the Lives of Women in Northern New England, 1650–1750*. New York: Alfred A. Knopf, 1982.

———. *A Midwife's Tale: The Life of Martha Ballard, Based on Her Diary, 1785–1812*. New York: Alfred A. Knopf, 1990.

U.S. Department of the Interior. Topographical Map of Richmond Area. SE/4 Gardiner 15' Quadrangle, N4400-W3945/7.5. U.S. Geological Survey, 1980.

Wallace, Mary Anne. "Days of Joy and Fear: Nineteenth-Century New England Family Life at Sea." Master's thesis, University of Southern Maine, 1993.

Watkins, F. W. *Watkins's Commercial and General London Directory and Court Guide for 1855*. London: Longman, Brown, Green, & Longmans, 1855.

Webster, Henry Sewall, and Alfred Johnson. *Vital Records of Gardiner, Maine, to the Year 1892: Part II, Marriages and Deaths*. Gardiner, Maine: The Maine Historical Society, 1915.

Webster, Henry Sewall, and Joseph Williamson. *Vital Records of Gardiner, Maine, to the Year 1892: Part I, Births*. Gardiner, Maine: The Maine Historical Society and the Reporter-Journal Press, 1914.

Primary Sources, Diaries, Contemporaneous or Limited Edition Publications, Unpublished Works, and Ephemera

Bray, Mary Matthews. *A Sea Trip in Clipper Ship Days*. Boston: Richard G. Badger, Gorham Press, 1920.

Brown, Anne Augusta Fitch. *Diary for 1870: The Diary of My Grandmother, Anne Augusta Fitch Brown, Wife of Capt. Jacob Bartlett Brown*. Privately published by Agate Brown Collord, 1959.

Chapman, Angie H. *Windjammer Bride*. Damariscotta, Maine: Chapman-Hall House, 1979.

Goodwin, Sarah A. P. *Sally and Captain Sam.* Edited by Martha Vaughan. Wiscasset, Maine: Lincoln County Publishing Company, 1992.

Gould, Annah Maud. *A Tempestuous Voyage: The Diary of Annah Maud Gould's Trip Aboard the Ship Berlin.* Edited by Laura Penny. Bowie, Maryland: Heritage Books, 1987.

Hathorn, Susan L[ennan]. Diary, 1855. Special Collections Library, Duke University, Durham, N.C.

[Hathorn], Susan H. Lennan. [Letter to Emily L. Whitten, of Topsham, Maine], manuscript, 1852. The Mount Holyoke College Library Archives and Special Collections, Massachusetts.

[Hathorn], Susan H. Lennan. "A Three Years Voyage on the Ship Graduate," student essay, manuscript, 1852. The Mount Holyoke College Library Archives and Special Collections, Massachusetts.

Illustrated London News 26, May 5–June 30, 1855.

Libby, Abial. "The Cholera in Richmond." Report to the Maine Medical Society. Archives of the Richmond Historical Society, n.d.

Libby, Abial. Civil War Diary. Maine State Archives, Augusta.

Mariners' Museum, American Steamship Notes. Mariners' Museum, Newport News, Virginia.

National Archives and Records Administration. RG 36, 41, 59, and 84, Washington, D.C.

Phelps' Strangers and Citizens' Guide to New York City: With Maps and Engravings. New York: G. Watson, 1857.

Shipping and Commercial List and New York Prices Current. New York, 1854, 1855, 1856, 1861.

Shipping Articles of two voyages of the brig *Josephine*, of Richmond, Maine, 1846 and 1847. Maine Maritime Museum Archives, Bath.

Sinnett, Charles M. "The Sturdy Hathorn Family of Mass., Maine, N.Y. State, and the West." Typewritten genealogy, Retyped and indexed by Virginia T. Merrill, Solon, Maine, 1946.

Spear, Laura Jernegan. "A Child's Diary on a Whaling Voyage." Edited by Marcus Wilson Jernegan. *The New England Quarterly* 2, 1 (1929): 125–39.

Sturtevant, Walter H. Notes for *Richmond on the Kennebec*. Richmond Historical Society, Maine. Typescript.

U.S. Bureau of the Census. Returns for Richmond, Maine, 1830, 1840, 1850, 1860, 1870, 1880; Dresden, Maine, 1830, 1840, 1850.

U.S. Geological Survey, Washington, D.C. Map of Richmond, Maine, 1974–80.

Vincent, Edward A. *Vincent's Subdivision Map of the City of Savannah, Chatham County, State of Georgia, Shewing All the Public and Private Buildings, Lots, Wards {etc.}.* N.p.: E. Vincent, {1853}.

Wallace, Mary Anne. "Ocean Sisterhood." Paper, Women and Society Conference, Marist College, Poughkeepsie, N.Y., June 4–5, 1993.

———. "Young Mariners: Nineteenth-Century Children at Sea." Paper, New England Studies Lecture Series, February 3, 1993.

Books Mentioned in Susan Hathorn's 1855 Diary

Acton, Eliza. *Modern Cookery in All Its Branches . . .* , revised by Sarah Josepha Hale ("Mrs. Hale's Cook Book"). Philadelphia: Blanchard and Lea, 1854.

Byron, George Gordon, Lord. *Poetical Works.* London: John Murray, 1851.

———. *Werner: A Tragedy.* London: John Murray, 1823.

Hilliard, George Stillman. *Six Months in Italy.* Boston: Ticknor, Reed, and Fields, 1853.

James, G. P. R. *Agincourt: A Romance.* London: R. Bentley, 1844.

McIntosh, Maria [Jane]. *The Lofty and the Lowly; or, Good in All and None All-Good.* D. Appleton & Co., 1854.

Moore, Thomas. *The Epicurean, A Tale,* illustrated by J. M. W. Turner. [London: John Macrone, 1838.]

———. *Poems,* "Lalla Rookh" [1817]. London: Oxford University Press, 1910.

Scott, Walter. *The Antiquary* [1815]. Edinburgh: Edinburgh University Press, 1995.

———. *The Black Dwarf and Old Mortality* [1816]. Philadelphia: Porter, [n.d.]

———. *Guy Mannering: or, The Astrologer* [1815]. London: J. M. Dent & Sons, Ltd., 1906.

———. *The Heart of Mid Lothian* [1818]. New York: Oxford University Press, 1982.

———. *Ivanhoe* [1819]. New York: Penguin Books, 1986.

———. *Rob Roy* [1817]. Boston: Houghton Mifflin Co., 1956.

Shelley, Percy Bysshe. *The Cenci.* London: C. and J. Ollier, 1819.

Stephens, Ann S. *Fashion and Famine.* N.Y.: Bunce & Brother, 1854.

Stowe, Harriet Beecher. *Sunny Memories of Foreign Lands.* 2 vols. Boston: Phillips, Sampson, & Company; New York: J. C. Derby, 1854.

Acknowledgments

❧✿❧

Thanks to the enthusiastic and generous help of many people, my work on this project has truly been an adventure. My greatest debt is due to Duke University's William R. Perkins Library, in particular the Special Collections Library, where Susan Hathorn's diary is held, and William Irwin and Virginia Daley there, and to the resourceful reference staff at Perkins and Rebecca Gomez of Duke's Interlibrary Loan Department. As librarians and Maine maritime historians themselves, Mary Anne Wallace of Wells and Nathan Lipfert of the Maine Maritime Museum, Bath, provided crucial insights during this project's early stages, thoughtful readings of the manuscript, and great personal encouragement throughout. Angie VanDereedt, of the National Archives Civil Records Division, plucked document after relevant document from government records. John A. Robbins Jr. opened the files of the Richmond Historical and Cultural Association to me and provided genealogical, legal, and geographical orientation and research on Richmond, Bath, Gardiner, Dresden, and Augusta. Elaine D. Trehub, formerly of the Mount Holyoke College Library Archives, unearthed Susan Hathorn's essay and letter there. Fred Auten, Lizzy Libby Auten's grandson, loaned me his family pictures and provided additional family information. Alice Scales, of the Graphics Communications Program at North Carolina State University, brought the computer to the rescue of some of the mid-nineteenth-century materials used to illustrate this book.

Others who extended themselves and their institutions to help include the Reference Department staff, Durham County Library; Norman Brouwer, South Street Seaport; Jeff Brown and Art Dostie, Maine

State Archives; John Fisher and Ralph Hyde, Guildhall Library, London; Jan Flores, Georgia Historical Society; David Jenkins, National Museum of Wales; Lynn Randall, State of Maine Law and Legislative Reference Library; and Irene A. Stachura, San Francisco Maritime National Historic Park.

I also owe special thanks to Jane Garrett, Joan Druett, and Rebecca Goz, and to Dr. John Harland, Stanton Crapo, and other members of Marhst-L, the Maritime History List-Serve on the Internet. To John Weingartner, this book's editor, I am most grateful for the pleasure of a shared vision.

To Mary Stirling Groom, my late mother, I owe thanks for the voyage that made me first wonder about women writing at sea.

To my daughter, Karen, my thanks for her unflagging encouragement and experienced critical and editorial help. To my son, Stephen, my thanks for enduring with his usual dry humor my disappearances in Maine, and for his help with the databases.

And most of all to my husband, Henry, more thanks for more things than I can begin to count.

Illustration credits

Maps of *J. J. Hathorn* routes drawn by author; Morro Castle from *Getting to Know Cuba: A Travel Guide*, by Jane McManus; rigging and sails of a bark, "reefing a topsail," hemstitching and fagoting, 1855 map of Richmond, and Hathorn Block computer-enhanced and adapted from nineteenth-century materials by Alice Scales; *J. J. Hathorn* original enrollment, Santiago de Cuba Consular Return, *J. J. Hathorn* 1854 return crew list, *J. J. Hathorn* coastwise manifest, and *J. J. Hathorn* 1855 crew list reproduced from documents in National Archives, Washington, D.C.; Trinidad de Cuba photo from *Cuba*, by Erna Fergusson, reproduced in appreciation to Erna Fergusson; entries from Susan Hathorn's 1855 diary and 1855 map of Savannah reproduced with permission of Special Collections Library, Duke University; America Square adapted from collection of Guildhall Library, City of London; Crimean War medal ceremony from *Illustrated London News*, May 26, 1855; entrance to Bute

Dock from collection of Welsh Industrial and Maritime Museum, Cardiff; Savannah shipping arrivals from *Shipping and Commercial List and New York Prices Current*, August 29, 1855; embroidered slipper-tops adapted from *Treasures in Needlework* (1870), by Mrs. Warren and Mrs. Pullman; *Alabama* from *Early American Steamers*, by Erik Heyl; *Metropolis* from *Long Island Sound and Naragansett Bay Steam Vessels* (1895), by Samuel Ward Stanton; U.S. Hotel from Cantaloupo Collection, South Street Seaport Museum, New York; two views of Main Street, Richmond, from files of Richmond Historical and Cultural Society; photo of Susan Libby courtesy of Fred Auten, Cass City, Michigan; bark (cover) adapted from photograph courtesy of The Harland Collection, Dr. John Harland, Kelowna, B.C.

Index